Battlefield Bombers: Deep Sea Attack

Battlefield Bombers: Deep Sea Attack

Martin W. Bowman

Pen & Sword
AVIATION

First Published in Great Britain in 2014 by
Pen & Sword Aviation
an imprint of
Pen & Sword Books Ltd
47 Church Street, Barnsley, South Yorkshire S70 2AS

Copyright © Martin W Bowman, 2014
ISBN 9781783831975

A CIP catalogue record for this book is
available from the British Library.

Typeset in 10/12pt Palatino
by GMS Enterprises

Printed and bound in England by
CPI Group (UK) Ltd, Croydon, CR0 4YY

Pen & Sword Books Ltd incorporates the Imprints of Pen & Sword
Aviation, Pen & Sword Family History, Pen & Sword Maritime, Pen & Sword
Military, Pen & Sword Discovery, Wharncliffe Local History, Wharncliffe
True Crime, Wharncliffe Transport, Pen & Sword Select, Pen & Sword
Military Classics, Leo Cooper, The Praetorian Press, Remember When,
Seaforth Publishing and Frontline Publishing.

For a complete list of Pen & Sword titles please contact
PEN & SWORD BOOKS LIMITED

47 Church Street, Barnsley, South Yorkshire, S70 2AS, England
E-mail: enquiries@pen-and-sword.co.uk
Website: www.pen-and-sword.co.uk

Contents

Acknowledgements

I am indebted to all the contributors for their words and photographs. Thanks also go to my fellow author, friend and colleague, Graham Simons, for getting the book to press ready standard and for his detailed work on the photographs; to Pen & Sword and in particular, Laura Hirst; and to Jon Wilkinson, for his unique jacket design once again.

Prologue

Task For Coastal Command

Hector Bolitho

The newspapers give too much space to the glory and heroics of war and not enough to the misery; the days of slow starvation in dinghies, the horrors of mutilation and the cries of men being burned. The mass mind fights shy of these things, naturally preferring the heroism. There is too much limelight on the gallantry, which encourages war and not enough on the despair and pain, which might put a mute on the trumpeters who cry, 'He died a hero.' That he was a hero is merely incidental to the fact that he died in pain, that he was robbed of life and that he is lost to his generation. There is glory in living for an ideal as well as in dying for it.

'The times when the aircraft should return from their night patrols seem to become fixed in my mind and I find myself waking from sleep in a state of wordless prayer. There is no adventure in the war for those who sit on the earth like this, with the fear of being called in the morning and told that another aircraft has been lost in the Channel. It means the sudden obliteration of ten men; men with whom I have walked along the beach, or shared pints with at 'The Travellers' Rest.'

The aircrews themselves are resilient when the bad news comes, but they are also vindictive. Their hatred of the German is not emotional. It is terrible with purpose. They go about their business hoping that next day will give them the chance of revenge but knowing that the crop of deaths among themselves is inevitable. My older heart. starts when I see the dismal ritual; the disappearance of faces from the mess table, the packing of the dead man's possessions, the pile of his luggage in the hall; and the new man, fresh from his training, walking up the stairs to occupy the empty room.

The professional service man pretends that he has conquered these feelings. Perhaps he has developed a crust of hardness which helps him. But five years of life on the edge of the service, of crossing so many names out of my loose leaf address book that it becomes more simple to start a new page for each letter, have left me as vulnerable to grief as I was in the beginning. Only two of the eleven pilots who ate my birthday lunch with me before the war are now alive.

This loss dismays me, of a generation mown down before they have known the richness of summer, before they could ripen and feed the world. They are so unmean, so just and so kind. I sat in the mess last night with three of them, talking of the dullness of the mess food. We each imagined the dinner we would like to eat and I whispered, 'Twelve oysters, the breast of a roast duck with apple sauce, new potatoes and peas picked an, hour before they are cooked, followed by a fresh peach which you could peel in one piece, like taking off a vest.'

One of them said, 'Oh, that's cruel. I am hungry, let's make hogs of ourselves.'

They all went to their rooms and brought back tins of food which we took into the kitchen. Between the four of us we ate a tin of sheep's tongues from New Zealand, spread on slices of thick toast and crowned with mustard pickles. Then we shared a tin of honey, also spread on buttered toast, a tin of peaches, two tins of cream and a cold pudding. It was their hoard of gifts, saved for several weeks and we ate them in sheer vicious greed.

We all felt rather sick afterwards, like the man who said, 'I'll tell you what I had to eat, if I can.' We went to the edge of the cliff for air and my wretched conscience made me think of poor children who would have loved my share of the peaches. We sat in the moonlight and belched, looking down to the sparkling waves and watching the aircraft coming home. Then, for some reason, truth was released and I sat with my head in my hands, watching the three faces in the moonlight and listening to them talk without a hint of self-consciousness.

All three of them have had horrible experiences. One was shot down over the Mediterranean and he saved his aircraft and some of the crew in circumstances that won him the DSO. One had a fight against six Ju 88s and the other, who is a generous, good creature behind his noisy toughness, told us of a time when he switched on his torch in an aircraft and the light fell on what had once been a human face. These are the experiences which affect their thoughts, not the opportunities for glamour. Each one of them admitted that he finds himself recalling his horrible experience as he lies in bed. And each one of them admitted the menace of fear.

I think the popular picture of the aircrew dying for their country in the flash of heroism is false. It is a bad seed to sow for the future. I do not believe that they fight for nationalism or for that old carrot dangled before their nose in the name of freedom. They know that nationalism is a defunct aim and that freedom cannot be won with swords -it can be bred only within each man by the development of his integrity.

The real heroism of the aircrews of Coastal Command lies in their patience; in their capacity to survive the dark hours of vigilance. They loathe the false light that is shed on their occasions of victory. I saw this so clearly the other day when the broadcasting man brought his van here to make one of them speak. As a writer I felt that it was my duty to help the broadcasting man, but as a member of the service I knew it was my instinct to hold back. The pilot was not merely indignant. He was sick with confusion.

I am often alarmed when I hear Australians and New Zealanders talk anxiously of their chances when they return home. They seem suspicious of government promises that they will be cared for and taken back into commerce and industry. Also, Australians and New Zealanders seem unconscious of their value; of the store of experience and judgment they will take back with them, not only because their courage has been proved but also because of the widening of their mental horizon. Those who have been here three or four years realize that however independent the new countries have become, their roots lie in Britain. Some of them yearn to go home soon because they are poor travellers and unwilling to learn, but most to whom I speak realize that their language, their civic consciousness, their democratic intentions and their integrity owe a debt to the English system.

When they arrive here they are critical of the foibles of English life. One Australian was peeved when his host in Scotland scolded him for shooting a brace of grouse sitting on a fence and another was perplexed when he shot a fox and stretched the skin on the barn door; perplexed when his host begged him to bury the skin quickly before the neighbours saw it. Foxes are shot in Australia and it is no crime to kill sitting birds. These superficial differences cause embarrassment 'at first, but this passes as the visitors realize that England still has some lessons to teach the world. 'The English know how to live,' they say. 'They are not as restless as we are.'

After four years here they learn more than how to fly and fight. They are going through an intensified education, feeding their new country vigour on the old wine of England's experience. They are growing rich, through action and thought and when they go back to their dominions they will be ten times as valuable as when they came away.

English pilots and aircrews are no less enriched and the problem for their employers after the war is not, 'How can I fit them in?' but, 'How can I translate the value of what they have learned into terms of civilian life?'

I thought of this again yesterday after a meeting which had an amusing beginning. I wished a few days ago to find out something about the migration of Huguenots to this country and as there are no books of reference in the mess I went into Newquay in search of a library. There was none so I tried a bookshop. 'Have you any book of reference that would tell me the early history of the Huguenots in England?' I asked. The poor girl answered, 'You want a *Who's Who.'* I came back defeated.

A little time afterwards I went up to the aerodrome and met a pilot, Flight Lieutenant Gilbert Potier, of 53 Squadron, who made an attack on a U-boat two or three weeks ago. Within five minutes I found that he comes from Huguenot stock and he was able to tell me all that I wished to know. Two weeks after D-Day Potier was on his third operational patrol with 53 Squadron when he contacted a U-boat, at night, three miles away; too close for him to get down from 500 feet and home accurately. He flew on until the contact was astern and then he lost it. It was in 'the quiet loneliness just before dawn.' He turned directly towards where he thought the target was but still there was no contact. Suddenly, after passing astern of the supposed U-boat, the contact was picked up again, at short range. The Leigh Light[1] was switched on to reveal what he called 'a fat, juicy U-boat,' dead ahead. The crew drill of the months of training went like clockwork and he did not have to give an order. The bombs were dropped and Potier flew over the spot many times, but neither bodies nor wreckage appeared. Four hours after, they again flew over the scene of the attack and there was a big patch of oil on the sea. The ambiguous judgment of the attack is, 'Insufficient evidence of damage,' but this does not mean that the U-boat got away unharmed.

A few notes should be written on the Americans fighting with Coastal Command. They began their contribution in the summer offensive against the U-boats in 1943 when United States Army Air Force squadrons hunted and sank U-boats with us, from a base in Cornwall and later in Devon. Then three US Navy squadrons took their place, quickly fitting into the pattern of the U-boat war in the Bay. The American Wing is operated under the direction of the RAF Group Headquarters but there are two fundamental differences in their background: first in the length of their operational tour which is 800 hours for RAF aircrews and thirty sorties or about 300 hours for the Americans; second, in their training. They have had no equivalent of our Operational Training Unit and new American crews have therefore trained and operated at the same time. It is a tribute to the spirit which the Americans bring into the fight that just before the invasion it was possible for them to check out about thirty new crews in a few days, so that they could take their place in the D-Day sorties.

Each of the three American squadrons has been able to operate six aircraft a day and recently seven, over the South-Western Approaches. The crews had to fly ten and a half hour sorties every other day to achieve this high average.

It is often chance that places a U-boat across the path of an aircraft and the Americans have not always been lucky. Their persistence has been all the more admirable. Of one hundred U-boats seen by the Group in June, the Americans sighted sixteen. June was their great month. Lieutenant Koskinen sighted a surfaced U-boat in the Bay and it is possible that he damaged it; certain that his attack sent it under and delayed it from its task. On the 13th, Lieutenant 'Champ' Johnson attacked a U-boat and stayed long enough to see the escape of high-pressure air making a foam bath about 50 feet in diameter; enough to suggest that this U-boat had also been damaged.

It has always impressed me to arrive at Dunkeswell and see the way in which the Americans throw themselves into a corner of the war which must seem very remote from their own troubles.

This has been a long list of exploits for the laymen to read and one cannot hope that he will follow the details of these continuous attacks with the interest of a trained U-boat killer. But what matters is the effect of such a terrific experience of war, over an entire hemisphere, on a pilot who once saw his horizon within the pages of a ledger.

He will go back into peace with something of great value, if only the big business man will be far-sighted enough to use it. But perhaps the sight of the world and the maturing of his heart and mind will make Potier restless with the idea of adding up the fortunes of others and he may prefer, when it is all over, to go into the spaces of the world and make his own.

It is not whimsical nonsense to say that I love my pen. Any writer who cares about good paper, good ink and a quiet, smooth pen must understand what I mean. I enjoy a page of clear, patient writing, but to achieve this I have struggled with many belligerent or dreary pens, that spluttered with the crossing of t or leaked disgusting smears on fingers and paper. About a year or more ago I was standing in the hall of the Savoy Hotel when a ferry pilot bought one of my books from the stall. The clerk, an old friend of mine, said to the pilot, 'There is the author. I am sure he will sign it for you.' I happen to like autographing books. It is a pleasant fillip to my vanity so I took the ferry pilot's pen and wrote something in the book. The pen was a Sheaffer and it stroked the white paper as gently as a moth's foot. I said to the pilot, 'This is a beautiful pen.' This story throws a bouquet at myself, but it must be told. After I had autographed the book the pilot said, 'Will you have a drink?'

We parted at one in the morning, after dining and gossiping the night away. He had flown the Atlantic many times. He was a kind, trusting American with photographs of his wife and son in his pocket. Next morning, he had returned to his base, but he had left a parcel for me. In it were the Sheaffer pen and a note, asking me to accept it as he had liked my book so much. He had read it all the way through before he went to sleep.

I went off to the Air Ministry, purring with vanity and with the pen next to my heart. It has been there ever since. The pen has flown fairly high and it has seen the coast of France. It has never failed me. I can truthfully say that it was the first pen that made the act of writing a pleasure to me. Yesterday, I dropped it on a concrete floor and chipped the end of the nib. When I tried to write with it, it demurred and threw a dozen minute blots over the paper. I felt as a violinist might feel if his fiddle broke into pieces in the middle of a phrase. I took the pen to one of the RAF instrument makers. It seemed hopeless for one half of the nib was beheaded and I thought it would never write again.

The instrument maker is a craftsman and he re-shaped the nib, making it dumpy, of course, but out of the wound he made a new point which writes as perfectly as before. Again the pen purrs in my hand.

I am writing this because I love craftsmanship and hate moulded plastics and things made out of stuff never intended of them. I don't want a chair made out of petrified cheese and cups made out of dehydrated carrots. I want objects which show signs of a craftsman's talent and devotion. For this reason I wish to bow to Mr. Sheaffer and to the RAF instrument maker who repaired my pen and made it whole again.

This morning, lying in bed, I felt so miserable that I decided there was no joy in thinking, so I had a cold shower and went down to the kitchen for a cup of tea. The mess servants were just arriving so I sat with them and talked as they stoked up the fire and made the tea. But it was no escape from my inwardness because one of them, a quiet, kind man, began to talk of the crews we had lost. He has been in private service for many years and he said that working in the mess has taught him the value of gratitude. He said that the aircrews make less demands on the servants than anybody else he has ever worked for. 'They are always grateful,' he said, 'and for people doing a job like ours, gratitude is a very nice thing.'

I suppose this is why the servants here are so much kinder than any I have met in houses or hotels. I feel a little conscious of my wingless state as I enjoy the privileges that should belong to the aircrews alone. One's clothes are pressed and garments are taken away, washed and ironed and put back in the drawer without a word being said. Yesterday a waste-paper basket appeared without my asking. The batman said he imagined that authors should always have a waste-paper basket - I didn't tell him that he was guilty of a piece of very penetrating literary criticism.

Footnotes

1   Very early in the war Coastal Command had realised that its anti-submarine aircraft would need something more reliable than the quickly consumed flares they were using at night to illuminate U-boats during the last mile of the approach when ASV metre-wavelength radar was blind. As a result, in 1940 Squadron Leader Humphrey de Verde Leigh a personnel officer in Coastal Command was encouraged by the then Chief of Coastal Command, ACM Bowhill to develop the idea of an airborne searchlight. A pilot in WWI, Leigh had flown many anti-submarine patrols and had experienced the frustrations of searching for the elusive underwater craft. Locating the U-boat had become considerably easier since the introduction of ASV radar; nevertheless, the difficulties of the last mile or two of the approach remained. The target simply dropped off the radar screen, leaving the aircrew literally in the dark. Despite early difficulties, Leigh had his prototype installation ready by January 1941. The Leigh Light went into production but eighteen crucial months had elapsed between Leigh's original suggestion and the first use of the device on operations.

Chapter 1

Saviours of Shipwrecked Men At Sea

Lifeboats found at sea - poignant evidence of the U-boat terror - increased in numbers ever since 1939. Saviours of shipwrecked men, protectors of merchant ships and the scourge of German submarines - such are the giant Sunderlands which roar away each day at dawn to go about their lawful occasions. By the time they pick up their moorings at dusk they may have sunk a submarine, flown a thousand miles on convoy patrol or saved from death some of the victims of Hitler's foul submarine campaign.'

'Action stations! U-boat attack! Our ship is struck by two torpedoes. She splits in two and sinks in less than two minutes. There were very few survivors.' So said Kenneth Cooke GM LM, who on 18 March 1943 was a carpenter on board the newly-built tramp *Lulworth Hill* homeward bound from Mauritius via Freetown with a cargo of 413 tons of rum and no less than 11,000 tons of sugar. It was a pleasant tropical evening - nearest point of land 950 miles west of Loanda, in Portuguese West Africa off the starboard bow. There were no ships in sight; none had been seen for a few days, so it seemed that they had the ocean to themselves. But they had soon found how wrong they were. The Italian submarine *Leonardo da Vinci* commanded by Capitano di Corvette Gianfranco Gazana-Priaroggia had surfaced and the *Lulworth Hill's* guns had opened fire, driving him down. At 0340 Gazana-Priaroggia's second attack succeeded. The tramp had sunk in 90 seconds. Captain W. E. McEwan and 42 men were killed.

How long Cooke was in those dark depths of the sea he had no idea but he thought it was the end. He remembered saying goodbye to all at home. At the point of giving up hope he suddenly shot up to the surface. He felt himself being drawn down again and attempted to swim away; but it was a losing battle. This time he was sure his last hour had come, but he fought for his life by swimming under the water. After what seemed ages he found himself on the surface. The *Lulworth Hill* had disappeared. He saw a red light so he knew someone else had managed to avoid being sucked down. He reached him and found it was one of the ship's gunners. They swam around looking for a lifeboat or raft when suddenly the sea was lit up all around them by a powerful light. It was the enemy submarine and it very soon had them spotted in its light. They swam toward it, the gunner ahead of him. When Cooke got alongside he heard an enemy officer asking questions. He spoke little English and they had a hard time making themselves understood. Cooke naturally assumed that he was German and that he was captain of a U-boat but he was the SS liaison officer, temporarily assigned to the submarine to stiffen the Italian crew's resolve, which at that stage was showing signs of crumbling. Cooke answered his questions truthfully. Name of ship; where from; what cargo, how much, where bound, how many crew and where is your captain? What is your rank on board?

How long Cooke was in those dark depths of the sea he had no idea but he thought it was the end. He remembered saying goodbye to all at home. At the point of giving up hope he suddenly shot up to the surface. He felt himself being drawn down again and attempted to swim away; but it was a losing battle. This time he was sure his last hour had come, but he fought for his life by swimming under the water. After what seemed ages he found himself on the surface. The *Lulworth Hill* had disappeared. He saw a red light so he knew someone else had managed to avoid being sucked down. He reached him and found it was one of the ship's gunners. They swam around looking for a lifeboat or raft when suddenly the sea was lit up all around them by a powerful light. It was the enemy submarine and it very soon had them spotted in its light. They swam toward it, the gunner ahead of him. When Cooke got alongside he heard an enemy officer asking questions. He spoke little English and they had a hard time making themselves understood. Cooke naturally assumed that he was German and that he was captain of a U-boat but he was the SS liaison officer, temporarily assigned to the submarine to stiffen the Italian crew's resolve, which at that stage was showing signs of crumbling.[2] Cooke answered his questions truthfully. Name of ship; where from; what cargo, how much, where bound, how many crew and where is your captain? What is your rank on board?

Cooke said: 'Carpenter.' The gunner replied: 'Gunner.' This might have been his undoing, as he was immediately taken aboard and Cooke was left to his fate. The *Leonardo da Vinci* started its engines and made off. Cooke was washed off by the water which almost broke his arm and he was half-drowned by its wash. Suddenly the submarine stopped and he swam toward it. He got close by and could see some men on an upturned lifeboat. The submarine liaison officer was waving his arms and shouting 'Now you shall drown because your Air Force has killed many people in Germany.' The submarine then made off and turned off its lights. It was very dark now and Cooke failed to find the men in the lifeboat. He called out many times, but got no reply. He was now all alone and feeling very sick from swallowing fuel-oil. He swam around as best he could, still calling out.

So began fifty days of hell. It was the kind of hell that hundreds of shipwrecked crew men were fated to endure after being sunk by enemy submarines. Sometimes aircraft such as the Sunderland came to the rescue before the men drowned or slowly died of thirst.

The Sunderlands' work of mercy started in the war with the rescue of the crew of the *Kensington Court* which was lumbering home with 8,000 tons of grain, on 19 September 1939. An SOS from this torpedoed tramp steamer which was seventy miles from the Scillies brought three Sunderlands to the scene just before she went down. The position of the sinking ship had been accurately given and the three flying boats converged upon her almost simultaneously. Flight Lieutenant John Barrett on 204 Squadron piloting L5802, had commenced anti-submarine search at 1215. At 1337 the crew intercepted a signal from the *Kensington Court* - 'gunned by submarine' 100 miles away from aircraft's OR position. It was learnt that a submarine had opened fire on the *Kensington Court* without giving a warning. Barrett made for the ship's position immediately and found *Kensington Court* down by bows, with one Sunderland on 228 Squadron from Pembroke Dock waterborne half-a-mile from the ship. There were 34 survivors in two ship's boats. While two of the Sunderlands flew round to hunt for the U-boat, Flying Officer Thurston Meiggs Wetherall Smith, the captain of a 228 Squadron Sunderland, alighted safely on the surface and taxied up to the ship-wrecked men. A shuttle service of rubber dinghies was established and twenty survivors were put aboard Smith's flying boat. By skilful handling he succeeded in taking off again, despite his heavy load, whereupon Flying Officer John Barrett alighted and picked up the other fourteen men in the boat, while the third Sunderland kept guard above. The promptitude with which the call for help was answered and the skilful way in which the Sunderlands were navigated to the spot, led to the rescue of every member of the crew of the *Kensington Court*. [3]

That same month the SS *Blairlogie*, under fire from a U-boat, sent out an SOS. A Sunderland went to the rescue. Four and a half hours after leaving base and 300 miles from the nearest land, the Sunderland found not the ship, which had sunk, but the crew in the boats. The aircraft brought an American vessel to the scene and stood by until the rescue had been made, returning late in the evening after a flight of more than 1,300 miles. These rescues were the first of many similar errands of mercy which the Sunderlands carried out as the war progressed. On 2 December 1939 a Hudson sighted seven people adrift on a raft over a hundred miles from the East coast of Scotland. In fog and mist it guided a Danish ship to the spot. A little later a Hudson found six survivors of the Swedish ship *Listor* clinging to its cargo, a quantity of timber, strewn over the surface of the sea. The Hudson and subsequently its relief remained above them for five hours until a destroyer arrived to pick them up.

The SS *Domala* (*Empire Attendant*) of the British India Line bound from London and Antwerp to Calcutta on 2 March 1940 was attacked by a Heinkel bomber in the English Channel, 20 miles from St Catherine's Point and set on fire. Four bombs struck the *Domala*, causing heavy casualties and the German aircraft then strafed her with its machine guns. On board, apart from her crew, were 143 Indians who had been repatriated by the Germans, her total complement being 295. The captain was killed, along with 36 members of his crew and 63 of the Indian passengers. [4]

The *Domala* was taken in tow for Cowes while the Dutch steamship, a Royal Navy destroyer led by an Anson to a raft, the only one of four with anyone on it and boats from the shore, picked up survivors from the water and the few lifeboats and rafts that had been launched.

On 2 July 1940 a Sunderland was dispatched to find the survivors of the *Arandora Star* which barely two months earlier had been converted into a troopship. The *Arandora Star* was torpedoed 75 miles west of the Bloody Foreland, County Donegal by the U-47 under the command of Günther Prien, who on 14 October 1939 had entered Scapa Flow and sunk the *Royal Oak*. The *Arandora Star* was proceeding without escort and was carrying German and Italian internees and prisoners-of-war, in addition to her crew of 174 and a military guard of 200 men, for internment in Canada. Thirteen lifeboats packed with survivors were picked up soon after 1100 hours. Nearby, scattered over a wide area, were rafts, pieces of wood and other wreckage to which survivors were clinging. 'Of these there were many score,' reported the Sunderland, which dropped Mae Wests, first-aid outfits and packages of food. Two hours later it found the destroyer *St. Laurent* of the Royal Canadian Navy and brought it towards the lifeboats. The Sunderland then flew round and round for more than three hours guiding the destroyer's boats by means of flares to where the survivors were floating. A total of 805 people lost their lives. Of the enemy aliens, 243 Germans and 470 Italians perished. In addition 37 soldiers and 55 members of the crew died, including her master. [5]

On Monday 15 July Sunderland P9063 on 10 Squadron RAAF, Mount Batten, captained by Flight Lieutenant H. M. Birch, while on convoy protection patrol at 1430 hours, south of Bishop Rock sighted a ship being attacked by five He 111s. Birch climbed the Sunderland up to 2,000 feet in an attempt to interrupt the attack, but was unable to do so. After completing their attack the Heinkels turned to the Sunderland whose front gunner opened fire causing one of them to turn, exposing its underside to further fire before reached the safety of cloud. The other Heinkels came in to attack the flying-boat, but were discouraged by fire from the four guns in its rear turret. They retired to a safe distance and shadowed the Sunderland for about ten minutes before leaving the area. While the Sunderland had suffered no damage one of the ships in the convoy, the 1,359 ton motor vessel, *City of Limerick,* sank later as a result of the Heinkels' attack. RAAF men took part in their first rescue of survivors of a U-boat attack on 28 July 1940, when Flight Lieutenant Birch, who was later awarded the DFC, brought his Sunderland down beside four lifeboats full of survivors from the 13,200-ton motor vessel *Auckland Star*, which was sunk by U-99 commanded by 30-year old Fregattenkapitän (senior commander) Otto Kretschmer. Birch offered to pick up any injured survivors and then, finding there were none, directed a trawler to the lifeboats.

It was nearly two hours since Kenneth Cooke had been cast adrift after the *Lulworth Hill* had been sunk that he heard someone call back to him. He made his way toward the cry and found one man on a raft which had broken adrift when the ship went down. This man helped him aboard and he found it was 21-year old Able-seaman Colin Armitage. A few minutes later they picked up the Chief Steward Herbert Thornton who had been in the water for three hours, had swallowed a great deal of oily water and was in bad shape.[6]At daybreak they saw much wreckage around them; also another raft with no one on it. They rowed toward this raft and managed to grab hold of it. Thornton got aboard just as it was torn from Cooke's hand by the sea. They quickly drifted away, leaving Thornton on the other raft. Next a cry of 'Help!' was heard and they saw Basil Scown the Chief Officer not many yards away. They rowed to him and picked him up. He was violently sick with the oil and sea-water he had swallowed. Cooke too, was sick, but felt much better afterwards. After two hours' very hard work they managed to reach the other raft and lash it to their own. They rested and decided to let one raft go. After removing food and water they cast it off. They now searched for the men on the upturned lifeboat. After two hours they spotted them, which meant that there were fourteen men on the raft. The raft was built to carry twelve men. That night all were very tired, cold and wet. One of the young boys talked in his sleep and called for his mother. This made Cooke feel very miserable and downhearted as he thought of home and parents. He dropped off into a fitful and exhausted sleep.

The second day on the raft everyone was suffering from the cold night and hunger. All were very thirsty, so they decided to have some of the precious water. Chances of making land or of being picked up by a ship was discussed. Then they raised the sail and set off on their long voyage - not knowing of the hardships and deaths that were to overtake this band of brave men.

After a week everyone was suffering from thirst. Salt-water boils were beginning to break out on their bodies and feet from the chafing of the brine-soaked clothing against their skin. One young man started drinking sea-water. Hunger had almost left them: all that was desired was water. Already the members of the crew were looking very gaunt. Second Engineer Eric Ledger's feet were very bad (gangrene) and he could only moan and curse when someone accidentally knocked them. It was very depressing to see fine youngsters suffering from thirst and hunger. Six were under nineteen years of age. The ninth day on the raft Cooke was feeling ill and weak; his throat was terribly parched; his lips cracked and bleeding. He had many salt-water boils which caused him much irritation and restless nights. Thirteen long days adrift; the Chief Officer had almost lost all reason. He wanted his knife to cut his throat and end his suffering. He raved wildly until his last bit of strength was used and he fell unconscious. Four men were drinking sea-water quite often. One young boy was looking very ill and had not the strength to sit up. During the night Basil Scown called Cooke. He talked quite a lot and said he couldn't last much longer. He gave Cooke his ring, saying if he got through he had to give it to his wife. Also a message, which he had to repeat to her.

Eighteen days and death paid its first visit. Basil Scown passed away and ended his terrible sufferings. A short ceremony was held and then two of the crew slid it over the side fully clothed. The body floated astern -

sharks had not been following them for nothing. All bowed their heads to avoid seeing the ghastly spectacle which followed. The rest of the day the survivors sat in gloomy silence.

Twenty days on the raft and conditions were terrible. Everyone was covered with large salt-water boils, lips split and blackened, finger-nails turning black from lack of blood. Three men were now very ill; all having taken to drinking the deadly sea-water, knowing it would mean their deaths. Faces were getting thinner, the bones standing out in bold relief, eyes sunken and glazed. Sharks were with them again. Rescue now looked hopeless and the survivors were asking each other who would be the next to go. Everyone's will-power was weakening.

Twenty-four days had now passed; days of living hell. Four of the little band had passed away. The last two days the youngest boys, Deck Boy Fowler aged seventeen and eighteen year old J. Arnold an apprentice, known and loved by everyone of their late ship's crew who went by the name of Little John, passed away. No living man could describe the terrible sights they faced daily. Faces were covered by uncut beards, hair unkempt and matted with brine. Men lost their reason. Eyes glassy and glazed, always staring out to sea looking and searching the horizon for the ever-expected ship of rescue. Men were suffering terrible and indescribable agonies, losing all hope of rescue and faith. Unable to overcome the lure of the salt death four more died. Eric Ledger passed away after suffering unbelievable agonies from gangrene. One took his own life by drinking sea-water and going over the side where he was soon pulled to pieces by the ever-waiting sharks. The other two slowly choked to death from thirst. On 22 April only Cooke and Armitage were left; their minds tortured in delirious moments by the return of the dead - who they could hear moaning and moaning in agonizing death. Most of the day Cooke and Armitage were unconscious, but returned to sanity in the cool of the evening.

On the 41st day they saw an aircraft and they fired a flare. On Sunday 2 May another aircraft was right on their course and dropped four packages, they were so weak they could only retrieve two of them; one of which contained a wireless. They used this for the first time on 4 May and sent an SOS. Next day, after 47 days at sea a RAF seaplane spotted them and dropped many packages of food and water. Finally, on 7 May Cooke and Armitage were rescued by the destroyer HMS *Rapid*.[7]

A rather unusual case in which a submarine and a Sunderland were both involved was the rescue on 3rd and 4th September 1940 of the Norwegian crew and the crew of the British steamer *Haxby* from the Norwegian steamer *Tropic Sea*. The *Haxby* was sunk by a German commerce raider three months earlier and the survivors of her crew were placed on board the *Tropic Sea* - which had been captured eight days out from Sydney - on which the Germans put a prize crew and ordered the Norwegians to carry their precious cargo of wheat to Germany. But the submarine HMS *Truant* was on guard off Cape Finisterre. Lieutenant Commander H. A. V. Haggard signalled the *Tropic Sea* to stop, which made the Germans scuttle her by exploding mines in her before they took to the boats. The commander of the *Truant* took on board all the British survivors of the *Haxby* and the captain of the *Tropic Sea*, with his wife, but owing to the limited space in the underwater craft it was impossible to pick up any more without jeopardizing the safety of the submarine and all on board. However, the commander of the *Truant* notified the position of the other boats to base so that a Sunderland could be sent out to pick up the remainder. As the sea was flat calm, there was no immediate risk for the men in the boats.

Before dawn on 4 September, the crew of a 10 Squadron RAAF Sunderland (P9603) captained by Squadron Leader 'Hoot' Gibson made ready to depart. Rifles and revolvers were served out to them in case the Germans should cause any trouble and while it was still dark the Sunderland took off, climbed to 1,000 feet and settled down on her course to the south-east. The second pilot, Flying Officer 'Vic' Hodgkinson RAAF saw Eddystone Lighthouse slide by underneath. The life-boats had sails and the Sunderland searching for them had a difficult task, for in the twelve to fourteen hours that had unavoidably elapsed the lifeboats could have travelled far.

As it grew light several small sailing ships, flying the French flags with white flags above them were noticed. In the course of the morning the Sunderland came to the point in the Bay of Biscay where the Truant had left the survivors. The seas were empty, so the Sunderland began a square search and after a time saw three lifeboats bunched together with brown sails set. Coming up with them, those on board the Sunderland noticed that one of the boats was towing a raft which was painted grey. They kept on sailing when the flying boat swooped low over them and no attempt was made to lower their sails so the front gunner was ordered to fire a short burst across their course of the leading boat. They immediately hauled down their sails and the crew put down their oars. Taking a good look at the boats as he circled round, Gibson decided to alight. From a thousand feet the sea seemed quite calm but by the time the flying-boat was down on the surface the captain found there was a confused swell. On completion of the landing run Gibson was 60 yards from the smaller boat.

Moving over to the boats, Gibson ordered the drogues to be thrown out from the Sunderland to take the way off and steady her; after which he switched off two of the engines and left the other two ticking over. Beckoning one of the boats to approach and finding out the men were Norwegians the captain of the flying-boat ordered them to lower the mast to prevent damage to his tail planes and then told them to throw a line. In a few minutes the ten Norwegians in the boat were taken on board through the rear hatch and after placing them so as not to upset the balance of the aircraft, the captain got away and about six o'clock that evening landed the Norwegian seamen in Plymouth harbour. A call was made later at the police station and two boxes of handcuffs were borrowed in case the Germans should prove truculent when they were picked up next day. But by the time the Sunderland arrived, there was no sign of the other boats to be seen. During the night a strong breeze had arisen and there is not much doubt that, the Germans took advantage of it to reach the Spanish coast.

Perhaps one of the most dramatic rescues effected by means of Sunderland flying-boats was that of the survivors of the Ellerman Lines flagship *City of Benares*, which had departed Liverpool in convoy OB.213 on 13 September 1940 bound for Montreal and Quebec. Aboard the steamer, which before the war had sailed between Liverpool and Bombay via the Mediterranean, were 199 passengers, of whom 90 were evacuee children and a crew of 209. At that time British Government policy was to encourage the evacuation of juniors to the apparent safety of North America and South Africa for the duration, under a scheme managed on their behalf by the Children's Overseas Reception Board. On the night of Tuesday, 17 September 1940 when she was about 600 miles out into the Atlantic, only a matter of hours after the convoy's Royal Navy escort had been withdrawn, the *City of Benares* was torpedoed during a gale by the U-48 under the command of 31-year old Captain Heinrich 'Ajax' Bleichrodt. Of the nine grown-ups who worked hard to get their charges into the boats, seven lost their lives. One boat full of boys got away singing Roll out the barrel. But the rough seas and hail storms took grievous toll and the Havant class destroyer HMS *Hurricane* which came on the scene next day could only find 115 survivors scattered about on the rafts and in the boats.[8] Two out of the nine children picked up were too weak to survive. One boat was not picked up until 10 days later, on 29 September, when a Sunderland on 10 Squadron RAAF captained by Squadron Leader W. H. Garing sighted the lifeboat containing six children, two nurses and thirty-eight Lascar seamen. Garing dropped a note saying help was coming and marked the location with a smoke float. The survivors were picked up by a destroyer and landed at Greenock. In all, 258 of those aboard the *City of Benares* perished, including 77 of the 90 children. In fact only 57 of her passengers survived the attack. Immediately after this tragedy the Government terminated the child evacuation programme to prevent similar disasters.

An extraordinary thing was that on the night of Wednesday, September 23rd Mrs. F. Steels dreamed that her son Harry was safe in a boat, although all hope of further survivors had long since vanished. Her dream was true. Her son was safe. One day perhaps science may be able to reveal all the wonders of the human brain and the mystery of telepathy. Anyway, on Wednesday, September 25th a Sunderland flying-boat which had been on convoy duty far out in the Atlantic and had just been relieved by another Sunderland was starting on her homeward flight when a boat was sighted.

'Through my glasses I could see the people in the drifting boat were pretty well exhausted,' said the captain of the flying-boat afterwards. 'As I watched, a little chap who was lying down amidships suddenly stood up and began waving his arms. Then he picked up something white, probably a handkerchief and began to wave that. I could not understand it at first. Then it dawned on me that he was signalling, *'City of -'*. Weak as he was that kid signalled the ship's name, which told us the whole story. That was enough. We were off right away to get help.'Which they did from the Sunderland and a warship guarding the convoy they had recently left.

From that boat, with forty-six survivors in all, were picked up six more children to fill the hearts of their parents with joy. But there was nothing to lessen the sorrow of Mr. J. E. Grimmond, five of whose children were lost. The night before these children sailed, their London home was completely destroyed by a bomb, but the shelter in the garden saved them and their parents. The first reaction of Mr. Grimmond, who suffered the brutalities of the Germans in the last war, was to rejoin the army and in a message in the *Sunday Dispatch* he said: 'Many thousands of people have already had their loved ones killed in the war. They have the right to fight on until we have avenged them. I have never been a cruel man. I did not want this war or the one before it. All I wanted was a home, a family and a job. I think most people in this country felt the same. But the Germans would not leave us in peace. They are not peaceable themselves. I know them. I was taken prisoner in March 1918. Now I want the Germans to suffer. I want them to suffer as my children suffered. And what my children suffered and what my wife and I have suffered will give you an idea of the treatment we could expect if we gave in to Hitler.'

On 16 October 1940 a rescue of survivors of the *Stangrant* who had been in life boats on the open sea for three and a half days was made. Two days before, a lifeboat with 21 men in it had been seen by a Sunderland, which dropped a container with food and cigarettes, for the condition of the sea made it impossible for the flying boat to alight. Two days later the Sunderland set out again. 'It was still dark,' said the pilot, 'when one of my gunners reported a red light on the sea some miles away. Soon we could see the outline of a boat below us. We flew round for about a quarter of an hour waiting for daylight. I discussed landing with my co-pilots. We decided that it could be done and came down on what appeared to be the flattest area of sea in the neighbourhood.' The flying boat landed safely, reached the boat and took off the men. On the way back they were given a hot breakfast on board the Sunderland.

On 26 October a Sunderland helped naval units to pick up survivors from the *Empress of Britain*, one of the largest liners to be placed on the Southampton to Quebec service before being taken over as a troopship. She was returning to the United Kingdom from Canada after a long voyage that had commenced in Cape Town, when a long-range German bomber attacked her about 100 miles north-west of the Irish coast. She was hit by high explosive and incendiary bombs and left damaged and burning. She was abandoned by all but a small party of her complement of 643, the survivors being picked up by naval escorts. During the operation three Blenheim fighters gave protection from enemy air attack. The Polish destroyer *Burza* took the *Empress of Britain* in tow but on 28 October she was hit by two torpedoes from the U-32 commanded by Leutnant Jaenisch and blew up. The loss of life in the two separate attacks is variously put at 45 or 49. She was the largest British merchant ship lost in the Second World War. A few days later, on 3 November, a Sunderland gave similar protection when all the survivors from the *Laurentic*, a Cunard White Star Line passenger liner converted to an armed merchant cruiser, patrolling the

Western Approaches, were picked up. She had gone to the aid of a sinking ship and was torpedoed and sunk by the U-99 off the Bloody Foreland, County Donegal. Three torpedoes sent her quickly to the bottom with the loss of 49 lives.[9]

'Bruce Sanders' wrote *Bombers Fly East* for the Air Ministry in 1942 and he detailed some ASR operations in a chapter called *In The Ditch*. 'The men who go down to the sea in aircraft have to be ready to face anything in the way of adventure. The crew of one Sunderland, after being shot down into the Mediterranean, arrived back inside the British lines with a company of Italian prisoners. The adventure reads like something out of a sensational novel. ['Bruce Sanders' was the pen name used by Leonard R. Gribble, a thriller writer of such works as *The Scarlet Widow!*]. It was way back in December 1941 when the flying-boat was attacked over the Mediterranean by a couple of Messerschmitts. One German plane was shot down and the other was damaged before it made off. But the cost of victory to the Sunderland was its starboard, engines. Both were knocked out. One gunner was killed and another member of the crew wounded. Land was in sight, but the Sunderland could not make it. The captain had to put his aircraft down on a rough sea. The flying-boat ricocheted twice, bouncing forty feet the first time and came to rest with one float broken off. But for two and n half hours the Sunderland remained afloat, drifting in a fresh breeze towards land. However, the flying-boat was fast breaking up. The captain decided that he and his men must swim the remaining distance to shore. The wounded man was put into the only serviceable dinghy and, two at a time, the others slipped into the water. The second pilot was all but drowned as a strong undertow caught him, but the captain, who was a powerful swimmer, reached him in time. All got ashore.

It was noon and they found themselves on a rock-strewn beach, as they estimated somewhere not very far west of Apollonia. While they were taking stock of the situation - they were well behind the Italian lines - a score of armed Italian soldiers appeared from behind a ridge of rocks. The Sunderland captain went forward to surrender, for his party were without arms. He walked towards the Italian soldiers with outstretched hands. To his utter amazement the nearest soldier lifted his rifle above his head and threw it as far away as he could.

Before the truth of the strange situation could be fully understood another party, of Italians arrived. These were more truculent and gave the British to understand that they were prisoners. A stretcher was constructed from the dinghy's oars for the wounded man, who could not walk and then, in a long, straggling procession, the party moved off along the rocky beach. Three of the British party were without boots and it came on to rain. Then darkness fell and in the wet night the British were without provisions or blankets and the Italians would not allow a fire to be lit. They were afraid of Arab sharpshooters. Dawn brightened the east and another start was made, but the procession had not gone far when it was accosted by another party of Italians, this time twenty officers. They were very angry officers. Their allies the Germans, they said, had stolen their vehicles and told them to get to safety as best they could. Now there were more than a hundred Italians and the tired, weary crew of the Sunderland - or, rather, what was left of the crew.

The Italians proposed an amazing offer to the Sunderland captain. No less than a gentlemen's agreement, whereby, in return for the Italians' aid, the Italians themselves should receive favoured treatment in the event of the party being overtaken by the advancing British. At this stage another group of Mussolini's army arrived, fifty men with an Italian major in command. He was a middle-aged man with a face tanned and wrinkled like a piece of old leather. In his belt he had, stuck a cat-o'-nine-tails, which he used as a fly-whisk, but when one of the British airmen complained that an Italian soldier had stolen the wounded man's flying-boots the cat-o'-nine-tails was laid across the thief's back with a will.

The strange company moved on and towards the end of that day the wounded airman died. The Italian major at once set about preparing a military funeral and burial. When the dead airman was lowered into his last resting-place on the rock-girt African shore the major burst into uncontrollable tears.

Eventually they all reached the Arab settlement of El Hamia, where food was purchased. The British bought macaroni and coffee; and for a two-shilling piece and a wrist-watch secured three eggs - not very large ones. An Egyptian pound bought a bag of dates' in that rather blacker than usual black market. One of the Sunderland's crew had an idea. He told an Arab that if he would take a note to the British, who apparently were only fifteen miles away, he would get a substantial reward. The Arab was agreeable and when night came disappeared with the note. But when morning came the major sent for the Sunderland's captain and said he proposed to set out for Benghazi. However, he did not know who held the town - British or Axis troops. The discussion ended in a side-bet between the two leaders and the major agreed to press on with his troops, while leaving the British airmen with the Arabs.

The Italians started off. Some while later the Arab sheikh produced guides and. pack-horses to conduct the British to their own lines. They too set off. After an hour they overtook some of the major's men who were straggling badly. The Italians, nearly thirty of them, hailed the appearance of their erstwhile companions with cries of delight and without more ado surrendered themselves and joined the trek towards the British lines - wherever they were. And in due course the few Sunderland airmen arrived inside their own lines, with their bag of prisoners and one of the most incredible stories of the war began to circulate.

The motto proudly used by one of the RAF's Air-Sea Rescue squadrons was 'By Searching We Save.' Since 1 January 1942, when that particular squadron was formed, until the time of the launching of the first airborne lifeboat, the squadron had searched for and saved nearly a hundred bailed-out airmen in the ditch. Most of them had been Allied personnel, but some had been enemy airmen. The squadron's commander, Squadron Leader A. S. Linney of York, had been one of the RAF's gallant band who covered the

Dunkirk fighting. He had been shot down himself and rescued by two Frenchmen in a rowing-boat. He knew both sides of the Air-Sea Rescue Service from experience. There were no braver airmen in the world than the pilots and crews of that service. They snatched helpless airmen from under the very nose of the enemy. They braved the German coastal batteries to effect a rescue. They were prepared, if driven to it, to fight off E-boats and Focke-Wulfs to get the men they had rescued back to a hospital bed and safety. They even came down in the midst of enemy minefields and when the need was urgent did not shy from taxiing back with an overloaded aircraft through their own.

Before the war a well-known Australian radio singer used to imagine himself doing something as hare-brained as flying an aircraft, but not once in his wildest imaginings did he see himself performing the feat accomplished on a memorable occasion by Pilot Officer T. E. Hilton, of the Air-Sea Rescue Service. But then in those days he did not see himself as Pilot Officer Hilton. The Air-Sea Rescue Service airmen were men who flew ready to risk the mischances of other airmen overtaking themselves. It was so with this Australian who had given up radio singing for piloting a Walrus in dangerous waters, close under the guns of the enemy and bringing back men who would fly again in the battle of the narrow seas.

On this particular occasion Hilton was patrolling a stretch of the English Channel about eight miles out from Cap Gris Nez. He was looking out for a tell-tale trail of fluorescence on the surface of the waves or the speck of a dinghy containing a British or Allied airman who had had to ditch after raiding enemy territory. He found such a dinghy. But it was drifting in the middle of a German minefield. On each side of the dinghy, as Hilton scanned the sea below his amphibian, he saw a line of mines. The dinghy was occupied, but the occupant appeared to be in no position to do anything to save himself from what appeared to be certain death. At any moment the lift of a wave or a vagary of the wind might carry the light rubber dinghy a few feet and toss it against the horns of one of those bobbing mines. It might even be that the airman in the dinghy was unconscious and completely unaware of his peril.

Hilton put down the nose of his aircraft and skimmed lower to have a closer look at this problem the sea had suddenly presented to him. On closer inspection he saw that the occupant of the dinghy, if not unconscious, was exhausted by his ordeal. The man made no stir to hail the plane. Circling round, Hilton had to make up his mind quickly. Going in was a risk, but he knew just what he could do with his Walrus, which was a manageable craft. If he did not go in, the chances of the airman ever coming out of the trap into which he had fallen were slim.

The Australian decided that he had to go down and get the airman out of the dinghy. That would mean surfacing between the lines of mines, which would not be an impossible manoeuvre. But on the other hand getting away again, lifting the Walrus clear of those bobbing dots would be a very different proposition and might well prove to be impossible. That was a hazard; but Air-Sea Rescue work was full of hazards. He prepared to take this one.

Keeping his fingers crossed, he went down. Judging his distance to a nicety and taking advantage of the pull of the wind, he drifted neatly between the two rows of mines and came to rest on the sea with as little flurry as a duck. It was a pretty piece of flying. He then began to taxi forward slowly towards the rubber dinghy. As he moved his wake disturbed the mines. They oscillated with what seemed to be dangerous vigour to the Australian. But the Walrus at length came safely to rest alongside the dinghy. The airman in it grinned at him and stirred a hand. He could not do much more. So Hilton set about getting him aboard the Walrus. That took time. He dare not risk hurried or forceful movement, for fear of sending the dinghy on to a mine, but eventually, after the expenditure of a great deal of patience, he got the airman into the hull of the amphibian. He went back to the controls and prepared to take off. This was the really dangerous part. He lifted the Walrus as gently as he could, but even so the floats sent clouds of whirling spray before the fresh wind. The spray eddied round the lifting nose of the Walrus. Then Hilton got a shock. He caught sight of something he had missed before - the dark shape of a mine, not in either of the two defined lines, but on its own and barely fifteen yards ahead, right in the path of the sluggish Walrus. There was no time to think. No time to drop down and consider the position. He was skimming the waves and the mine was rushing towards him, a bobbing danger it did not seem feasible he could avoid. With split-second judgment he contrived to lift the Walrus like a jockey raising a mettlesome horse. He saw the horns of the mine flash underneath the Walrus, missing the amphibian by bare inches. Then down he came on the other side with a resounding splash that bounced the aircraft badly.

Up went the Walrus again and down once more, bouncing and hedge-hopping across the minefield, missing death time and again by a hand's-breadth. Hilton flew more by instinct than by sight and judgment, until he realized that he was airborne and that the sea was at last, after what had seemed ages, rushing away from him instead of at him. He got back to base with his rescued airman and made out a normal report. Hedge-hopping a minefield, to the Air-Sea Rescue Service, was merely one of the day's - or night's - hazards.[10]

The wall-of-death daredevil riders at circuses and gymkhanas have nothing on the men who pilot the aircraft of the Air-Sea Rescue Service. Their job, they know, is to rush in where in good truth angels might well fear to tread.

The exploit of three Air-Sea Rescue sergeants has become famous in a Service where bravery is accepted as a part of every man's normal make-up. On 14 December 1942 they took a Walrus through mine-fields, ten miles east of Dover, to rescue some Germans clinging to a raft in a very rough sea. The pilot was Sergeant Tom Fletcher DFM from Manchester, the front gunner Flight Sergeant Glew DFM from Washington in Durham and the rear-gunner Flight Sergeant Healey DFM from Watford. The three sergeants, between them, already had a record of forty lives saved.

When they spotted the raft with the men clinging to it, Fletcher realized that the sea was too rough for the Walrus, once down on it, to hope to take off again. But he did not hesitate to go down. His plan was to taxi all the way back to port. He dropped on the sea and sidled up to the raft, while Glew got ready with a boat-hook. However, the Germans were desperate and filled with fear. Instead of making the boat-hook fast to the raft the nearest German clutched it and tried to get on board the Walrus. He was dragged into the rear hatch as the raft was swept by on the high-rising waves.

This selfish action left Fletcher with the difficult task, if he was to continue rescue operations, of turning round and taxiing back to the raft's fresh position. He managed to get round by skilful work at the controls and next a rope was flung to the Germans to make fast. But they missed the snaking coil and at that very moment a large wave lifted the Walrus and pitched it heavily on to the raft. One of the five Germans was injured seriously and two of them hurled into the dark waves. One of these managed to get his fingers to the rope and the other tried to grasp the Walrus's wing-float. Both were too weak to hold on. Another wave caught them and they were tossed aside by the force of water like two pieces of flotsam. But Healey had been working in the meantime to get one of the other Germans head first into the rear hatch. Just as he succeeded, the RAF machine was brushed off the raft by another large wave.

Again Fletcher employed all his ingenuity as a pilot to taxi round and back to the raft, on which, as he drew close, there remained only one German. The Walrus smacked against the raft and at the moment of impact Glew, reaching out, hauled the last man aboard.

While all this was happening night had come down. Fletcher, reluctant to lose the three men who had been washed away, spent some time trying to find them, but it was time wasted. He at length started back with a smashed windscreen and a foot and a half of swilling seawater in his hull. The Germans lay prone, too exhausted to help and Glew and Healey worked the pumps without aid. Next, the electrical equipment commenced sparking. Smoke rose from the radio. The Walrus began lagging. Fletcher, realizing that their position was becoming graver with each passing minute, risked disaster and opened wide the throttle. The Walrus responded by racing across the surface of the sea in a series of drunken staggers. The water rushed into the hull and Glew and Healey had to redouble their efforts. But Fletcher kept on till he was spotted by a trawler, which guided him to port. Only when he stepped ashore did he realize that in his desperate race across the sea he had charged headlong through several minefields. But he had made the journey knowing that it was impossible, at any stage of the way, for him to get his overloaded craft airborne. Frequently, however, rescue is not achieved by one aircraft, but by a relay of rescue planes, all taking it in turn to bring safety a little nearer to the unfortunate occupants of a dinghy. Closely co-operating with the aircraft are the high-speed launches of Air-Sea Rescue. What the crew of the one cannot handle, the crew of the other usually manages. Between them the personnel of launches and aircraft find few rescue tasks beyond their ability to tackle with success.

A splendid example of this co-operation was given by the crew of a Walrus and the airmen manning an RAF rescue launch. The Walrus sighted a Lancaster bomber floating, surprisingly, on the sea and not far distant a rubber dinghy containing the crew. The twenty year old pilot of the Walrus, who was from Horley in Surrey, went down and landed in a very heavy swell close to the dinghy and took the seven bomber men aboard. Including the Walrus's crew of three, that meant there were ten RAF men crowded into the small rescue plane. The pilot had no hope of ever getting airborne with such a load. All he could do was remain on the sea surface until help came in reply, to his radio signals. But there was something aboard the still floating bomber which might be valuable to the RAF's Intelligence officers - the camera which had recorded the results of the raid on which the Lancaster had flown. This is what went down in the Walrus's log afterwards: 'We taxied towards the bomber in the hope of getting alongside so that someone might climb aboard for the camera. The swell made this difficult and, after we had been carried against the front guns of the bomber - one of which ripped into the fuselage of the Walrus - I abandoned the idea. Soon a high-speed launch reached us and we transferred four of the bomber crew to this. All came back OK, some by sea, some by air.'

Frequently it is a mere detail that, gets a bomber's crew back to Britain and ensures their flying again. Early in 1943 the crew of a Coastal Command Hampden torpedo-bomber, after a successful attack on an enemy convoy off the Dutch coast, had to ditch. They were forty-three hours in their dinghy before a Walrus caught a gleam in the trough of the waves. It was a speck of sunlight touching a lead pigeon container. The Hampden had, been manned by Canadians and one man from the Channel Islands. The pilot reported the adventure colourfully. 'We found the convoy,' he put on record, 'but had bad luck to be hit almost immediately by AA. A hole in the fuselage under the port wing did not stop us from attacking a fairly big merchant ship. I headed straight for it and dropped a torpedo at seven hundred yards' range. Then all hell broke loose. Red, green, white and yellow tracer came from every angle. We were hit repeatedly. The port engine, wing-tips, elevators and rudders and the main-plane were damaged.

'We headed for home, but the aircraft started to vibrate violently. It was all I could do to hold the steering column. 'The damaged engine caught fire. I ordered an SOS to be sent and told the crew we would have to ditch. We didn't hit the water hard, but the aircraft was so badly riddled that she broke into three pieces and sank within eight seconds. We all had to swim for the dinghy. The pigeons, which had been thrown into the water, were floating away. The rear-gunner picked up one of them as he swam to the dinghy. I saw the other pigeon about twenty-nine yards away, so I went back and got it.'

The pigeons were released, with messages for help attached to them. But they must have been injured in the attack or the subsequent crash, for neither of them reached home. The airmen, not knowing this' waited patiently in their dinghy as the hours slipped by and then began dragging with terrible slowness.

'Wet through, we huddled in the dinghy and took stock of our position,' the pilot relates. 'We had a quart of water and eight ration tins. The next morning we saw a couple of Beaufighters - but, they didn't see us. In the afternoon we sighted a Hudson, but it was too far away, so we settled down for another night.'

There is no need to try to picture the feelings of men in that condition. On the following afternoon three Beaufighters approached on patrol. 'One of them spotted us,' the pilot 'adds, 'and flew low. The other two dropped food containers. We knew then that rescue was at hand. An hour or so later a Walrus aircraft appeared and sightedus first of all by the glint 'of the sun on one of the pigeon containers. It alighted and took us aboard.'

Not that all danger was over. That was the very moment when an E-boat dashed up from the Dutch coast to prevent the rescue. The Germans opened fire on the rescue aircraft, but the skipper of the Walrus had been in similar situations before. He knew a trick or two and he left the Nazis firing at the clouds. Even so, it was a pretty close call; as close as any of the Hampden crew ever wanted to make.

During the North African campaign the RAF's Air-Sea Rescue Service was in full operation and over grey salt-marsh and blue sea kept up a consistent programme of rescue and aid for stranded airmen. But farther out in the Atlantic and the Bay of Biscay bomber crews who have had to ditch badly damaged aircraft cannot hope for succour from the Service's high-speed launches or the small amphibians flown by its daring pilots. When possible, Coastal Command has to rescue its own airmen who have gone deep-sea hunting and through the luck of war have had to ditch their aircraft.

On 9 July 1942 a Sunderland flying-boat made a brave and successful attempt to pick up the survivors of a Whitley which had been forced down. The Whitley developed engine trouble on a U-boat hunt and it became obvious to the crew that they would have to ditch their aircraft. The radio operator, Sergeant George Barfoot, who before the war was in the King's employ at Buckingham Palace, sent out a message of distress just before the Whitley touched down on the waves. The dinghy was launched with great difficulty, for a very high sea was running and a considerable amount of water was shipped. At intervals the stranded bomber men let off Very cartridges and that evening a second Whitley sighted smoke from a Very cartridge on the distant horizon, some hundred miles from the Spanish coast. Search was made and the dinghy spotted. The pilot of the Whitley climbed, to gain altitude enough to send out an SOS to base, giving the position of the dinghy. By that time dusk was closing down over the Bay and when the Whitley dropped again the crew were unable to spot the men they had located. But the search went on. Other Whitleys went out to seek for their fellow-airmen and the following morning the castaways were again discovered. The dinghy was drifting towards the Spanish coast. More reports were flashed to base and a Sunderland flying-boat [on 461 Squadron RAAF, piloted by the unit commander] Wing Commander N. A. R. Halliday of Liphook, set out to attempt to pick up the Whitley survivors. The Sunderland's navigator, Flying Officer Frederick Gascoigne, an Australian, checked and rechecked his navigational calculations, until the search was narrowed down to an area of thirty miles square. Methodically the Sunderland began cutting up this square of sea into smaller squares. It was an exacting process, for a moment's relaxation might have meant missing the stranded crew and for the Whitley men that may well have been the end. Wing Commander Halliday has described the rescue bid.

'We had been searching for one and a half hours,' he said later, 'when we saw a puff of smoke. It came from the dinghy, which was then three miles ahead. We circled it and although the swell looked ominous, we decided to try and land. We had our fingers crossed as we went down. There was a bump and for a moment I thought we had broken the starboard float - it went right under the water. But we landed successfully. Then came the tricky job, either of getting the Sunderland to the dinghy or the dinghy to the Sunderland. We manoeuvred for ten minutes without getting nearer than about fifty yards, so my first pilot took off his clothes and prepared to carry a line to the dinghy. Before he could do so the second pilot got up on the wing, which was pitching heavily and climbed along it with a line. He heaved the line from the wing-tip to the dinghy crew, who picked it up. The pilot crawled back along the wing, towing the dinghy behind him and we soon had all the crew aboard.'

Fortunately the take-off was managed without mishap and the Whitley crew, who had been in their dinghy for just under twenty-four hours and were down to their last Very cartridge, arrived at the Sunderland's base to partake in a celebration supper thrown by an American Intelligence officer to mark the occasion.

RAF crews based in West Africa have an additional danger to face when they come down in the ditch - the sharks that infest tropic seas. The nightmare experience of one Hudson's crew reveals the kind of fortitude possessed by the men of the RAF who scour the less-frequented sea-lanes. This particular Hudson force-landed in the South Atlantic many miles from the West African coast. The men had scarcely half a minute in which to get clear of their aircraft before it sank under the waves. The dinghy was only half inflated when it was thrown out and the men jumped after it. One thought alone gave them some cheer in their desperate predicament. The wireless operator had received an acknowledgment to his SOS. Their plight was known. Aid would come. The only question was-would it be in time?

The four members of the Hudson's crew swam over to the dinghy, which was floating upside-down. Before they could reach it they discovered with horror that they were not alone. One of them raised a cry and pointed. Cutting like two blades through the sea were the fins of a couple of sharks that had witnessed the disaster. One of the crew got to the dinghy, seized the paddle and began beating the water furiously. The fins turned away. The next instant the paddle slipped from the hand of the men wielding it and drifted away. The captain ordered his men to cling round the dinghy, holding it for support and whenever the threatening fins approached to kick out violently with both legs and make as much disturbance in the water as possible. With some trepidation the plan was put into execution. For how long they kept up this simple defence none of them ever knew, but it proved sufficient to keep the white teeth of the sharks at some distance - until they saw an aircraft flying in the clear sky. It was a Hudson and it came to within four miles of where they floated. They could do nothing to attract the pilot's attention as their distress signal in the' dinghy had become water-logged and useless. They waved, but all their efforts succeeded in achieving was tilting the dinghy enough to cause their emergency rations to slip from their fastenings into the ocean. As the only food they had disappeared the Hudson circled and faded, like a mirage.

Those men might have been forgiven for giving way to despair. But the men of the RAF who flyover the great waters are not given, even in such extreme circumstances, to despairing until the last hope has flickered out. Theirs had not. They still had the all-but-immersed dinghy. Valiantly they set to work to turn it over. They found the inflating tube and began blowing down it, one by one, taking it in turns and. while one used up his precious breath the others splashed and kicked to keep away the glinting fins which were still circling them.

But the dinghy was inflated and they climbed in, only to find that they had to plug a couple of holes in the floor. This they did with the epaulettes from their tropical shirts. There they sat in the temporarily watertight dinghy, four men, very tired, with four life-jackets, one useless distress signal, one sea-anchor, an empty tin and one precious flask of brandy as night was falling - and the flashing fins went round and round their tiny rubber island.

The night passed with two of them on watch and two sleeping, in turns. Every half-hour the dinghy had to be bailed out. A Sunderland roared by in the distance some time about dawn and once on the horizon they saw the flash of a naval vessel's searchlights. The search was on, but they could not help the searchers to find them. Throughout the next day they lay there rocking and pitching in their dinghy while searching aircraft continued to miss them. A tiny speck in thousands of miles of ocean, missing them was the simplest matter in the world. One Hudson came within a quarter of a mile of them without spotting the dinghy. It was towards the end of that day, when they were churning the sea around them to whiteness and waving frantically with their life-jackets, that they finally succeeded in attracting the attention of a searching Hudson. The bomber swooped over them and down parachuted three very welcome bottles of lime-juice and a brief note, which read, 'Help coming. Navy on the job.' They had to wait the better part of another day before a destroyer, guided by a Hudson, hove in sight. It was not long then before a launch was lowered and they were picked up, more than forty hours after they had gone into the ditch. As the launch sped away the flashing fins were still slicing the water.

However, there are the exceptions to every rule and even in the case of ditched aircraft there are those remarkable examples of skill and daring which defy chance and misfortune alike. One Sunderland which was ditched far out in the South Atlantic was actually sailed by its crew; who refused to abandon it. The flying-boat ran into a violent tropical storm while returning from a special patrol and by the time the two pilots had mastered the worst the elements could do they were down to their last few drops of petrol. The captain jettisoned his bombs, made for the nearest coast and at the very last moment, when the tanks were dry, force-landed on the sea.

Fortunately the storm had abated. The crew set to work ingeniously rigging a dinghy oar to the mast and the cockpit awning was fitted to it as an improvised sail. The wind, as luck would have it, was blowing in the right direction for them. Then they adopted a device known as the Dutchman's log which was simply dropping a piece of wood from one turret and timing how long it took to pass the next turret. From this figure they were able to calculate that they were sailing at about one knot. They then made a signal, giving their speed, an estimated that they would arrive at the coast in three days' time. But before that period had passed they had been picked up by a naval vessel.

Another Sunderland forced down hundreds of miles from land was actually towed, through a period of seventy-four hours back to base; that despite an electrical storm and a high running sea. The feat provided a record, even in the annals of that record-breaking organization which is Coastal Command.

The captain of the Sunderland has put his own story on record.

'The first night was the worst,' he reported when he arrived back at base. 'There was a strong wind, with several rainstorms and a fair bit of lightning. Sometimes we could not see the corvette which was towing us, although she was only three hundred yards ahead. In the morning the wind and swell dropped noticeably and throughout the following day and night - our second night on the water - we made a good speed. During the morning of the third day, though, the wind freshened and the Sunderland began to plunge very heavily and to make water forward. That night, with a rough sea and a strong wind, we had to reduce speed and just crawl along and the flying-boat really took a terrible buffeting. We put out three dinghies on the main-plane, in readiness if the Sunderland sank. The fourth day the going became a lot easier, but by then we were wondering just how much strain had been put on the Sunderland and whether she would stand very much more. However, she came through splendidly and the corvette handed us over to a pinnace when we reached our base. On the last day the first lieutenant of the corvette came aboard to help us. The whole thing, indeed, was a magnificent piece of work by the corvette.' Quoting the Sunderland captain's own words, it was also a magnificent piece of work by the Coastal Command crew.

Probably the best operational stories of the war will be those told by the men who go down in the ditch when their luck is out and come up again when that luck changes.'

On the night of 11/12 August 1942 a Leigh Light Wellington on 172 Squadron piloted by an Australian Flying Officer A. W. R. Triggs was on an anti-submarine patrol over the Bay of Biscay. In the small hours of the following morning the tail gunner suddenly saw 'excessive sparks passing behind like a cluster of stars', the oil pressure fell to zero, the aircraft lost height and in a few minutes the pilot was forced to ditch. The crew carried out their drill correctly, including the transmission of an SOS, but when the aircraft struck the water the dinghy failed to blowout of the stowage. This the pilot remedied by prising off the lid of the stowage with his bare hands, while the rest of the crew stood on the wing up to their knees in water. The dinghy then began to inflate and despite the high seas the drenched crew managed to climb aboard. For the next three hours all six men baled furiously. Then the search aircraft began to appear. No less than eleven of them passed over or near in the course of the morning, but all the efforts of the distressed crew could not attract their attention. There were only two marine signals in the dinghy and both of these were fired in vain.

Throughout the morning a total of 11 aircraft were spotted, obviously searching for the dinghy, but none found it. In the early afternoon, however, a Whitley on 51 Squadron saw the dinghy and released a Thornaby Bag and a spare dinghy near the ditched crew. The Whitley crew saw the crew retrieve the bag and then sent off a signal giving the survivors' correct position and turned for home. Within a short time Sunderland 'B-Baker' on 461 Squadron RAAF, piloted by Wing Commander N. A. R. Halliday escorted by three Beaufighters was hastening towards the scene. The flying-boat survived an encounter en route with a Focke-Wulf Condor; but another Whitley, on 77 Squadron, which spotted the dinghy and signalled 'Sunderland coming', was shot down on its way home. Halliday's instructions were to alight and pick up the survivors if the state of wind and water permitted. The conditions were far from good. Halliday circled the dinghy, sizing up the conditions for landing. There was a heavy swell, whipped by a 25-knot wind, but after jettisoning all depth charges and 500 gallons of petrol, Halliday decided to make the attempt. Triggs in the dinghy watched in agony as the Sunderland touched down. The flying-boat hit a wave, bounced, hit the water again and at once the starboard wing dipped into the water, dragging the flying boat down at the nose. The main hull step shattered. A second later a starboard engine burst into flames. The whole episode lasted less than a minute. Unseen by Triggs, six men on the flying boat crew managed to evacuate the sinking Sunderland and clamber into the only dinghy, but this promptly burst. Flying Officer John H. F. Watson, the navigator, remembered seeing a derelict dinghy nearby (the spare dropped earlier by a Whitley) and could now see it, 400 yards away. Watson voluntarily swam to retrieve this dinghy but, having already suffered concussion in the aircraft crash, his efforts to reach the dinghy, though successful, weakened him so much that as soon as he climbed into the dinghy he collapsed into unconsciousness. When he regained his senses shortly after, there was no sign of his five comrades. They had been engulfed by the waves.

So 12 August passed. Wet, cold and uncomfortable the six men from the Wellington now faced another night. The next day two more Whitleys arrived over the spot, only to be intercepted and driven off by German aircraft. At one point a French fishing boat passed within 400 yards of the dinghy but Triggs and his crew remained silent, not wishing to become prisoners of war - such was their faith in eventual rescue. Then the weather closed in. Throughout Thursday 14 and Friday 15 August most of the search aircraft were grounded. Meanwhile on 14 August the six men took their first meal - a biscuit, a Horlicks malted milk tablet, a square of chocolate and a small mouthful of fresh water. They also beat off a shark which showed an unwelcome interest in them. Towards the close of the day they tried to improvise a sail - for it was not until later in the year, after a number of fighter pilots had been picked up dead in their dinghies, that proper sails were included in the packs - and that evening drank a tin of tomato juice 'celebrating' the Friday night party usually held in their Mess back in England. While the Wellington crew thus kept up their spirits the single survivor from the Sunderland in the other dinghy was without food. Watson consoled himself by drinking water and chewing at the strap of his wrist-watch.

Throughout, weather conditions deteriorated, with rain showers and clinging damp mist obliterating the sky, while the sea surface broke up in heavy surging waves which constantly threatened to over-turn the tiny dinghy. On Saturday night torrential rain added to the crew's misery until daybreak on Sunday 17 August. That morning the bad weather left them, leaving clear bright skies and their morale was uplifted. Then at mid-day a Beaufighter appeared and signalled to the Wellington crew: 'contact other dinghy - injured man aboard'. Guided by the aircraft the six men began to paddle the half mile or so which separated them from the survivor of the Sunderland. While they were doing so a Hudson on 279 Squadron arrived over the scene and dropped a Lindholme gear. Triggs' crew paddled for five hours to close the 1,000 yards between them and Watson. They then managed to get him aboard their own dinghy, rubbed him down and gave him a malted milk tablet and half a can of tomato juice. His first words were: 'I'm all for the open air life, aren't you?' This the crew of the Wellington countered with another question: 'You wouldn't be an Australian, would you?'

By then a British destroyer, accompanied by launches and Beaufighters, was fast approaching. But so were German aircraft. Soon the Beaufighters were shooting down a Ju 88, only to be attacked by FW 190s. Night fell. The seven men were still in the two dinghies, now lashed together. Early the next morning a German motor launch, escorted by three Arado 196 float-planes and two FW 190s was seen heading towards the dinghies. But two Beaufighters were back on the scene and they at once dived at the enemy. Under cover of their attacks HM Launch Q180 was then able to approach the dinghies and take aboard the exhausted survivors. Then began the journey northwards, escorted by three other naval launches but their adventures were not yet over. The tiny convoy was immediately attacked by a pair of FW 190s but the gunners on deck held all attempts at bay and these were chased away by the hovering Beaufighters. Later that evening Q180 finally reached Newlyn Harbour and put the survivors ashore, where they were immediately rushed to hospital.

On 29 May 1943, a grey day, the Bay of Biscay was no ideal landing spot for a flying-boat; a heavy swell and a buffeting wind made the operation hazardous in the extreme but it was the only hope of rescue for stranded men. Flying Officer Gordon O. Singleton peered through the murk of sea and sky beneath his Sunderland and suddenly spotted the two dinghies with their load of survivors. Singleton approached dead into wind, keeping the nose well up and the swell at right angles to his bow. Then he brushed from crest to crest, stalled correctly into a trough and pulled off a magnificent landing. The survivors came in through the rear door. They were wet and cold and shaken, yet they were cheerful and full of gratitude. But then came the problem of take-off. There were now twenty-seven men on board, five hundred gallons of fuel and eight depth charges. All added together produced a sum total of dead weight which the Sunderland could never be asked to lift. Singleton looked at H. E. Winstanley, his navigator and said. 'We've shot ourselves with science. We can't take-off in this swell. We'd be smashed to matchwood.'

It was almost a case for Providence. Providence had to calm the seas or send along a ship, whilst conveniently diverting all enemy aircraft which might be roving through the area, for the Sunderland was a sitting target. Singleton suspected his order was too tall. Their only solid hope was a Free French destroyer which was known to be in the Bay of Biscay somewhere. Would it be near enough and how could they contact it? Providence answered by sending a Sunderland on 10 Squadron. Singleton heard it coming and had a crewman up on the mainplane to meet it. He signalled with an Aldis lamp: 'Inform group of our condition. Contact Free French destroyer and lead it to us.' It seemed an age until the Free French destroyer came on the horizon, then another age till it closed in. The destroyer lowered a whaler and soon the survivors were being transferred to the destroyer. But on its second run-in the whaler punched a hole in the Sunderland above the waterline. Singleton reconciled himself to the fact that he couldn't take-off. The destroyer would have to tow him home. He couldn't drift along for ever awaiting calmer conditions: the threat of enemy fighters was far too real.

His crew inflated a small dinghy, passed it out through the rear door and dropped a drogue into it to act as a stabiliser. A tow rope was then made fast to the Sunderland's nose and the operation began with the Frenchmen starting off at ten knots. The effect was instantaneous and startling. When the bow-hands tried to close the nose turret it fouled the rope and no power on earth could have prevented the seas from flooding in through the opening. Within seconds they knew they'd have to man the pumps and within a minute they were at it, pumping hard by hand, while the engineer worked like a man possessed to start the auxiliary motor. Finally he got it going and the engine took over from the men, pumping the water out while it continued to pour in. Singleton was profoundly disturbed. His aircraft was being pounded by pile-driver blows. The seas even crashed high over the mainplane and into the engines. Water was everywhere, streaming and thudding and pounding. He got a man on to the Aldis lamp and flashed for reduced speed. The destroyer cut it down by half to five knots. That was better, but there were still the sudden shocks and unceasing shudders. And then the drogue, that anchor which had held them straight, was torn from its moorings and the Sunderland swung hard to starboard. The destroyer stopped and Singleton started his starboard outer engine. He would have to use power on that side to make up for the drogue, to counter the tendency to swing into wind. They moved off again and Singleton played on the solitary throttle, countering the vagaries of the wind, holding his aircraft straight. The sea wasn't moderating as he had hoped and the aircraft could not continue to survive these shocks undamaged. And now hanging over his head was the certainty of trouble in that engine. Sooner or later it would overheat. Sooner or later it would have to be throttled back and then the future was anybody's guess.

Then a movement near the destroyer's stern caught Singleton's eye. A peculiar object was moving in the water, passing the ship and swinging in towards the Sunderland. Suddenly an excited crewman rocketed up the companion way screaming, 'Skipper, a mine.' By then the aircraft was almost on top of it. Sweating with fear, Singleton rammed his starboard throttle wide open. The thrust of the engine lifted the wing and float high above the water and the mine bobbed beneath and passed astern. Singleton breathed again. But only for a moment. The engineer came up from his instrument panel and tapped the captain on the shoulder. 'Temperature's rising on the starboard outer, Skipper. You'll have to nurse it.' Singleton tried to throttle back, but the aircraft immediately veered to starboard and he had to open the throttle again and the engineer yelled, 'Switch off! Danger point!' Singleton closed the throttle and pulled the cut-out. The aircraft swung hard to the right, the destroyer continued to go forward and the rope stretched out, suddenly taut, but it didn't snap. No. It tore the aircraft's bollard clean away from its mounting and the Sunderland was on the loose on the open sea.

The destroyer hove-to and requested instructions. There were only two things Singleton could do: abandon his aircraft or take-off. He decided to take-off. The perils before him were enormous. He selected an into swell run, seventy degrees out of wind. That alone was a major hazard, but the other way, into the wind and along swell, would have been suicide. He took a deep breath and opened three throttles. The fourth he held back, because with full power the Sunderland would have swung immediately into wind. Slowly speed built up and to keep the aircraft straight was a supreme challenge. It was like controlling a team of horses all bolting in different directions. The seas almost, swamped them. The boat plunged and reared and smashed through waves which enveloped its bows completely, which poured in rivers over the hull and the windscreen, but at last they staggered into the air. And at that moment an urgent call came over the intercom:

'Galley to Captain. We've been holed. I think you'd better come and take a look.'

Singleton clambered down to the galley. He recoiled. In the hull bottom was a jagged hole seven feet long by four feet wide. The wardroom was wrecked. Debris was piled up against the rear wall. The lavatory hung in the slipstream. Now Singleton was faced with the appalling fact that he could never alight again. The moment he put his aircraft to water she'd fill up and go down like a thirty-ton tank. And they couldn't bail out: the squadron hadn't carried a parachute for months. They couldn't alight, they couldn't bale out and without a belly they couldn't even belly-land. There was, of course, only one thing left and Singleton did it. High on the cliff-tops near St. Ann's Head in Wales was a landplane base at Angle aerodrome. At eight o'clock that evening Singleton was circling it at a thousand feet. He was going to try to land his flying-boat on the ground.

The runway came up on his beam. Singleton turned in towards it into wind and ran out full flap. He lined up the flying-boat's long nose on the grass beside the runway and began to close off his throttles. He came in over the cliff-top low and flattened out just above the fence and solid earth was beneath him coming up towards the keel. The Sunderland hit. Twenty-six tons of flying-boat hit the earth and the step cut in like a blunt knife. Singleton held on, straight and level and the ground tore past and parted in a furrow behind him. For a hundred and fifty yards the great boat ploughed on, then turned gently to port and slid over on to one float. The float collapsed and the wing-tip buckled quietly into the earth. The flying-boat without a belly had come safely to ground.[11]

At Benbecula in the Outer Hebrides on the afternoon of 10 June 1943 Fortress pilot Wing Commander Ronald B. Thomson DSO commanding 206 Squadron decided that he would fly the anti-submarine patrol between the Faeroe Islands and Iceland detailed to take off at dawn the following morning. He woke early and joined the crew of 'R for Robert' for breakfast, where he sat with the station armament officer, Flight Lieutenant A. Barratt, a former bomber pilot who had been grounded following a serious crash. Barratt asked to join the Fortress crew 'for some coastal experience' and Thomson readily agreed. After a detailed briefing Thomson took FA704 off at 07.10 hours and headed for the patrol area NW of Faeroes, 350 miles distant. Using powerful binoculars to scan the sea and protecting their eyes against the sun with special anti-dazzle glasses, they kept up a continuous search, flying at 1,500 feet to make as much use of the cloud cover as possible. But, as was forecast, the clouds were small and offered little protection. Thomson continually monitored his engine instruments and had just looked up from a routine check when he and his co-pilot, Flight Sergeant A. Chisnall, both sighted a surfaced U-boat seven miles dead ahead. It was U-417, eight days out after leaving Kristiansund on its first patrol and commanded by Oberleutnant zur see Wolfgang Schreiner. The gunners immediately went to their positions and the wireless operator sent a sighting report as their skipper turned into the attack. Thomson reported later: 'When I saw the U-boat dead ahead, I went straight for her, ordering all guns manned and the bomb doors opened. I came down to sea level and held steadily towards her. The U-boat opened fire at 400 yards and I could feel her stuff hitting us, but carried on over her at about 50 feet, dropping the depth charges and turning off as soon as the conning tower was below. As I turned the U-boat was at right-angles to its original track, but forging through the depth charge scum and I thought to myself that I'd missed. Suddenly things started to happen. The plumes rose high as a flash of light seemed to ripple over the surface and then the bows rose straight up - it was the reverse of a crash-dive. The U-boat started to sink back and I yelled at the top of my voice through the intercom, 'For Heaven's sake, take photos!' Within one minute of the attack the U-boat had entirely disappeared - that was one U-boat which was certainly killed. I flew over the spot and saw 20 to 30 Germans lying in the water looking up at us. Some were covered in oil; some were shaking their fists at us but the majority were prone'. I was just saying 'Poor blighters, they've had it' - as it was pretty cold that far north and there wasn't a ship within miles that could pick them up - when my second pilot broke in and shook me stiff, saying, 'Don't look now, skipper, but oil and petrol are coming out of No 3 engine.' I did look and saw that the engine appeared to be falling out of its mountings. I didn't get time to worry about it, as No 1 and No 2 engines then started shaking and refused to answer my controls. Only No 4 engine responded - it was clear I'd have to ditch. All this happened within about five minutes and the sight of the U-boat crew in the water, some of them shaking their fists at us, was still clear in my mind as I put her down. Thank the Lord it was a sweet landing and nobody was seriously injured. We all clambered into the only dinghy that would inflate, but unfortunately the store-packs came adrift so we had no food, water, distress signals or paddles.'

During its run-in to attack 'R for Robert' had been hit in the nose, wings, bomb bay, cockpit and rear turret and three of its four engines; though none of the crew had been wounded by some stroke of sheer luck. Once ditched, Thomson had dived into the sea to recover the only inflatable dinghy to be seen, but the rough seas meant that he could only hold on to it while the rest of his crew swam over to clamber into it. Just before ditching, however, an R/T SOS had been sent to base, where the rescue operation immediately swung into action. At about 1900 that day the first would-be rescuer - a USN Catalina from Iceland - circled the dinghy and then attempted to land for a pick-up. As one of the ditched crew said later: 'The chances were all against him. We saw him circling and thought he was 'fixing' us for other aircraft or ships. Then we saw his wing floats go down and realised he was going to try a landing. All our hopes went out to him for his as well as our sakes. His first touchdown was near-perfect but a big wave hit the Cat, the starboard prop flew off and she buried her nose straight into the sea. We watched the crew taking to two dinghies and within half an hour the Catalina had disappeared.'

For the next 24 hours both ditched crews remained in sight of each other, but could not link up due to the heavy seas. Thomson's WOp/AG, Flying

Officer J. L. Humphreys, described the conditions:

'It was heart-breaking. We had no paddles and they couldn't reach us. We could only wave at each other. Then in the evening the wind freshened to about 45 knots and we knew we were in for a rough night. Seas rose to about 45 feet high and, although we hauled the cover over our dinghy and clipped it down, plenty of water got in and we had to bale hard all night, using a pair of shoes. It was bitterly cold.'

During the second day a Catalina and a Fortress [flown by Flying Officer Hill] appeared and dropped supply boxes but these fell too far from Thomson's crew to be retrieved. When the next day dawned the American crew had vanished. They were rescued many miles away but there was only one American survivor. Thomson's account continues:

'On the third day, in the afternoon, another Fortress found us and accurately dropped two supply packs. We got them both and these contained water, corned beef, milk tablets and other necessities. It was the first food we'd had in 50 hours - up to then we'd been too seasick to bother with the thought of food. Half an hour later a Catalina arrived and dropped two more containers, comprising more food, plus cigarettes, matches, medical kit and some very welcome chemical hot-water bottles. Our armament officer who had come along 'for the ride' was grey with cold - after our rescue he went down with pneumonia. In mid-afternoon we had another visitor - a Sunderland on 330 Norwegian Squadron - which made two valiant attempts to land. It was heroic and each time the flying boat came in it hit heavy seas and was thrown 20 feet into the air. We hid our eyes, thinking it must crash. The Sunderland's captain, however, realised that he hadn't a hope in such a heavy swell and, thank God, abandoned the attempt.'

Unknown to Thomson's crew they had ditched in the middle of a mined area and though High Speed Launches (HSLs) of the Air Sea Rescue Service were already speeding to the spot, the mines would obviously prevent speedy rescue. At Group Headquarters Squadron Leader J. A. Holmes DFC on 190 Squadron, a veteran Coastal skipper, volunteered to fly a Catalina for a pick-up attempt. With a crew of five and his aircraft (FP102/L) stripped of all unnecessary gear, Holmes took off:

'We set course very carefully and had a minimum petrol load in order not to lose time. After about three hours we located the dinghy - a tiny yellow dot on a vast grey sea. Flying low to size up the state of the sea and the best position for landing, I ordered my crew to prepare our own dinghies in case we crashed and then turned in to land. Throttling back I came in slow with the nose high, cleared one big lump of sea by a touch of engines and then stalled onto the water. The Catalina bounced twice, hovered and then fell back onto the water with an impact which shook the whole aircraft. Luckily there was no damage and I then caught sight of the dinghy.

'We taxied towards it, crabwise and it was a slow job because every time I tried to turn the aircraft dug its nose in and we took green over the bows. At last we managed to throw the Fortress crew a line and when we hauled the dinghy in it seemed incredible that eight people could be crowded into so small a space. They looked weary and bedraggled and hung on to our line for dear life; yet they managed a grin and a word of thanks as they came aboard. We took the weakest of them on the bunks and the others sat on the fuselage floor as we made ready for take-off. None of us were quite sure just what might happen in the next 60 seconds - there were 13 of us aboard. We shouted to the passengers to brace themselves and to expect some bounces before we became airborne. A clear lane opened up in the seas ahead, so I pushed the throttles fully open and we surged forward. I'd decided to haul back everything at 50 knots, relying upon power to hold us in the air. We rushed over one swell, down into the trough, then up the side of another. Then we were thrown into the air as the needle touched fifty. There we stayed - she came off like a bird.'

Two months after their ordeal, it was announced that Wing Commander Thomson and navigator, Flying Officer J. Clark, who had sustained a damaged back and Humphreys had each been awarded the DFC. For his gallant rescue flight, Jack Holmes was awarded a Bar to his DFC. Thomson remained in the RAF and added the CB to his decorations before retiring as an air vice-marshal. Holmes also remained in the service, retiring as an air commodore in 1967.[12]

In the Bay of Biscay on 2 September Ju 88s shot down two Liberators on 224 Squadron. Flying Officer J. V. Gibson took off at dawn and failed to return. At 10.30 am Canadian Flying Officer G. H. Wharram took FL938 'P-Peter' off from Gibraltar's runway on a later patrol, which was uneventful until they were 100 miles north of Cape Finisterre, where the murky weather experienced off the Portuguese coast had cleared to leave a thin layer of cloud at 5,000 feet. After investigating a small ship flying the Irish flag, a fast-moving contact was detected on radar and moments later the gunners reported that four Ju 88s were approaching. One pulled away to make a frontal attack. Whahram turned to reduce the attack angle as he started to climb for the cloud, but the Junkers' first burst exploded in the cockpit. Whahram cried out and collapsed dead within seconds. Flight Sergeant Ron 'Jack' Foss, the second pilot, immediately took control of the badly damaged Liberator and ordered Pilot Officer D. Johnstone to drag Wharram clear of his seat and take up his place to give assistance.[13]After a struggle, the captain's body was pulled clear and Johnstone was able to help Foss with the aircraft's controls and to give him instructions as the German fighters turned in for further beam and rear attacks. The first phase of the attack lasted about 20 minutes. Foss was able to ward off some attacks by using the sparse cloud, but the Liberator was hit repeatedly. The mid-upper turret soon became unserviceable. Sergeant E. A. Maloney the rear gunner, claimed to have hit one of the fighters, which left the scene trailing smoke before he was killed by a further burst of fire from the German fighters. 'Jack' Foss recalled the subsequent events to Hector Bolitho:

'The weather was just the type that Coastal Command boys hope for; a steady wind, a warm and pleasant atmosphere, with just enough cloud to protect us in case enemy fighters found and attacked us over the Bay of

Biscay. Everyone was in high spirits. We wished to find and destroy a U-boat, which our crew hadn't done up to then. This coupled with the ideal weather, was the reason for our feeling joyful and pleased. At one o'clock in the afternoon everything was going fine. We were travelling fairly close to the Spanish coast. It looked peaceful. We sighted a few small Spanish fishing vessels, busy hurrying to and fro. The navigator came through on the intercom, telling us to alter course westwards. Our Skipper did this with alacrity. Like the rest of us, he was anxious to get into the real patrol area where U-boats are most likely to be found and we hope, sunk.

'At two o'clock, as we flew westwards, the clouds began to thin out and the wind gained in strength until there was no cloud to be seen. The wind had reached a speed of about thirty knots and the sea was no longer the calm pond that it was. It was a rough medley of white horses, chasing each other frantically across the ocean. The waves must have been up to thirty feet in height. We felt sorry for any sailor who might be down there roughing it, little dreaming of what was soon to come. At a quarter past two we had just altered to a northerly course when the observer sighted something to starboard. I thought 'is this the chance we've been waiting for at last.' The skipper was all smiles and he immediately altered course and I gave the order to open the bomb doors. At the same time I increased the revs so that we would have more power should we need it.

'As we got nearer, everyone on the flight deck was craning their necks. The observer was craning his neck out from his little compartment and asking if it was a sub. At first it seemed as if we were to be lucky. We could see a thin trail of smoke going back with the wind, as of a U-boat recharging his batteries. Everything was set. The bomb-aimer was in position, the bombs selected and the radio operator was ready to dash out the sighting report on his keys. We were quite close before one of the gunners shouted over the intercom. 'It's a 'bloody' little fishing vessel.' And so it was. A little fishing smack with *Eire* painted along the side. The things we said about fishing smacks in general I don't think need repeating. Anyone with half a thought can easily read between the lines.

'We circled the boat once at about 200 feet, getting various details about it, such as weight, markings, course and speed; etc. We were close enough to see the fishing lines over the side. Then we climbed away on course. At ten minutes past three we had just levelled off at about 3,000 feet, everything ship-shape, when we saw what was to prove a very fatal, solitary cumulus cloud. As we approached it, one of our gunners shouted, 'Aircraft dead ahead just entered cloud.' The skipper immediately altered course to starboard, as he didn't like the idea of an aircraft dodging into cloud. Then, out of the corner of his eye he sighted another aircraft attacking in a dive from the port bow. He immediately shouted over the intercom, 'Look out boys! Junkers! Jettison bombs.'

'While he shouted that, he was turning into the attack, hoping to get out of the enemy's sights. We both looked up and were just thanking God that we had foiled his attack when I saw flames spitting from the leading edges of the Junkers' wings. It was but a second later that the skipper turned round to me and said, 'They've got me' and then seemed to go stiff.

'As I took over the controls, I glanced around at him. A very upsetting feeling came over me because I could see the hole in his chest where the cannon shell had passed through. I shouted over the intercom that the skipper was hit but got no reply. It was several minutes later that I realized that the intercom was unserviceable. Then a horrifying dryness came into my throat. I couldn't swallow or part my tongue from the roof of my mouth because I realized that without fighter control from one of the gunners it was really a matter of time, unless clouds came along, before we were shot down. Because if the pilot doesn't know they are attacking from behind he can't do much about it, until it is really too late.

'At twenty minutes past three we knew beyond all doubt that there were four of them attacking us. And we knew that we would be very lucky indeed if we got away from them as there was still not a cloud in the sky. The little cloud the Junkers had been dodging in and out of was far away behind us. In any case, it was far too small to conceal our Liberator. For the next two or three minutes the four Junkers circled around us while I was busy keeping the aircraft doing everything that they teach one not to at training school. Five minutes after, the second attack began, from the same Junkers as before. The other three were getting into position to attack. They were out of the range of our guns.

'This time it was a starboard frontal attack. I immediately turned into the attack, undulating fiercely. But this time he really had us fair and square in his sights, I had just pushed the aircraft over into an almost vertical bank when I looked up and saw flames coming from his wings again. My heart almost stopped beating, because this attack was identical in position to the first attack when the skipper had got his. But I was lucky again as regards to myself not being hit, but poor [Pilot Officer J. R.] 'Jimmy' Wilcox in the mid-upper was hit badly. He had bullets in his foot, leg and in his rear and scratches all over his face and neck. He fell more than climbed out of the turret. I shouted for someone else to get in the turret quickly as that turret has 0.5 guns and Jerry doesn't like those. [Canadian Flying Officer J. C.] 'Jack' Miller [the navigator, whose back was crushed and had bullet wounds in back and feet] was just about to get into the turret when Jimmy called to him and said 'It's no use. The turret feeder block is busted.' It was well and truly busted, putting the turret absolutely unserviceable.

'While I had been throwing the aircraft about I had noticed that the controls were getting difficult to move. It wasn't until I glanced around at the skipper's seat that I found out why. The skipper had somehow got jammed in the controls during the first part of the action. I would have got him out earlier had I been able to. I shouted to Flying Officer Thornton [sic] behind me, who was a passenger, to get him out of the seat and sit there himself. After a bit of hard struggling he did. I was still throwing the aircraft about the sky as if it was a fighter and it is no easy job to keep one's balance in an aircraft when it is being flown like that.

'Thornton [sic] had no sooner sat in the seat behind the armour plating when a hail of cannon shells came screaming through the aircraft, smashing every instrument on the panel except the air-speed indicator and thudding into the armour plating at our backs. It was a good job that he moved into that seat otherwise he would have been smashed to pieces later. It was in this third attack that our tail turret was smashed to pieces. The tail gunner got a cannon shell through his backbone. Even though he was fatally wounded he crawled out of the tail turret, just in time to get to one of the side guns. Then he got a good burst in at one of them, just as he died. Although none of us saw, we believe that Junkers crashed into the sea because from that moment, there were only three attacking us.

'Suddenly the engineer came rushing out of the bomb bay. He knocked my hand off the throttles and shouted as he was feathering the prop that our No. 2 engine was on fire. Luckily for all of us the fire went out when the engine stopped turning. But by that time they had got a really good burst into our No.3 engine. It was set on fire and throwing a 30 foot flame alongside the aircraft. It was in that attack that I think everyone in the aircraft got wounded as the bullets and cannon shells absolutely raked the aircraft from tip to tail. It was in this attack that I got wounded in the arms and legs.

'I went to feather No. 3 engine, but there were no levers there to pull. When I tried to get to the engine fire extinguisher alongside me I found that it was covered with twisted bars of metal which the cannon shells had done in one of the attacks. From that time on they just did attack after attack. As I was getting weak I told Thornton to push or pull the control column with me, so that I could keep the action fierce.

'The controls by this time were getting fairly mushy. The aileron control was almost unserviceable. The flames were beginning to cook the petrol, the port wheel was hanging limply down, the flaps were unserviceable, two engines had gone and the outer two were starting to seize up. So I decided to ditch. I shouted to the boys, 'Emergency hatch open, ditching.' It wasn't easy for them to move because everyone of them was wounded.

'When the boys were in their places, I started the aircraft into a shallow dive as I was only about a thousand feet up. I cut the throttles right back and dived to a speed of about 200 knots before levelling out just above the tops of the waves. It wasn't a case of landing with wind. We had to go along the swells of the sea, until the aircraft was down near stalling speed. Then I sat her down before a wave could knock us down. This was done more by good luck than judgment. The aircraft immediately sank and we went down with it twenty feet under water - completely dark. The terrific impact with the water had broken its back and almost ours as well. It was like hitting a brick wall at a hundred miles an hour. It wasn't a case of helping one another under the water. For one thing, it was far too dark to see anything. I just breathed in water and thought, 'Here it is.' We all must have been under there nearly two minutes before any of us struggled free. No one can realize the horrible feeling it gives one, to be jammed in an aircraft under water and slowly drowning. But we did struggle free and floated to the surface.

'When we finally got to the surface, that is, all except the skipper and Pat [Maloney], I suddenly saw daylight and took in a breath of air. We looked about and were appalled to see only one dinghy. The rest had gone down with the aircraft, except the one we used [which was designed to take five men only] and one small one-man dinghy. This one sank as soon as it was undone as it was riddled with shrapnel.[14] It wasn't easy getting seven of us into the two-man dinghy. Our Mae Wests had been riddled and didn't keep us up. Some could not swim and their wounds made it difficult to hoist them aboard. The sea was rough. We were sick over the side from the rough sea and from swallowing so much sea water.

'We hadn't been in the dinghy more than an hour when we sighted smoke on the horizon. Somebody said, 'Surely we're not saved already.' The wireless operator started to wave the telescopic flag frantically. It was one we had found in the dinghy. The smoke came nearer and we saw the shape of a vessel. It was altering course towards us. We all started talking and cheering like wildfire as we thought we were going to be picked up by some boat and saved from the dinghy experience with only Horlicks tablets to eat and two small tins of water between the seven of us. As the craft got nearer we recognized it as a 517-ton U-boat with a modified conning tower. It was dirty yellowish in colour. The navigator gave the order not to answer any questions but just say 'water,' which we did. The U-boat came to within twenty yards. We saw the Germans quite clearly. They were clean-shaven and wearing uniforms. One of them called, 'You British. You Allies?' We did not answer. We just shouted, 'Water!' When the commander of the U-boat gathered from our unresponsiveness that we didn't intend saying anything, he gave orders to his men to carry on, which they did, roughly in a westerly direction. 'Ben' [Johnstone, who had shrapnel wounds in hands and feet] said, 'Would you sooner be taken prisoner, rather than risk your chance of being picked up.'

We all said, 'No, we'd sooner take the chance.' We were all highly thankful as none of us wished to be taken prisoner, especially on board a U-boat. We were thankful also because we were all expecting to be raked with machine-gun bullets at any moment and we were ready to dive into the water as soon as any of the Germans got behind a gun. Although some of us were badly wounded and dying, there still remained the thought that life is sweet and we were determined to live as long as possible. Had they fired on us, I don't doubt that we would all have been killed, even if we had dived under the water. We couldn't have stayed underwater forever and they would be certain to have got us when we came up. When the U-boat had passed on, we really gave vent to our feelings: a very lurid description of what we thought about U-boats and Germans in general. The description certainly isn't befitting to write on paper. There were some really choice words: among them, 'The bastards have gone.'

'Later on in the evening, we took stock of what we had and what we didn't have. The results were not very encouraging. We only had two small cans of water, one small tin of orange juice, a green lemon and the usual Horlicks tablets and chocolate which we carry on our persons for such emergencies as this. As you can see, this was not going to last us long between seven of us. And there was no knowing when we may be picked up, if ever. 'Ben' said, 'Well, boys, there isn't much chance of shipping being this far down in the Bay.' Our morale was very low for a short while, but in true English fashion we soon got over our low feelings and started licking our wounds and seeing how badly wounded each of us was. 'Ben' had wounds everywhere; a lot of them being caused by the ditching and the rest by bullets and shrapnel. Jimmy Wilcox had bullet wounds in his face and leg and also his rear. We had to lay him down in the bottom of the dinghy, as he was in so much pain. Then there was Jack Miller, he had the front part of his leg blown off by a cannon shell. He said, 'Even if we are saved I suppose I shall have to have my leg off when we get back.' Dick Bareham had a bullet right between the shoulder blades. [Sergeant M. W. 'Mike'] Dilkes [the radio operator], Jerry Wilcox and myself were the most fortunate of us all. Mike only had a cannon shell blow a piece out of the side of his knee. 'Thornton' had a scratch on one of his fingers and myself a bullet in the wrist and shrapnel in the knees. The officer was a bit aloof at first but we called him by his Christian name the second day. When we had finished bandaging ourselves with odd bits of torn shirt and handkerchiefs, we settled down as best as possible along the walls of the dinghy bracing ourselves so that we wouldn't fall back into the water. It was terribly cramped. Had any of us fallen out I doubt if the rest of us could have got him back again because we were beginning to feel the reaction from the attack and the ditching; also from the experience of being jammed in the aircraft under water.

'That night the sea calmed down slightly and we managed to get a drogue out to keep us headed into the waves so that the dinghy would not be turned over.

'That night was hell to us. The biting wind went right through us, like a knife. We were soaked through and through again. There was no covering to protect us in any way whatsoever. Our wounds were paining us horribly because our circulation was still fairly good. As the night went on each of us wanted to turn around or move our legs because of a cramped feeling we kept getting, because of the lack of space to stretch out comfortably. This in the dead of night with the sea throwing us around was no easy matter. We didn't talk much. Just mumbled 'Bloody cold,' or 'For heaven's sake keep still' when someone moved. Never before were any of us so thankful as when the dawn came. It meant that soon the sun would be up, the wind would perhaps drop and the possibilities of being seen by an aircraft would be far greater.

'All that day we kept a watchful eye out for aircraft or ships and as the day went by we were all getting lower and lower in ourselves. We just looked at each other. We were chilled to the marrow of our bones. We had not even seen as much as a bird or a bit of driftwood. After we had had our meals of Horlicks tablets and a suck of the lemon all round, the lemon being finished after this, we began to settle down for another night. We wondered if we could stand another day. It was getting late in the day and soon the sun would be down below the horizon and we were just about to give up hope when someone, I believe it was Mike, sighted a Sunderland a few miles away. We said, 'Good boy, Mike, nice work.' Everyone cheered and began waving frantically. But it was all to no avail as the Sunderland didn't see us at all. One could then read the thoughts of everyone quite easily as it was so plain to be seen. I thought of my wife and the little baby she is going to have. And of my people who are not in very good health. I wondered how they would be now as they were sure to have been told I was missing. That thought was more horrible to me than anything I was suffering in the dinghy.

'That night again was a horror. We had had no food or anything warm to drink that would help to keep out the bitter cold. All that night was just one long nightmare and by the time dawn had come, we were so cold that the pain from our wounds had ceased. But another pain was coming, that of immersion feet and legs caused by the continual soaking from the sea. This meant that to bend or unbend our legs was sheer agony and torture. And we had to keep moving every now and then because of cramp in our bodies. We had plenty of pain and agony.

'All that day we kept watch for aircraft until we felt, that our eyes would drop out from staring. It wasn't until about six o'clock in the evening that we sighted an aircraft in the distance. But it was even too far away for us to recognize what it was, let alone signal to it. So we just gave that one up as a bad job. We had our meal which was the usual Horlicks tablets and the tin of orange juice this time. Then we settled down as best we could to wait for the night of horror that was soon to come. That night the sea was very rough. The ones that could took it in turns all night to keep the dinghy headed into the sea with an oar which we had found under the rubber seat. It was torture anew for us, because to do this we had to sit upright in the dinghy and face the full blast of the weather. By the time the next one's turn came the one who had been guiding the dinghy was frozen stiff.

'The following morning when it was light enough to see; we took stock of ourselves. Everyone was blue with cold and it was almost impossible for any of us to move our legs. Poor Jimmy and Jack; their wounds were beginning to go gangrenous. They could see it and it turned them slightly hysterical. We managed to quieten them down though, with such things as: 'We are bound to be seen today' and giving everyone a piece of chocolate, which is part of the small emergency pack. I can say, with the deepest of sincerity, that a piece of chocolate to us in our condition, was thought greater of and treasured more than a home-cooked dinner would be to people who had plenty. The mere thought of a home-cooked meal was nearly enough to send us mad. Our condition was so low by this time and our nerves so frayed that we began to be snappy and quick-tempered towards one another. We barked at each other, 'Watch my foot,' or 'Look out for my arm.' I think if it hadn't been for the fact that two aircraft passed nearby four or five miles away, we would probably have started fighting. They missed us of course; the aircraft, but they gave us hope. The slightest thing anyone did or said that didn't quite suit the other person nearby, then an argument started straight away. All that day it was just one argument after another and by the time nightfall came we each and every one of us were utterly exhausted.

'That night again was the same as the other nights, just one long torture. The wind was getting colder than ever, for we had been drifting in a northerly direction all the time. In one way this helped us, because of the greater possibility of seeing ships. But in another way it was worse for us, because the water was getting colder. As I have said before, the wind, coupled with the fact that our resistance was now very low, had rather drastic effects on our will to live.

'Early next morning one of the boys started muttering to himself and flinging his arms about. Jack and I gave him some morphia. Then Jack cuddled into him to keep him warm and I think that was one of the main reasons why he kept going that day, as he was able to get some warmth back into his body. But it also meant that Jack was getting worse, as he had nothing with which he could replace the heat. In the afternoon of that day we had luck at last. Dick sighted a Sunderland and we all waved our hands and the flag as best we could. When it saw us and altered course towards us, none of us could speak. We all had a lump in our throat as we were so happy to think at last that we were going to be saved, that we were almost crying. We signalled frantically for the aircraft to land as the sea was smooth enough. The captain realized what we needed for he dived over us and dropped Horlicks tablets and water in some Mae Wests to which we frantically paddled. When we got the water in the dinghy we all went crazy for a while because instead of trying to save it for as long as possible, we just drank tin after tin until the whole dozen tins had gone. Soon after dropping the water the Sunderland made off for base, as his fuel was probably getting low by this time. That night Catalinas came over with searchlights to keep in touch with us. But we had nothing to signal back. One of the flame floats they dropped fell near to us. The flame was five or six feet high and we had to paddle away or it would set us on fire. Although the searchlights swept across us several times, they didn't seem somehow to see us and just before midnight they gave it up and went away.

'The next day never seemed to be coming as we were all so eager to have another aircraft around us to show that they were still in touch with us. Though we strained our eyes continually that day, we never saw an aircraft anywhere. It wasn't until late in the afternoon that we gave up hope and resigned ourselves to our fate. Late that evening we decided to try fishing with bent hairpins and a piece of string. We bought the hairpins in Gib for our wives. We used chewing gum for bait. We tried for over two hours but we had no luck and gave it up as a bad job. We tried a piece of rag as bait and the fish came up to the surface. But they would not bite. If we had caught any fish, it wouldn't have been fried either, as by this time we were hungry enough to eat it raw and really enjoy it. In any case there wasn't likely to be any frying-pan on the dinghy with which to fry the fish, so fried fish and raw fish were to us just a thought.

'After we had given up fishing, we tried knocking down seagulls which were flying around us, fully determined to eat them raw and suck their blood. There were about twelve of them, crying and swooping.

'We beckoned them with our fingers and said, 'Come nearer my beauty.' But they were far too quick for us to hit with the oar and so we had to go hungry again, only having one Horlicks tablet each that day.'

During the morning of their sixth day in the dinghy they were sighted by a Sunderland and a Catalina, the latter dropping more supplies. They were too weak to recover all the supplies, but amongst those they were able to haul aboard were 12 tins of water and some distress signals and flares. They spent the afternoon alone. Sergeant D. H. 'Dick' Bareham the engineer had become very weak and delirious and Pilot Officer W. R. 'Bill' Collins, who had a deep wound in the left leg was weakening. During the night a Catalina was heard and Foss and Johnstone let off some flares; the aircraft flew overhead and dropped a circle of flares around the dinghy.

'As the night came' continues Foss 'we began to get very thirsty and try as we could to resist it, in the end we were drinking sea water like ordinary water. When the first one [Miller] drank it, we said, 'Stop, you'll go mad.' But he did not stop. We all drank it in the end: I think that was one of the main things that hastened his death, because just around midnight he died. [Miller became delirious and sank into a coma. They gave him two injections from the first aid ampoules. Wilcox was also showing signs of collapse and they gave him more water, but during the night he became delirious, went over the side of the dinghy and sank out of sight. Miller died just after dark and they put him over the side after saying a few prayers]. 'We stripped him and took his personal effects and then we buried him at sea. Jack said a little prayer for him, the rest of us closing our eyes and placing our hands together. Early the following morning [Wilcox] died and we did the same again and I think those two prayers were the sincerest I have ever heard, as every word was meant and it came from the bottom of all our hearts.[15]

'Early the following morning two Sunderlands arrived, but we were far too gloomy to shout or cheer. We just acknowledged them and when they dropped their supplies we picked some of it up, being far too weak to get it all. They dropped a first-aid kit on a parachute, but although we tried hard, the remaining five of us, we just could not get it aboard. We were too weak. So we cut the parachute away and used it to break the wind. In one of the packs we picked up there were some distress signals and our eyes glistened when we saw these, as it meant we could keep in touch with the aircraft that night.

'The dinghy by this time was leaking badly at the valve and we had to pump it up about every hour. This was using up all our remaining strength, but we managed to keep going somehow. That night Catalinas came over again with searchlights. This time we were prepared and we let off distress signals every now and then and kept in touch with them until they left for their base.

'Early the following morning one of them went delirious and after trying to bite everyone for about half an hour, he collapsed in the bottom of the dinghy. He tried to bite at Bill Collins' jugular vein, to suck his blood.

'After this little bit of trouble we settled down in a more or less dopey condition. About an hour later two Sunderlands came along, one of them circling us and the other one going off in one direction and returning again. We knew what this meant, but by this time we were far too gone to even trouble about being saved. We agreed to pump the dinghy up once more and if we weren't picked up by the time it deflated, we would go down with it, as our will to live had long been extinguished.

'Luckily, about twelve minutes after we had made this decision, HMS *Wild Goose*[16] appeared on the horizon. Instead of cheering or shouting with joy we all just sat there with tears in our eyes, for at last we were saved.'

The Sunderlands guided the sloop to the dinghy. At 9 am a whaler was lowered with Surgeon Lieutenant G. Stewart RNVR on board. The doctor found the airmen huddled close together, very wet, with their feet immersed in water, but surprisingly alert and fairly lively, except for Bareham, who was described as 'comatose and unbelievably cold'. Only Foss was able to transfer to the whaler, which took the dinghy in tow to the sloop where the remainder were transferred individually. Foss recalled being taken below 'into the marvellous warmth' and given boiling coffee'; 'which we drank as if it were only lukewarm. All our feelings had gone out of our bodies. The doctor took charge of us then and as there wasn't room for all of us in his ward I was taken aft to a cabin. Later that night another [Bareham] died and sometime later Bill [Collins] died as well. [Collins appeared to respond well initially, although he had suffered badly in the dinghy and the gaping wound in his leg needed urgent treatment. He spent a fitful night and started hallucinating the following morning. At 1.30 pm he suddenly collapsed and died a few hours later]. The doctor did not tell me until about a week later, as he wanted me strong enough to be able to take it, in case it had a fatal effect on me. All that day I lay in bed thinking of them, what they had gone through, how they had suffered and when they were safe aboard ship to suddenly pass away and to have suffered in vain. The Navy gave them a military funeral at sea and there they lay at rest, two men, who gave their lives for their country, so that it may be free and beautiful to live in for years to come. [The three survivors slowly improved and when *Wild Goose* docked at Liverpool on 21 September they were admitted to hospital where they spent the next few weeks making a full recovery]. So out of the nine of us who started from Gibraltar that fateful day, only three of us are now living to tell the tale of an experience which makes us have a hardened outlook on life; not smiling or laughing like we used to, but remembering those seven horrible days as if it had only just happened.'

Within a few weeks, it was announced that Flying Officer Johnstone had been awarded the DSO. Dilkes, who had tended the emergency radio throughout the ordeal and helped his colleagues without complaint, was awarded the DFM. Ron Foss received the Conspicuous Gallantry Medal (CGM), an award for gallantry in the air second only to the Victoria Cross. He was also commissioned and eventually retired from the RAF as a squadron leader.[17]

On 3 September Sunderland DD861 'P-Peter' on 422 Squadron RCAF captained by Flying Officer Jacques de le Paulle was airborne at 0100 hours from Castle Archdale for an anti-submarine patrol on the western edge of the Bay of Biscay with an ETA at base of 1425 hours. Generally known as 'De Loop' Jacques de la Paulle was born in New York to a French family. He was educated in France and at the outbreak of the war he was studying medicine at the Sorbonne in Paris. He volunteered to be an ambulance driver and for his gallantry after the German advance into France he was awarded the Croix de Guerre. After the fall of France he escaped back to the United States, crossed the border into Canada and joined the RCAF to train as a pilot in April 1941. By the middle of 1943 he had flown ten anti-submarine patrols as the captain of a Sunderland flying boat.

Three hours into the patrol and without warning, the starboard outer engine caught fire, exploded and dropped into the sea, taking with it the float and part of the wing. It also severed the fuel lines to the starboard inner engine, which started to fail. With the combined efforts of de la Paulle and his American co-pilot, the Flying Officer Romeo Freer RCAF, it was just possible to keep the Sunderland circling long enough for three SOS signals to be sent as urgent preparations were made to ditch the huge flying boat. The sea was rough and the starboard wing dug into the sea as the Sunderland alighted, allowing water to rush in through a large hole that appeared in the bows. Flight Sergeant Ken Middleton the flight engineer had removed the astrodome and together with the captain and the wireless operator he pulled the 'H' dinghy through the opening. As it fell off the wing, it pulled de la Paulle into the sea. The other two left the aircraft with Romeo Freer, who by this time was up to his neck in water and unable to grasp the emergency radio. De la Paulle opened the dinghy (No.1) as he floated in the water and it inflated immediately. Four of the crew climbed in as de la Paulle swam after the emergency pack, which had become detached and started to float away. The pack did not survive intact and the Very pistol was lost. Almost immediately the dinghy deflated, probably because it had been torn by some of the wreckage. The other seven members of the crew were on the lower deck of the Sunderland when it hit the water. Most had been able to brace for the impact and only minor injuries were sustained. There had been insufficient time to jettison the depth charges and the second navigator, Sergeant Joyce, had the presence of mind to tear the fusing wires away from them. One of the wireless operators released a pigeon, which flew away.

Third pilot Don Wells recalls: 'Barely a minute passed from the time the engine caught fire until we were in the drink. The hull was badly crushed and the plane started to sink; there was a lot of shouting of orders but no panic. I went aft to see if the rear gunner was all right and to release the dinghy which was stowed by the rear door. The aircraft was sinking by the nose and by the time the dinghy was pushed out of the rear door we were almost 40 foot high in the air. I dived feet first, came up spluttering and heard someone shouting about the DCs not being defused, but it was a false rumour. We counted heads and found that everyone was on the surface. The whole crew of twelve had survived; the only injury being to navigator

Pilot Officer A. Bolton, who had a nasty cut on the head. One dinghy was torn and had to be repaired before we were all out of the water. The skipper was cool and confident as though this sort of thing had happened to him lots of times. He set about taking stock. We knew that we were about 250 miles from the northern coast of Spain and although an SOS had been sent it must have been short. Skipper calculated that our rations should be apportioned on the basis of a 14-day voyage; this worked out to half a pint of water, one Horlicks tablet, half an ounce of chocolate and one stick of chewing gum per day, per man. We were also equipped with a couple of spray sheets, canvas pails for baling, flares, paddles and some small lines which were used to lash the two dinghies together. The portable radio transmitter had been left in the aircraft, jammed under the navigator's table. The rubber dinghy is not a comfortable place to spend time especially in rough water. With six men in each rubber ring there was little room to move; the only worthwhile occupation was talking. Considering that we had crew members from England, Scotland, France, Canada and USA, I feel we were reasonably civil.

'By mid-afternoon we were adjusted to our situation and I managed to doze off in the night despite the discomfort of having a wave break over us every little while. Time tended to drag, baling was a constant chore, the cigarettes had all disappeared; we took turns watching the horizon for ship or plane.'

That first day they tried to dry their clothes and rations were apportioned on the basis that they could be at sea for at least twelve days. The mast was erected and used with the dinghy apron to sail in an easterly direction. All twelve Mae Wests were inflated and tied together to make a long tail to increase the chances of being sighted. Most of the crew were seasick, when none of them drank or ate. The next day they rationed themselves to a teaspoon of water and three Horlicks tablets each and some chewing gum.

'The second day was quite warm' continues Wells 'but a stiff gale came up in the night and we had to hold on to avoid capsizing. Two separate aircraft flew over that day. We fired off flares but were not seen. We were somehow cheered by this and there was a general discussion about what we would do when we next got leave in London. Just after noon on the third day, a Liberator with USA markings [possibly sighted a flash from the base of the first-aid tin which Don Wells had used as a signalling mirror] flew right over us, turned and circled. Great excitement and useless shouting. After a few more laps the [6 Squadron USAAF Liberator commanded by Lieutenant Dudock] came over with flaps down and dropped a parachute bag with fair accuracy. The bag hit the water about 200 yards off and our skipper stripped off, dived in and struck out through the waves to retrieve it. After a longish swim he managed to bring the bag back and was pulled aboard. The bag contained a dozen oranges, three packets of American cigarettes and a note saying. 'Don't go away. Help is coming.' A couple of long hours later a beautiful Sunderland [homed by Dudock after sending a sighting report] appeared from the north and we cheered.'

The Sunderland was JM679 'R-Robert' on 228 Squadron captained by Flight Lieutenant Howard C. Armstrong who was airborne at 0855 hours on 6 September for an A/S patrol before sighting the dinghies at 1728 hours. Armstrong sought permission to alight and Headquarters 19 Group agreed for an attempt to be made at the captain's discretion. The survivors waved the flying boat away as they were aware of the heavy swell but, after jettisoning the depth charges and making two attempts, Armstrong found the right trough and dropped it 'like a real pro'. Armstrong bounced 50 feet into the air due to the heavy swell with 45 knots IAS and just managed to remain airborne after sinking to sea level and gaining 60 knots IAS. The swell was such that the crew of 'R-Robert' frequently lost sight of the two dinghies as they taxied towards them. Eventually Armstrong managed to get close and the twelve men paddled to meet the aircraft, where they were dragged on board.

Don Wells continues: 'We were all rather weak after three days of soaking in salt water and had to be helped into the aircraft. I was given a cup of tea and placed in the bomb bay with my back to the wall.' The four engines were restarted and Armstrong started the take off run. 'The take-off was awesome' [the aircraft was virtually thrown into the air at 50 knots and it staggered just above the sea, slowly gaining speed]; 'we were sure the aircraft would come apart but the pilot finally got it into the air and set course for home. The flight was not entirely uneventful as we came a bit close to Brest (it was dark at that time) and the AA gunners had a go at us. Not too long after we were landing at Pembroke Dock. The aircraft was out of fuel and the tide was out as well. After an interminable wait we were towed to the pier and managed to climb to the top of a lot of steps and walk a very long way along the pier to dry land. The day after, we met the 228 Squadron crew briefly and on 8 September our own CO [Wing Commander Skey] flew to Pembroke Dock and took us back to our base at Bowmore.'

The two pilots, plus the five Canadians and five Englishmen that made up de la Paulle's crew, arrived back at Pembroke Dock at 10.45 pm. As the Sunderland taxied on to its moorings, it ran out of fuel.

The survivors were loud in their praise of their captain, Jacques de la Paulle. One commented: 'The skipper was a model of leadership. The crew certainly had a great deal of respect for his abilities.' The crew returned to complete a tour of operations. Jacques de la Paulle was awarded the DFC in April 1944, when the citation made particular mention of his leadership during the ditching episode. A few weeks after the rescue, Flight Lieutenant Armstrong was also awarded the DFC, but shortly afterwards he and six other members of his crew were killed when their Sunderland hit Blue Stack Mountain in County Donegal.[18]

On 8 October 1943 destroyer HMS *Mahratta* happened by and rescued the six crew of a Halifax on 58 Squadron flown by Flying Officer Eric L. Hartley, who was shot down on 27 September attacking U-221 in the Bay of Biscay, 420 miles South-west of Cape Clear. Hartley, who was on his 28th anti-submarine patrol, dropped eight depth charges that sank the submarine which was commanded by Kapitänleutnant Hans Trojer, the holder of the Knight's Cross. One of the most experienced U-boat captains; Trojer was on his fifth patrol as a captain. Hartley's rear gunner, 19-year old Sergeant Bob Triggol, flying on his first operation, saw the U-boat rear almost vertically before it slipped beneath the waves with the loss of all 50 hands, but he was immediately ordered to his ditching position. Return fire had hit the starboard fuel tank and set the Halifax on fire. Hartley struggled with the controls and had to crash land on the sea just three miles beyond the attack position. The tail broke off the Halifax and Triggol went down with the aircraft. Sergeant M. Griffiths was dazed and, despite gallant efforts to rescue him, he floated away and was lost. Group Captain Roger C. Mead DFC AFC, station commander of Holmsley South airfield, who had been acting as second pilot to gain experience and Hartley and four crew were able to scramble into the inflatable life raft, which had inflated on impact.[19]

Due to the speed of evacuation from the sinking Halifax, the emergency rations and survival aids could not be recovered. With few provisions, 700 miles from home and with the likelihood of their SOS going unheard due to the low altitude of the bomber, the six survivors settled in for a long wait. Over the next two days they tried to make themselves as comfortable as possible in the overcrowded life raft. They took stock of their situation and found that they had five pints of water and some emergency rations, which included Horlicks tablets, a few barley sugar sweets, chocolate and a tube of condensed milk. On the second full day they were able to dry out some clothing and each had two Horlicks tablets at 6 pm and a mouthful of water, an event that became a nightly ritual. In order to conserve their meagre supplies they had decided not to eat or drink anything for the first 48 hours.[20] Roger Mead's notes vividly describe their 11-day nightmare.

'First day: Decided to eat and drink nothing for two days. All badly shocked. I was knocked about a bit. First wireless operator/air gunner burned on face. All seasick, But none seriously hurt and all in pretty good condition. First night cold and wet.

'Second day: Drizzle. Crew's condition excellent. All chirped up a lot and kept our heads, convinced we would be picked up.

'Third day: Drizzle at first, but we dried our clothes when weather cleared up. Tried some fishing. Made lines out of some odd earth and aerial wires and fish-hooks with safety pins. No luck. Found some chocolate spoiled by water; ate half an ounce and two milk tablets each. Bad night - cold, wet and very uncomfortable. Between us kept watch all night, guessing the hours. Those nights were hell.

'Fourth day: Issued one small piece of chewing gum apiece; given back at lunch-time for bait. Again no fish, Two milk tablets each. Said morning and evening prayers. Another bad night - cold and wet. Water slopping over into dinghy.

'Fifth day: Nice, fine day. Clothes dry. Decided on one milk tablet each, four times a day. Had my shoes and socks off when sea rose to real Atlantic swell and overturned us. Kept our emergency rations but lost a lot of clothes. Difficult now to keep warm, especially feet, but all lucky to get back into dinghy. Thoroughly done in and badly shocked after that - Special issue of barley sugar - one each. Bucked us up. Sea rough all night; all wet and miserable. Dinghy water-logged all the time. Kept baling out.

'Sixth day: Poor weather, drizzle. Caught rain-water in our hands and drank it. Weather improved in afternoon. Sun-bathed, dried our clothes and Mae Wests. Dinghy doing extremely well. Ration still four milk tablets a day. In the evening opened first tin of water, shared round carefully. Determined to have a comfortable night, but very cold and all stiff and miserable. At 0200 saw a light on the horizon. Fired a signal; then found it was only Mars.

'Seventh day: Warm. Dried everything out and bathed in the afternoon, one after the other. Frightened by a couple of whales basking and bellowing 400 yards away. All wounds healing well. Had a discussion on what action to take. Decided to reach patrol area of the Bay (of Biscay). Still trying hard to catch fish. Made fishing net from half a mast and a seat of old pair of pants. No fish, but at about 1800 caught an unlimited number of jelly fish, all sizes and what looked like baby octopi. Tried to make a drink out of them. Foul. Seemed to be mainly water. Dubious stuff altogether. Kept it in case we got thirsty. Night warm and dry. Sea calm.

'Eighth day: Low cloud, turning to warm sun. Made and shipped a two-sheet sail. Most effective. Crew now breathing through sea- wetted handkerchiefs and keeping hair and faces wet to reduce evaporation losses. Hope still high but night bad. All getting tired easily. Most of the crew lying all the time on the floor. Sea rough but maintained a good speed all night.

'Ninth day: Very rough. Great strain on all. Shipped water continuously. Night an absolute nightmare. Very rough, raining hard. Afraid of being tipped in the water at any moment. Everything soaked.

'Tenth day: Crew very tired. Special issue of chocolate - two small cubes each. Weather improved in the afternoon after three distinct storms. Using pocket compass; hope to reach patrol area in two days. Night: no notes.

'Eleventh day: Weather cleared mid-day. Divided one tin of water among us - two ounces each. A little chocolate.'

At that stage Roger Mead became '...too dopey' either to write or even read his notes.

The crew had offered a prayer every night during their ordeal, but on this terrible night an additional prayer made for speedy deliverance, since they felt that although all four of them could manage another three or four days, the position of the other two was becoming critical. The dinghy continued to ship water for the next 24 hours but the four fittest managed to keep it reasonably dry and maintain a constant watch. Suddenly at 1430, Flight Sergeant Kenneth E. Ladds the mid-upper gunner, who had been on his 47th sortie and who was on watch, sighted the mast of a ship. Three Very cartridges were fired and three Royal Navy destroyers turned towards them. Twenty minutes later the *Mahratta* was alongside the dinghy and the six survivors were carefully lifted on board where they were cared for by the ship's doctor and crew at the end of their 11-day ordeal. Twenty-four hours later they were taken ashore by stretcher to the Royal Naval Hospital at

Plymouth. The crew could not have survived for much longer, but their determination was rewarded by what was a very lucky sighting. The destroyers were returning to England from Gibraltar and happened to pass close enough to the tiny dinghy for it to be spotted. The destroyer had discovered the dinghy by pure chance - they were not actually looking for it.

The survivors took a few weeks to recover but all returned to duty. Eric Hartley received an immediate DFC for sinking U-221 and for his leadership during the dinghy ordeal. Flight Sergeant Ladds was awarded an immediate DFM for his conduct. The ordeal did not seem to affect Mead greatly. When in June 1944 the Group Captain addressed Coastal Command personnel in the base theatre Hector Bolitho, one of the assembled throng, observed that Mead was 'thirty-five but looked twenty-five, which was strange as he spent eleven days in a rubber dinghy last summer, drinking three ounces of water in six days and ending with such a thirst that the crew squeezed the liquid from jelly fish to drink.'[21]

Hector Bolitho spent an hour one afternoon with Flight Sergeant G. R. E. Robertson, who was in the dinghy with Group Captain Mead. 'Robertson said that the painful memories of being in the dinghy had left him, but sometimes when he lifts a pint of beer he recalls that during all the eleven days he had less than that quantity to drink. He said that during the first days in the dinghy he worried about his parents but when anxiety, fear and hunger left him, he considered, quite calmly, whether it would be better to die slowly of thirst, dive over and be drowned or drink salt water and go mad. He said, 'But I was quite happy about it. He said also that his memory is still confused as to what he saw and what he imagined. During the hours when they were fishing over the side of the dinghy, using pieces of their scabs and the soft skin between their toes as bait, he stared into the water and thought he saw big fish swimming below, 'like dolphins, staring from the depths.' They had fished for days without catching anything Out jelly fish and he still does not know if the 'dolphins' were really there.

'We talked then of the power of imagination in people who fly and of the temptation to exaggerate what happens to them., The sailors of the old days no doubt believed that they saw sea serpents and mermaids because, in the loneliness of staring into the eternal spaces of sky and sea, their gift for fantasy was encouraged. They came home with 'sailors' yarns' and the phrase crept into common use. We agreed that the same gift sometimes makes airmen decorate their stories with a few thrills from their imagination. I quoted an engineer who told me that when his aircraft dropped its depth charges the U-boat was blown clean out of the water so that he could see moonlight between the hull and the sea. It is impossible for depth charges to, blow a 740-ton U-boat into the air like this, but he faithfully believed it had happened. He had been so astonished by the might of the explosion that he expected to see moonlight between the hull and the water and nothing would convince him that he had imagined it. It seems a little like the child who has read stories of lions and tigers and who comes back from the garden convinced that he has seen them walking among the trees.'

Sometimes disasters at sea happened just off-shore, as Hector Bolitho recalled when he returned to the officers' mess at Watergate on the Cornish coast on 12 July after a visit to an Australian Sunderland squadron. 'I came back to find two solemn stories. The treachery of this northern coast of Cornwall did not die with the wreckers and the smugglers. When the sun shines it is glorious, but when the gulls fly in, crying on the wings of a gale, a dark cloud falls on the land. The cliffs crumble in the storms and the waves groan and threaten. An aircraft crashed into the sea on Monday, while I was away and only a few of the crew were saved. Yesterday, two WAAF servants from the officers' mess were drowned. One was just married and her sad husband arrived to arrange the funeral. The bodies were washed ashore at Newquay. The sea looks horrible to-night. The cliffs are sullen and dark and the gulls cling to the crags, startled and silent.'

Three U-boats surprised a 58 Squadron Halifax by remaining on the surface and fighting back just after midnight on 21 August. The captain of the Halifax, Wing Commander J. B. Grant, the CO, was flying the aircraft off the mouth of the Gironde River when the first U-boat was contacted. Flares were dropped and the German was seen, a mile and a half away. Almost at once, two more were seen 300 or 400 yards apart, no doubt making for the shelter of the river. All three fired on the Halifax, but Grant lost them in the darkness. About two o'clock in the morning, Grant was flying over the supposed track of the U-boats again, still seeking for them, when there was a violent explosion within the aircraft. It lost height rapidly and all engines were opened up, but the controls were ineffectual and the Halifax struck the sea in a series of violent shocks. The crew were so dazed that their recollection of what followed is hazy. Water rushed in over Grant's legs and he escaped through the emergency hatch, followed by two other members of the crew. Two more got out through the rear escape hatch. The dinghy did not appear so the captain climbed on to the port wing, but he was soon swept off by the heavy seas. Half an hour passed, in anxiety and darkness, before he made his way to the surviving members of the crew in the water. Then the aircraft began to burn, possibly because of the ignition of the flame floats. Only five of the crew of nine escaped and they passed through a grim ordeal, in a sea covered with petrol and oil and with waves breaking over them so persistently that they could barely breathe. After about two hours, one of the survivors disappeared. Rain began to fall and the sea became more turbulent. One of the navigators then became very weak, still imagining that he was flying and asking for the course and airspeed. He died about six o'clock in the morning.

Dawn came and the men tried to cling to what little wreckage there was. They were ill and weak and the only substantial support they had was the piece of a wing to which they clung, hoping it might attract any aircraft passing by. The sun was hidden, but the survivors knew that land must be about twenty miles to the east so they set course with a compass and decided to do their best to reach the coast. During the morning a Sunderland came towards them and they enjoyed a few moments of hope, but the aircraft flew on without seeing them. A Liberator and another

Sunderland also passed them and they tried to wave a piece of dull metal as a reflector to catch the stingy morning sun. It was apparently enough to attract the attention of the captain of a warship steaming by. The ship was the frigate Saint John. Some of the sailors had seen the wheel of an aircraft in the water so they had searched the sea for survivors. The three men from the Halifax were taken on board after ten and a half hours in the water, but even then their misadventures did not end. The shore batteries opened fire on the Saint John and one rating was killed and another injured, before the frigate could turn out to sea.

There had not been a disaster like this for some time and it was a reminder of the horrors possible when a big aircraft is lost at night.

A Wellington on 172 Squadron that was on anti U-boat patrol on the night of 26 August began to send a signal to say that it was attacking a U-boat, No more was heard and the aircraft did not return. The mystery was cleared, for three members of the crew, all injured, were rescued early on the morning of the 28th by a Sunderland flown by Flight Lieutenant Tilley. The Wimpy crew had seen a U-boat and had attacked it, but the flak had been too much for them and the port engine had burst into flames. They pressed home their attack, but the aircraft crashed into the sea and only three of the crew survived.

A Liberator on 53 Squadron piloted by Flight Lieutenant Cameron McA Forbes also crashed into the sea, about three o'clock in the morning of the 27th, without the satisfaction of attacking a U-boat first. Cameron Forbes recalled: 'It was very black and the moon had gone down, not the blackness that is full of colour, an unpleasant blackness. There was a haze. The radar got a contact and we flew in, but there was nothing to see. The contact was vague but still on the screen so we flew in again, but still there was nothing. It was a nervous strain, keeping exactly on the right bombing run, seeing nothing, then going away and not knowing what the contact was. Perhaps it was a fish. Then I heard a harsh New Zealand voice over the intercom. It cut through my head. He said he thought he saw something, a slick or a swirl, so we decided to go in as it might be from a periscope. We turned and let down to 100 feet. It calls for accurate flying because you can't see the horizon and you can't see the sea. Then you dash in. There was no more talking on the intercom. I might have been by myself. Then the voice said, 'Level.' The bomb doors were open and the Leigh light was turned on. The beam was sweeping out in front of us: purplish light. And the light on the altimeter, red, green, amber. Mostly amber. Then there was a tug on the aircraft and I had the sensation of something being wrong. I can't describe it but you know when you feel it. Then a long, tremendous crash. It is rather like being on a scenic railway when you come to the top and see a tunnel far below you. You don't know when you'll pull out. That's the sensation I get on a homing run.

'I have an extraordinary recollection of the period between the crash and the realization that I was out of the aircraft, under water: the feeling of being swung forward and pressure on my right side. I remember saying to myself, 'Well, Forbes, you've gone a complete circle.' I thought of a surrealist picture by Dali, of myself curled up in the prenatal position. It was passing through my mind. 1 was curled up and I had completed a cycle. It was dark and I had my eyes closed. I was at the end of something and I expected that I would be given an awful smack. Then I was in the water and I thought, 'Which way is up?' because I was under and it was dark. I inflated my Mae West, kicked away and came up. It seemed- ages, but it must have been only a second or two.

'I want to paint it, when I am on leave, that moment when I came to the surface of the water. But I couldn't do it the way that I felt it that instant. When I broke surface I saw nothing at first. But we had dropped flame floats before we crashed and they made an eerie light on the water in the night. There seemed to be two of them. I struck out for the dinghy. It was inflating, upside down, hissing; a long, steady groan. That's the picture: just the dark sea, the two flame floats and the dinghy, upside down. I'd like to paint that, with pieces of the aircraft floating, pieces of wreckage and the flashes of the light on the water: I struggled over to the dinghy.

'I thought a little. The front part of the aircraft where I had been must have broken off, just like a broken biscuit and with me in it. And I must have gone down with it and been released when it was deep, so that I rose to the surface. The flame floats were still flickering on the sea.

'I got to the dinghy. I don't know what time it was. It must have been about three in the morning. My hand was cut and something must have grazed past and taken my watch with it. I yelled, 'Dinghy, dinghy, here' and I heard two voices, one calling, 'It's Al' and one calling. 'It's Ted,' [Sergeant B. A. A. Coombes and Sergeant E. R. A. Steer] but I didn't know then how many of them were in the water. I and Ted swam towards the dinghy and I got there too and found it was upside down. Al had his watch on his wrist but something had grazed it and taken off the glass and one of the hands and buckled the other one, so we still could not tell the time. I didn't feel the hurt in my hand where it had been struck when I lost my watch. It was my left hand that had taken a bang and it was swollen. The three of us did not say much. I said, 'How the devil do you get this right way up?' but it sounded as if somebody else was saying it in the darkness - like your voice coming back to you when you speak through a microphone. That was the only thing any of us said until we got the dinghy over. I managed to crouch on the piece of aircraft to which the dinghy was still attached by a cord and to help to turn it the right way up. One of the boys hadn't much joy in his arms as his collar bone was broken. The other one had not got much joy in his legs. I felt the piece of aircraft shudder under me. I couldn't tell how big it was. I kicked it away and jumped into the dinghy. Al said, 'Give me a hand with Ted,' so we hauled him in. I wound the cord around my hand, to break the dinghy away from the piece of aircraft. The cord broke easily and we were free. It's strong cord but it broke all right that night.

'Just as I broke the cord the last of the aircraft went down. I could see it, white in the light of the flares. It seemed small and insignificant. We were much bigger than it. I had flown it once before and never liked it. It was very final when it went down.

'We paddled with our arms and legs as best we could and gathered all we saw from the water, while the flares were still alight. We found two 'K' type dinghies, still in their packs, some wreckage, a cushion and some flame floats. We took all these into the dinghy. The flame floats were of inestimable value so we got them in. We grabbed everything. We found a damaged Mae West and took it in; anything might be useful. There was no sign of anyone else and that meant seven lost. I felt terrible about it. One of my usual crew had been sick that day and a friend of Ted Steer had come with us as wireless operator. I felt very badly about it because he needn't have been with us. He was Sergeant Tatum and he was not saved. Then began our five hours in the dinghy. Some aircraft passed near us in the darkness and we could hear them throbbing in the black. We had some of the distress signals that fire two red stars and used them, but the aircraft did not see us. They just flew on into the night.

'I never lost control of my thoughts. That is what I was afraid of, because I did not know how much the other two were damaged. The co-ordination in my mind was good: maybe it was not one hundred per cent but I knew what I wanted to do. We just sat there. The sea was very, very kind. It had taken seven of us so I suppose it was ashamed. It was quite calm and gentle, just rocking us gently. We'd hear the aircraft coming closer, closer. Then I'd screw the cap off a star cartridge, quickly and fire it when the aircraft was near us. Then I fired a second one just as the aircraft went away. It was difficult to screw off the caps as my hands were oily and I hadn't an awful lot of pull in them. The cartridge would go pop and nothing would happen. It was a crushing feeling because only five out of thirteen went off.

'It is not easy to see a little light and a little dinghy in the sea, like that. I can't remember how many aircraft passed us.

'We also had some flame floats and we threw them out at intervals so we could tell which way we were drifting and to attract any aircraft. Then we fixed up the weather curtain because the wind was cold. We snuggled together and got down as deep into the dinghy as we could. I tried to keep doing something all the time so that I would not pass out. I was the only one fully serviceable and I could have swum somewhere if I had had to. I told the others to go to sleep and they closed their eyes, but I do not think they slept. We had lamps and we switched them on to see each other's faces as we waited for the first light of morning to come. We had talked while we were baling out the dinghy, nattering to keep up our spirits, not that we seemed to need it. It was good to see the flame floats alight on the water. Sometimes we heard the splash of fish which were attracted by the flames.

'We weren't too badly off really, although the coast we were near might still be in the hands of the enemy. The worst that could happen was for us to drift on to the rocky shore and not be found. So it was best for us to keep on the area of patrol and hope to be picked up when morning came. We knew that there we e naval vessels to the west of us, but it wouldn't be easy to get to them because there was a cross wind.

'Then came the first glimmer of light. It was quite pleasant. We could see each other better. They both asked if I was hurt. I didn't think I was and I thought it better to convince them that I wasn't: Ted's jaw was broken in two places and his eyes were puffed up. He had two gorgeous circles under them. We said to him, 'Where were you last night?' and 'What was her name?' He couldn't laugh because of the breaks in his jaw; Al had lost his shoe and sock and he asked me to cover up his foot as it was bad. Ted had lost the sole from his shoe. He put his shoe on Al's injured foot and Al asked him politely, 'Do you mind? Can you move your shoe a wee bit, Ted?' 'That's all right, it's only my foot.'

'It was a slow dawn. I thought the sun would never rise. It wasn't a good dawn, in technicolor. It was pale but we could see the sea. Then I saw something floating and we paddled towards it with our hands. We had no paddles, they are stowed separately. But we had water and four emergency food packs and I had a pound note which was very wet.

'Then it was light and with the light we pepped up again. We were two or three hours overdue and we wondered whether they would tell our people we were missing. We wondered if they would be panicking at home and we hoped we would be picked up before the Adjutant got to his office in the morning so that no news would be sent to our families.

'It was good to see the water; cool, bluish, with glints coming off it. We then compared our faces in the morning light. It was something to talk about. And there was enough light then for us to see Les Sept Isles. But we didn't want to go there because there would be shoals and reefs to puncture our dinghy and we did not know whether the Germans were still there. We could see the sun rising up, with a little bit of cloud which the light picked up, deep blue becoming green and then yellow. The sea looked cold then and a swell began to come up so that we rocked a bit more. We stared at the islands. We had often seen them through binoculars but were never allowed to fly over them. I was looking at the dawn and Al was looking the other way. He said, 'What's that?' and I saw four dots that might have been more islands. We watched until one of them made some smoke. That cheered us up immensely. Then, 'Are they nearer?' 'Are they coming towards us?' 'Are they going away from us?' 'They can't be going away from us.' Then the dots seemed to alter course as they came close, three or four miles away and we saw that they were minesweepers. One aircraft had passed over us in the first light, but it had not seen us. It is difficult to see a little dinghy, even in the daylight. We called him a few odd things as he flew on. Then a second one came, a Liberator flying at 1,000 feet. It was one of our squadron and the pilot was Bob Dobson. He went on abeam of us and turned. I was not sure whether he was turning towards or away. Perhaps he was only going to investigate the minesweepers. If he did, he would have to do a circuit and he would surely see us. He turned towards us and flew over us, but he went away and we thought he hadn't seen us. Then he flew over the minesweepers and they 'seemed to be signalling because we could see the ship flashing back although we couldn't read the signal. Al started to wave the red sail and I waved the yellow weather apron. We waved like mad. Then the Liberator came back and flew between us and the mine-sweepers. The second one of the group altered course towards us and it was a bit awful to see a whole minesweeper bearing straight down on us. It came up and there was a slight swell so that we were disappearing a, wee bit into the troughs. Then they came alongside and somebody called, 'We'll throw you a line' and we called back, 'We'll have a shot at catching it.' But they didn't throw the line. They came alongside, hove to very nicely and put out a scrambling net.

'Then one of the fellows on board produced a new piece of rope with a horrifying, red four-pronged hook at the end. He cried out 'Catch' and when I saw the prongs I thought they'd probably go through us. But he was determined to throw it and he did. It came aboard and I saw that the prongs were turned so they could not hurt us. Then people came down the scrambling net to grab us and help us up. I saw the cushion we had picked up the night before and I shoved it between the ship and the dinghy, because there were barnacles on the ship. I felt we ought not to be outdone in seamanship. I used it as a fender until the other two were helped up. Then I scrambled up, but I was very stiff. I was on the deck and they led me to the Executive Officer's cabin where I got rid of my clothes because somebody was already waiting with a blanket to wrap around me. The others were taken to another cabin. Cups of coffee appeared, by magic. It is hard to express fully how kind they were to us. They took our names and flashed them back to the Liberator. I consumed pints of coffee and I didn't even taste the first three or four cups. They sent a whaler to one of the other ships for a surgeon and he came and checked us over. Those Naval types were kindness itself. 'How about some soup? Dozens of cigarettes appeared. I don't smoke them and I said, 'Sorry I smoke a pipe.'

''Have you got it?' one of them asked and I answered, 'Yes, it's in my battle dress.' Within a minute my pipe was cleaned, dried, filled, in my mouth and lit. They just couldn't do enough.

'It was a Canadian minesweeper, which pleased me no end, because I have been to Canada and I have very good reason for being enormously fond of almost everything that comes from Canada.'[22]

On 5 January 1945 there appeared in *The Aeroplane*, an article entitled *Crash In Labrador* about a Canadian Liberator and its crew who crashed while on patrol.

'The three airmen fought their way out of the tangled wreckage of what a moment before had been a huge, four-motored Liberator. A cry from their wireless operator-air gunner revealed him jammed beneath a fallen top-gun turret, unable to move but not gravely injured. The trio stumbled to his side, floundering up to their armpits in the 8 feet of snow that blanketed everything. With three motors dead, the fourth on fire and, further, dragged down by a 3-inch to 4-inch crust of ice under its wings, the Liberator had plunged headlong into the Labrador bush. The drooping starboard wing had clipped off a tree-trunk 18 inches thick. Slewing round with tremendous force, the tail had smashed against another tree and had been chopped right off the aircraft. A 100-yard semi-circular swath was gouged out of the forest before the heavy aeroplane came to a stop. The other gunner and a passenger were nowhere to be seen.

Then an odd scratching noise diverted the three from their attempts to release the trapped wireless air gunner. Twigs of a broken branch were gently scraping against the metal fuselage; puzzled eyes followed the branch along until the toe of a flying boot was discovered, protruding from the snow and hooked about the branch, at which it was frantically tugging. With a shout the three men hurled themselves on the flying boot, tugging and digging in the snow with their hands. The boot belonged to the other gunner, who had been hurled headlong and upside-down into a deep drift, his mouth and throat jammed with snow which threatened to choke or drown him. He was upon the point of asphyxiation when hauled out. Then the first WAG was released from the turret's clutches in the wrecked aircraft; but by the time the passenger was found, nothing could be done for him.

Thus did one man die and five men find themselves marooned in the bush in bitterest winter - six victims of that 'other war' the Royal Canadian Air Force has been waging for four years against the relentless twin enemies -weather and wilderness. Their story is typical of the high hazard constantly faced by hundreds of RCAF pilots far from any theatre of action. The survival of the five who escaped death in the crash speaks highly of their individual ingenuity, the emergency equipment and training provided for all air crew and of the search and rescue machinery which was thrown into action to save them.

The five survivors were Squadron Leader A. A. T. Imrie, pilot; Flying Officer J. D. L. Campbell, co-pilot; Flight Lieutenant G. R. Harland, navigator; Pilot Officer M. J. Gilmour, WAG (wireless air gunner), whose shoulder was injured by the falling gun turret and Warrant Officer A. C. Johns, the second WAG, who was almost buried alive in the snow. The passenger who lost his life was Flying Officer David Griffin, Public Relations Officer, who was home-bound from Iceland with notes for another chapter in the story of the RCAF, to complement his *First Steps to Tokyo*.

The five men realized their most urgent need was shelter against the extreme cold of a March night in Labrador. One man cut wood, the others hauled it to the fire and all were soon exhausted as they plunged to the waist in snow at every step. A sleeping place was tramped out beneath the wing; across it was laid a 12-inch layer of soft balsam boughs and for bedding a half-dozen spare flying suits, three layers of silk parachutes, greatcoats and extra flying equipment were piled on top. Fearful that a leaping flame might ignite the petrol-filled wing, they let their fire out the first night.

'The temperature fell to 45 degrees below zero and we were too cold to sleep,' reported the skipper. They were all up at first light and busy improving their shelter.

The navigator brought out his sextant when the sun rose and confirmed the high irony of their fate. They had been bang on course and had crashed but 13 miles from the great air base at Goose Bay, yet in the bush they might be miles from anywhere. Hundreds of aeroplanes would soon be searching for them and they should be easy to spot from the air, but the treacherous northern weather might fail at any time and wash out flying. They could hike out on foot, although it would be considerably more than 13 miles through the bush, providing they could fashion snowshoes to make walking possible and providing their strength held out. Yet the live survivors remained cheerful and figured that they had a 95 per cent, chance of survival.

That second day - a Saturday - they piled boughs around the wing as a windbreak for their shelter, rebuilt the bed and covered it with a tarpaulin motor cover, ten thicknesses of flight maps and small souvenir sheepskin rugs bought in Iceland. Everything possible was salvaged from the aircraft. Metal life raft covers became tins in which to heat food and melt snow for drinking water; twisted bomb doors made a metal base for the fire. They hunted endlessly for the 'Gibson Girl' - the portable radio. [23] This would have been a most valuable find, because ice and storm had prevented getting a distress signal away from the aircraft before they crashed, but it was never located. Only three of six emergency ration kits were located and having no idea how long they might be lost, the RCAF crew rationed themselves to three-quarters of a tin of corned beef, three squares of chocolate and three or four hard-tack biscuits per man per day. They had decided to stay beside the aircraft for four days and then hit the trail for what they hoped would be no more than a four-day trek to Goose Bay; so they knew they must husband their supplies.

Saturday night the mercury dropped to 55 degrees below zero. They took turns standing watch to keep the fire fed, yet guard against it spreading and to see that no one got uncovered and froze an arm or leg. But only one chap slept and two remained up all night. Sunday they concentrated first on making snowshoes. Sections of steel 'catwalk' chopped from the wreckage and a frame made from sections of cartridge-feed belts were tried and discarded and the next attempt was in real Indian style. Three balsam boughs, two long and one short, were lashed in a triangle as a frame for each shoe and parachute cord laced snugly back and forth across the frame. These snowshoes worked fine and another search was made for the missing radio, using dinghy paddles as snow shovels. In the crisp, frigid air they could hear aircraft taking off and landing at the airport just 13 miles away, but they saw few. A smudge was built, but a brisk wind whisked the smoke away at tree-top level; motor oil might have made a blacker smoke, but the oil was so congealed by cold it wouldn't drain from the crankcase. A machine-gun was dragged from the aeroplane and lashed to a stump pointing to the sky, from which it was planned to fire tracers to attract attention. But the gun seized after two shots.

On Sunday afternoon two DC-3s and a Canso went smack overhead. The co-pilot was standing by with a Very pistol ready for such a moment, but as he clicked and clicked the trigger, nothing happened. The cold had frozen the tiring mechanism and when he finally got a flare away the aircraft were out of sight. Then on Monday a native trapper heard the ring of their axe and found their camp. He agreed to take a letter to Goose Bay aerodrome and, good as his word, he made it to the base by Tuesday morning.

Meanwhile, a US Army Air Force DC-3 sighted their smoke signals on Tuesday morning, the breeze having died. Coming closer, the American pilot saw a 60 feet 'SOS' the boys had tramped out in the snow. A red marine flare spotted the survivors' exact position for the circling aeroplane, which sent a stream of rations, Arctic clothing, snowshoes, cigarettes and sleeping bags parachuting towards the five wildly waving fliers.

'Stuff showered down like manna from Heaven and it was just as welcome,' the co-pilot declared. Moments later the CO of the RCAF station at Goose Bay and his medical officer arrived in a ski-equipped Norseman aircraft, landing on a nearby lake. Squadron Leader Imrie's choice of the trees for a crash landing instead of the lake was justified when both the Norseman and an even lighter Piper Cub ski-plane which followed, 'mushed in' the treacherous snow - crusted on top but slushy beneath. The hurtling Liberator might have crashed right through the ice.

The five survivors were soon gulping hot coffee. They moved to a camp which their rescuers set up on the lake and that night slept snugly in the snow at 35 degrees below zero - in sleeping bags. On Thursday three dog teams arrived, one a team of native dogs to break trail and two US teams driven by who had been with Admiral Byrd at the South Pole. The US teams had been flown to Goose Bay for the job. The two wireless air gunners were flown out in the lightweight, ski-mounted Piper Cub, since one had an injured shoulder and the other had suffered from exposure, as soon as the weather cleared and a take-off became possible. The rest of the party set out on snowshoes for Goose Bay, mushing behind the dog sleds. On one sled were carried supplies for the trip and on the other was the body of Flying Officer Griffin. By forest trail, the journey to Goose Bay was 23 miles and leaving the scene of the crash on Friday - a week after they had been forced down - the party spent a night on the trail and arrived at Goose Bay at noon Saturday. Flying Officer Griffin's body was buried in the military cemetery at Goose Bay, Labrador. The five men who had won yet another battle in the war against weather and wilderness were soon completely recovered and were flown back to their home base in Newfoundland.

Footnotes

2   *War of the U-Boats: British Merchantmen Under Fire* by Bernard Edwards (Pen & Sword Maritime 2006).

3   Two of the pilots involved in the *Kensington Court* rescue were awarded the DFC - Flying Officer Smith on 228 Squadron and Flying Officer John Barrett of 204 Squadron - the joint citation reading: Acting Flight Lieutenant Smith and Acting Flight Lieutenant Barrett were, in September 1939, respectively in command of the first and second of three flying boats of Coastal Command which were engaged on patrol duty over the Atlantic when they intercepted messages from a torpedoed merchant ship - the *Kensington Court*. They proceeded to the scene to undertake rescue work. A lifeboat was seen in the vicinity containing thirty-four men and the first aircraft alighted and took on board 21 of the men. A thorough search was made by the second aircraft, which afterwards alighted and, in spite of the heavy swell, took on board the remainder of the crew from the lifeboat. Flying Officer Smith was serving in the Mediterranean off Tobruk on 4 August 1940 when he had the misfortune to be shot down and was taken prisoner by the Italians.

4   *Wartime Disasters At Sea* by David Williams (PSL 1997).

5   The Lloyds War Loss Records state that there were 176 crewmen, of whom 57 were lost, 254

military guardsmen, of whom 91 died and 1,178 aliens and prisoners, of whom 143 Germans and 470 Italians perished. *Wartime Disasters At Sea* by David Williams (PSL 1997).

6   *War of the U-Boats: British Merchantmen Under Fire* by Bernard Edwards (Pen & Sword Maritime 2006).

7   *50 Days of Hell* by Kenneth Cooke quoted in *70 True Stories of the Second World War* (Odhams Press Ltd)/ *The Real Cruel Sea: The Merchant Navy in the Battle of the Atlantic, 1939-1943* by Richard Woodman (John Murray 2004). The *Leonardo da Vinci* sunk only one more ship before being sunk by the destroyers HMS *Active* and HMS *Ness* off the Azores on 23 May 1943. *War of the U-Boats: British Merchantmen Under Fire* by Bernard Edwards (Pen & Sword Maritime 2006).

8   HMS *Hurricane* was sunk by U-415 commanded by Kapitänleutnant Kurt Neide on Christmas Eve 1943.

9   Her master, 51 officers and 316 ratings were saved. The former Blue Funnel liner *Patroclus*, another auxiliary cruiser, was also sunk by U-99 as she was standing by to pick up survivors. *Wartime Disasters At Sea* by David Williams (PSL 1997).

10   Adapted from *Hedge-Hopping A Minefield* by Leonard Gribble.

11   *RAF Flying Review*, February 1957, condensed from *They Shall Not Pass Unseen* by Ivan Southall (Angus & Robertson, 1956).

12   *Shot Down and In The Drink: True Stories of RAF and Commonwealth aircrews Saved from the Sea in WWII* by Air Commodore Graham Pitchfork (The National Archives 2005).

13   Johnstone (who Foss wrongly remembered as Flying Officer'Thornton') was a radar specialist who had been investigating signals emitted by German aircraft and submarines in the Mediterranean By the beginning of September 1943 he was at Gibraltar waiting for a courier flight to return to the United Kingdom. He was due to fly home on the night of 1 September, but hearing that a Coastal Command Liberator on 224 Squadron was due to return the following morning, he approached Whahram and asked if he could return with him and his crew. His main reason for the request was the opportunity to see the ASV Mark 5 radar in operation. *Shot Down and In The Drink: True Stories of RAF and Commonwealth aircrews Saved from the Sea in WWII* by Air Commodore Graham Pitchfork (The National Archives 2005).

14   Later they tried in vain to repair the single-seat 'K' dinghy.

15   *Shot Down and In The Drink: True Stories of RAF and Commonwealth aircrews Saved from the Sea in WWII* by Air Commodore Graham Pitchfork (The National Archives 2005).

16   The sloop, part of the 2nd Escort Group, had been searching for the past few days and the Catalina had called it to the area.

17   *Shot Down and In The Drink: True Stories of RAF and Commonwealth aircrews Saved from the Sea in WWII* by Air Commodore Graham Pitchfork (The National Archives 2005).See Shot Down and

18   *In The Drink: True Stories of RAF and Commonwealth aircrews Saved from the Sea in WWII* by Air Commodore Graham Pitchfork (The National Archives 2005) and *Short Sunderland; The Flying Porcupines' In the Second World War* by Andrew Hendrie (Airlife 1994 and Pen & Sword 2012).

19   *Hitler's U-boat War: The Hunted, 1942-1945* by Clay Blair (Random House 1998) and *U-boat Fact File* by Peter Sharpe (Midland Publishing Ltd 1998 and *Handley Page Halifax: From Hell to Victory and Beyond* by K. A. Merrick (Chevron Publishing 2009).

20   *Shot Down and In The Drink: True Stories of RAF and Commonwealth aircrews Saved from the Sea in WWII* by Air Commodore Graham Pitchfork (The National Archives 2005).

21   Roger Mead remained in the RAF after the war and retired in 1958 as Air Commodore Mead CBE DFC AFC. *Task For Coastal Command: The Story of the Battle of the South-West Approaches* by Hector Bolitho (1944). A few weeks later HMS *Mahratta* was sunk escorting a Russian convoy. There were just three survivors.

22   *Task For Coastal Command* by Hector Bolitho. The three survivors were taken to Cherbourg

23   The term 'Gibson Girl' is associated with this radio because of its 'hour glass' shape, which was attributed to the personification of the feminine ideal in the satirical pen-and-ink illustrated stories created by Charles Dana Gibson, during more than 18 years spanning the late 19th and early 20th centuries. The unit was developed for use in case of forced landings on water. It was designed to be held between the knees while being hand cranked, at which time a continuous tone went out so that ground stations could establish its position.

Chapter 2

Colonials for King and Commonwealth

The white Hudson flew down to one thousand feet and I could see the road running out of London towards the coast. But it was no longer a rolling English road for it was thick with jeeps, like beetles crawling along a yellow ribbon and an airfield over which we passed had Old Glory flying at the top of its flagpole. A few minutes later we were low enough to see some American sailors sitting on a gate and about 11 o'clock in the morning we passed over Gravesend, where Pocohontas is buried. I had the curious illusion of no longer being in England. Then we crossed over the coast, the white buttress of England and the illusion went. Across the water, in the mist, lay the coast of the enemy. We flew on and came to a gentle stretch of sand where children paddled in the old days, but now the beach was a labyrinth of barbed wire and the sea was bitter with almost five years of war. From Dover we looked across to Dunkirk. The war seemed very old then. The story of Mr. Churchill in France was like an incident in history. 'We will go on fighting,' he told them. 'What with?' they asked. 'I don't know,' he answered, 'I haven't had time to think about that yet.'
Hector Bolitho, *Task For Coastal Command*

By September 1941 the increased shipping losses again prompted the Admiralty to explore the possibility of employing bombers in the war at sea. Air Chief Marshal Sir Arthur Harris, Chief of Bomber Command had turned over large numbers of twin-engined bombers to Coastal Command but he steadfastly refused to allocate them any four-engined bombers. He was of the strong opinion that mining together with bombing shipyards and marine factories would prove to be the best method of dealing with U-boats. 'In view of the very small percentage of submarine sightings by patrolling aircraft' he wrote 'and the still smaller, indeed almost infinitesimal, number of kills awarded as a percentage of those sightings, it is apparent that the use of bombers on mine-laying and on direct attacks on submarine building yards and on submarine accessory factories inland and on the morale of the workers, is beyond doubt the most economical and effective way of employing aircraft in anti-submarine warfare, excepting only in the direct protection of shipping, in which task the aircraft, by forcing submarines to dive, frequently spoils an attack which might otherwise be successful.'

Ironically there was a four-engined bomber available to the hard-pressed Coastal Command - the American Consolidated B-24 Liberator.[24] But Coastal Command could only muster one Liberator squadron. Liberator Is first entered service on 120 Squadron at Nutts Corner in Northern Ireland in September 1941.[25] By January 1942 five of these had been converted into VLR (Very Long Range) aircraft whose range was 2,400 miles. (The Sunderland had a range of only 1,300 miles). [26]

The shipping losses in October and November showed a reduction over those of September, although the autumn gales and the redeployment of the U-boat packs to the Mediterranean were partly responsible. Hitler, worried by Britain's successful offensive on Axis convoys en route for Libya, sent packs of U-boats to the Mediterranean and although several were sunk, eighteen got through. In November the carrier HMS *Ark Royal* and HMS *Barham* were sunk and additional air cover was immediately sent to Gibraltar. On 14 December 1941 Convoy HG.76 sailed under escort from Gibraltar. By the morning of 17 December the convoy was out of air range of the Rock and over the next four days nine U-boats preyed on the convoy, sinking two merchant vessels, a destroyer and the auxiliary carrier HMS *Audacity*. However four U-boats were sunk and two Condors brought down. The thinned ranks of HG.76 carried on until at 10.54 hours on the 22 December when it was met 750 miles out from Nutts Corner by a Liberator of 120 Squadron. This aircraft immediately went into action, driving off a Condor shadowing the convoy and then, two hours later, sighting and attacking a U-boat. At 16.20 hours another Liberator took over and within three hours had forced three more U-boats to submerge. By the time fuel shortage forced the Liberator to turn for home the U-boats had been sufficiently discouraged and the convoy was molested no further.

In January 1942 six of Germany's largest U-boats arrived in North American waters to counter the USA's involvement in the war. Within three weeks forty Allied ships, totalling 23,000 tons, were sunk. American defences had still not been tightened up when Admiral Dönitz ordered all his U-boats west of the British Isles and several more lying off the Azores, to take up station on the North American and Central American seaboards. America responded by using B-24 Liberators of the 44th and 93rd Bomb Groups, which were earmarked for the Eighth Air Force in England, in anti-submarine patrols but by the end of May 1942 the U-boat packs had wrought havoc, sinking 109 ships in that month alone. However there was one consolation. With the U-boats otherwise engaged, the majority of convoys plying between North America and Britain escaped virtually unscathed for a few months. In waters protected by Coastal Command only nine merchant vessels were sunk in five months.

The Liberator was not the only American four-engined bomber to see service in Coastal Command. Although the Boeing B-17 proved less than successful during its short career on 90 Squadron in RAF Bomber Command, the Fortress was supplied in large numbers to Coastal Command, where it gave sterling service in the Atlantic and Bay of Biscay. Beginning in March 1942, forty-six Fortress IIA aircraft [27] and later, nineteen Fortress IIs (B-17Fs) and 98 Fortress IIIs (B-17Gs) were delivered to Great

Britain. The majority gave sterling service with RAF Coastal Command where they helped close the mid-Atlantic 'gap'. During March-July 1942 the first of 46 Boeing B-17Es were delivered to the UK as the Fortress IIA. [28] After August 1942 nineteen B-17Fs went to Coastal Command as the Fortress II. Originally the British had signed a lend-lease contract in June 1941 for 300 Fortress IIs for the RAF, but these aircraft were diverted to the USAAF when Britain decided not to use the B-17s as bombers but only for maritime operations. [29]

In June 1942 Coastal Command was helped by the transfer of a squadron of Whitleys and eight Liberators from Bomber Command in April and other aircraft were to follow. Advances too were made in the technical field. New depth charges, filled with Torpex (which was 30 per cent more effective than Amatol) were introduced. The fitting of the Mark XIIIQ pistol ensured detonation at 34 feet below the surface, although this was deeper than the ideal of 25 feet. Despite early misgivings at the Air Ministry a full squadron of Leigh Light Wellingtons was formed in February 1942 and by June they had proved so successful that Dönitz ordered all U-boats to proceed submerged at all times except when it was necessary to re-charge batteries, The morale of U-boat crews slumped with the knowledge that darkness no longer afford them protection. During July 1942 the Leigh Light Wellingtons chalked up their first U-boat kill and the following month the Air Ministry approved the formation of a second squadron. At the same time nacelle type Leigh Lights were ordered for all Catalinas and trial installation approved for the Liberators and Fortresses.

Wing Commander John Bernard Russell DSO, from near Barnstaple, flew

---

Fortress Squadrons Coastal Command 1942-1945

Squadron	History
59	Converted to Fortress II, December 1942. Used II/IIA on operations, January 1943-April 1943
206	Converted to Fortress II/IIAs August 1942. Used on ops, September 1942-April 1944
220	Fortress I, December 1941-July 1942. II/IIA from July 1942-January 1945
251 (Met)	Re-formed at Reykjavik, Iceland, 1 August 1944. Operated Fortress II/IIAs March 1945-0ctober 1945
517 (Met)	Operated B-17F September-November 1943
519 (Met)	Operated Fortress II, November 1944-September 1945
521 (Met)	Operated Fortress II/III August 1944-February 1946

N.B. Met - Metrological calibration

the first Leigh Light aircraft on operations. He had worked hard with the pilots and crews who had perfected the new night technique and it was largely due to his interest and encouragement that the squadron became operational so quickly. On that first sortie the squadron made two attacks on U-boats, which were picked up in the brilliant rays of the powerful searchlights. Russell was responsible for much of the subsequent development of the Leigh Light aircraft and it was for his work with these specially equipped Liberators that he received the DSO. He himself flew on numerous operational Leigh Light sorties after that first attack.

On one occasion early in 1944 he spotted a U-boat in the Bay of Biscay in the ray of his searchlight. The submarine commander crash-dived, leaving a tell-tale wake, which showed up clearly in the searchlight. Down went Russell's depth charges and the U-boat was forced to the surface again.

'It was a fine but cloudy night,' Russell set down in his log later, 'with moon obscured. I switched on the Leigh Light and illuminated a surfaced U-boat well trimmed down. It immediately began to dive and disappeared before we reached the spot, but I dropped a stick of depth charges ahead of the swirl. Five minutes later we saw the U-boat had re-surfaced about two miles away. As we flew over it opened fire, so we continued to shadow it while homing another aircraft to the scene. This aircraft attacked and the U-boat disappeared. I think it must have been damaged after the first attack; otherwise it would not have been likely to re-surface so soon. And after it disappeared an orange glow persisted for about ten minutes. I've never seen anything quite like it before and can only think it was caused by a fire in the U-boat.'

But the Germans were determined to counter continued Allied organisation and ingenuity and Admiral Dönitz managed to persuade Hermann Göring, head of the Luftwaffe, to let him have 24 Junkers Ju 88s for operation in the Bay of Biscay. He was further helped by the sudden appearance of large fleets of fishing vessels which began operating at night. The blip produced on the ASV screen by a tunnyman was indistinguishable from that of a U-boat. Each time Leigh Light operators exposed their searchlights to light up a fishing vessel they compromised their own position and were needlessly running down their batteries. By mid-August 1942 the French fishing fleet was so widespread that night operations against U-boats virtually came to a halt. Despite appeals, leaflet dropping and threats of capture or shooting up the vessels, only the end of the season brought relief.

A more serious problem was caused by the knowledge that the Germans had obtained an ASV Mark II set from a Hudson which had unfortunately crashed in Tunisia. By mid-September 1942 the Germans had developed the Metox 600, capable of receiving and recording ASV transmission from up to thirty miles and had fitted it to large numbers of their U-boats. This enabled them to dive well before they were sighted by anti-submarine aircraft. An attempt to flood the Bay of Biscay with ASV transmissions failed and by January 1943 Coastal Command aircraft had almost ceased to locate U-boats by night. The only answer was to replace the ASV Mark II, which had only a one and half metre wavelength, with the long overdue ASV Mark III of ten centimetres wavelength. This apparatus was already in operation having originated from an adaptation of centimetric AI. An American version, developed with the help of British scientists, had been tested successfully in May 1942. Within a few months USAAF Liberators on anti-submarine duties in the Western Hemisphere had been equipped with these or similar sets but by August 1942 it was evident that first British models would not be available until spring 1943.

Meanwhile, with U-boat packs prevented from finding any rich pickings

RAF 15 Group and 247 Group (Azores) Fortress/U-boat Actions					
Date	Aircraft	Sqn	Group	U-Boat	Remarks
27 October 1942	FL457/F	206	15	U-627	Pilot Officer R.L. Cowey Sunk south of Iceland
15 January 1943	FL452/G	206	15	U-337	Pilot Officer L.G. Clark Sunk south-west of Iceland
3 February 1943	FL456/N	220	15	U-265	Pilot Officer K. Ramsden Sunk 540 miles West of Malin Head
7 February 1943	FL459/J	220	15	U-624	Pilot Officer G. Roberson Sunk south-east of Greenland
9 February 1943	FL 195/L	206	15	U-614	Squadron Leader R.C. Patrick DFC Damaged
7 March 1943	FL459/J	220	15	U-633	Flying Officer W. Knowles Probable. Sunk South of Iceland
19 March 1943	FK203/M	220	15	U-666	Flying Officer W. Knowles Damaged.
19 March1943	FK208/B	220	15	U-384	Pilot Officer L.G. Clark Sunk 660 miles SE of Greenland
25 March 1943	FK195/L	206	15	U-469	Flight Lieutenant W. Roxburgh Sunk 80 miles SSE of Iceland
27 March 1943	FK195/L	206	15	U-169	Flying Officer A C I Samuel Sunk 180 miles SSE of Iceland
24 April 1943	FL451/D	206	15	U-710	Flying Officer R.L Cowey Sunk 120 miles south of Iceland
6 June 1943	FL458/A	220	15	U-450	Squadron Leader H. Warren Attacked in the Mediterranean
11 June 1943	FA704/R	206	15	U-417	Wing Cdr R.B. Thompson DSO DFC Sunk 120 miles NW of Faeroes
17 June 1943	FL457/F	206	15	U-338	Pilot Officer L.G. Clark DFC. Damaged
9 November 1943	FL459/J	220	247	U-707	Flight Lieutenant R.P Drummond Sunk 300 miles E of the Azores
6 January 1944	FA705/U	206	247	U-270	Flight Lieutenant A.J. Pinhorn DFC Damaged
13 March 1944	FA700/R	206	247	U-575	Flight Lieutenant A.D. Beaty joint action with a Wellington
	FL459/J	206	247	U-575	Flying Officer W. R. Travell 172 Squadron and USN. Sunk.
26 September 1944	FK191/P	220	247	U-871	Flight Lieutenant A. F. Wallace (Capt) Flying Officer E. C. W. Fields (pilot) Sunk 480 miles NW of the Azores

Sqn	Mark	Aircraft	Date	U-boat	Details
			RAF/RCAF Liberator U-boat Actions		
120	I	AM917/F	16 August 1942	U-89	Damaged by S/L T M Bulloch
120	I		18 August 1942	U-653	Damaged by S/L T M Bulloch
120	I	AM929/H	12 October 1942	U-597	Sunk SSW of Iceland. S/L T M Bulloch DFC
224	III	FL910/H	20 October 1942	U-216	Sunk Bay of Biscay. F/O D M Sleep DFC
224	III	FK225/G	24 October 1942	U-599	Sunk N of Azores. P/O B P Liddlington
120			5 November 1942	U-89? U-132?	damaged and/or sunk by S/L T M Bulloch
120			10 December 1942	U-611	Possibly sunk by S/L T M Bulloch S of Iceland
120	III	FK232/S	15 February 1943	U-225	Sunk west of Cape Clear. F/O R F T Turner DFC
120	III	FK223/T	21 February 1943	U-623	Sunk 540 miles N of Azores. S/L D F Isted DFC
120		FK223/N	5 April 1943	U-635	Sunk 440 miles SW of Iceland. F/O G L Hatherley
86	III	FL930/R	6 April 1943	U-632	Sunk 440 miles SW of Iceland. F/L C W Burcher & RN
120	III	FL923/V	23 April 1943	U-189	Sunk near Iceland. F/O J K Moffatt DFC
86	III	FL955/P	4 May 1943	U-109	Sunk 540 miles NNE of Azores. P/O J C Green
120	I	AM919/P	20 May 43	U-258	Sunk 530 miles SSW of Iceland. S/L J R E Proctor DFC
120	I	AM919/E	28 May 43	U-304	Sunk 360 miles SE of Greenland. F/O D C Fleming-Williams DFC
224	III	FL963/J	3 July 1943	U-628	Sunk in Bay of Biscay. S/L P J Cundy DSO DFC
53	GR.V	BZ751/G	5 July 1943	U-535	Sunk nr Cape Finisterre. F/Sgt W Anderson
224	GR.V	BZ721/R	8 July 1943	U-514	NE of Cape Finisterre. S/L T Bulloch DSO DFC*
224	GR.V	BZ721/W	28 July 1943	U-404	Bay of Biscay (with a 4th ASS USAF B-24)
200	GR.V	BZ832/D	11 August 1943	U-468	Bathurst near Dakar. Flying Officer L. A. Trigg VC
10 RCAF		BZ586/A	19 September 1943	U-341	Sunk 330 miles SSW of Iceland. F/L R. F. Fisher.
120	I	AM917/F	20 September 1943	U-338	Sunk 450 miles ESE of Greenland with HMCS ship.
86	GR.V	FL954/Z	8 October 1943	U-643	Sunk in North Atlantic. F/O C W Burcher DFC
120	III	FK223/T			F/O D C L Webber DFC
86	III	FL930/R	8 October 1943	U-419	Sunk 450 miles SSW of Iceland. F/L J Wright DFC
120	III	FK223/E	16 October 1943	U-470	Sunk 370 miles SW of Ireland. F/L H F Kerrigan
120	III	FK223/Z			F/L B E Peck DFC
59	GR.V	FL973/C			P/O W G Loney
59	GR.V	FL984/S	16 October 1943	U-844	Sunk 360 miles SW of Iceland. Both Liberators were shot down.
86		FL952			
86	III	FK241/Y		U-964	Sunk 500 miles ESE of Cape Farewell. F/O G Gamble
59	GR.V	BZ712/D	17 October 1943	U-540	Sunk E of Cape Farewell. F/L E Knowles DFM
120	I	AM929/H	17 October 1943	U-540	W/O B W Turnbull DFC CGM
224		AM929/Z	23 October 1943	U-274	Sunk 420 miles SSW Iceland. S/L E J Wicht DSO DFC
10 RCAF		'6A' 58	26 October 1943	U-420	Sunk 480 miles ENE of St John's F/L R. M. Aldwinkle
86	III	FL931/M	16 November 1943	U-280	Sunk 600 miles N of Azores. F/O J H Bookless RAAF
53	GR.V	BZ814/B	13 December 1943	U-391	Sunk in Bay of Biscay. S/L G Crawford DFC AFC
59	GR.V	FL984/S	25 May 1944	U-990	Sunk 120 miles NW of Trondheim. S/L B A Sisson
59	GR.V	FL984/S	27 May 1944	U-292	Sunk 90 miles WNW of Stadtlandet. F/L V E Camacho
53			7 June 1944	U-629	Sunk west of Brest. F/L J. W. Carmichael
224		FL984/G	8 June 1944	U-373 U-441	sunk W of Brest. F/L K. O. Moore RCAF
120		FL984/F	9 June 1944	U-740	Sunk W of Scillies. F/L A K Sherwood DFC
206	VI	EV943/K	10 June 1944	U-821	Sunk W of Ushant with Mosquitoes on 248 Squadron
86	III	FL916/N	26 June 1944	U-317	Sunk 106 miles NNE of Shetlands. F/L G W T Parker
311 Czech		FL916/O	26 June 1944	U-971	Damaged by F/O J Vella DFC. Sunk by destroyers

86	III	FL924/E	30 June 1944	U-478	Sunk off Norway. F/O N Smith DFC & Canso 162 Sqn
86	VI	EV947/E	15 July 1944	U-319	Sunk WSW of Lister. F/O D W Thynne (shot down)
86	III	FK223/U	17 July 1944	U-361	Sunk W of Narvik. P/O M G Moseley DFC
53	VI	EV877/C	9 August 1944	U-608	Sunk Bay of Biscay. W/C R T F Gates & HMS Wren
53	VI	EW302/G	14 August 1944	U-618	Sunk W of St Nazaire. F/L G G Potter & RN frigates
86	III	FK223/T	8 October 1944	U-643	Sunk in N Atlantic. F/O D C L Webber DFC
		FL954/Z			F/O C W Burcher DFC
311 Czech		FK223/Y & H	4 November 1944	U-1060	Beached after action NW of Namsos with two Halifaxes
224		KH340/O	29 March 1945	U-1106	Sunk NW of Shetlands. F/L M A Graham
86	VIII	KH224/V	23 April 1945	U-396	Sunk SW of Shetlands. F/L J T Lawrence
120	VIII	KH224/Q	29 April 1945	U-1017	Sunk 135 miles WNW of Malin Head. F/O H Oliver
311 Czech		KH224/L	5 May 1945	U-3523	Kattegat
224		KH347/G	5 May 1945	U-3523	Sunk E of Aarhus. F/L T H Gouldie DFC
86		KH290/K	5 May 1945	U-3503	Severely damaged in the Kattegat/scuttled.
					F/O M C Kay
86	VIII	KH290/K	6 May 1945	U-1008	Sunk in Kattegat. F/O M C Kay
547	VIII	KK250/K	5 May 1945	U-579	Sunk in the Little Belt F/O A A Bruneau DFC
RAAF					
86	VIII	KH347/G	5 May 1945	U-534	Sunk 13 miles NE of Anholt. W/O J D Nichol DFC
86	VIII	KH347/G	6 May 1945	U-2534	Sunk south of Göteborg

in waters five hundred miles from Anglo-American airbases, Dönitz was forced to concentrate his forces in the 'Greenland Gap' and the 'Azores Gap' where Allied air patrols could not penetrate. The only solution was to close the gaps using carrier-borne or very long range land based aircraft. In August 1942 there were no aircraft carriers or auxiliary carriers available for trans-Atlantic convoys while there were only five VLR Liberator Is (on 120 Squadron at Ballykelly in Northern Ireland) in the whole of Coastal Command. These aircraft had an operational range of 2,400 miles while the Squadron's remaining Liberator Mark IIs and IIIs could only extend 1,800 miles and 1,680 miles respectively. Air Vice Marshal John C. Slessor, Commanding Coastal Command, undertook a special mission to Washington to speed up the supply of Liberators.

At 2000 hours on 9 August, an unidentified ship sent a U-boat distress signal. It was subsequently believed that this signal was sent by the troop ship SS Letitia which had left the Clyde, bound for Halifax, Nova Scotia on 7 August with 600 troops on board. At 1922 hours on 11 August, two corvettes were detached from convoy HX201 to search for survivors, on the following and subsequent day's aircraft were also used in the search. Consequently, on the morning of 13 August Liberator IIIA LV341/Z on 120 Squadron captained by Pilot Officer Victor Dennis James RNZAF was airborne at 0533 hours and joined the search.

At 11.25 hours during the patrol the crew of Z/120 sighted a U-boat trimmed down on the surface. It was U-256, a Type VII U-boat commanded by Odo Loewe. As the Liberator went into the attack it was sighted by the submarines lookouts who mistook it for a Sunderland. U-256 crash dived to a depth of 110 metres, three depth charges were heard to explode, but U-256 suffered no damage. After this attack Z/120 sent a signal saying that a U-boat had been attacked but the results were unobserved. A further signal was sent at 1220 hours to say that they expected to arrive back at base at 1627 hours. On the flight home the crew of the Liberator were feeling rather pleased with themselves but disappointed at not seeing the results of their attack. Pilot Officer James and Sergeant Hector Vivian Francis Archer RAFVR, the second pilot, were in their seats. Sergeant William C. Gordon, one of the air gunners, who was off duty, was sitting behind them. Sergeant Frederick N. Hollies, another gunner, was standing behind the pilots. Flight Sergeant Kenneth Henry Watson RAFVR was operating the wireless. Sergeant Seymour 'Bill' Clare, flight engineer, returned from a routine inspection to report that there was a slight smell of petrol in the bomb bay. Gordon was getting on at Watson to take his turn in the rear turret so as to allow Sergeant Peter F. George, who was already in the turret to come up front for his stint on the wireless. Watson was not too keen to give up his seat until he picked up base, which for some reason he was having difficulty finding. Gordon insisted that he had over run his time on the set and at last Watson relieved George in the rear turret.

At about 1515 hours, Gordon was helping himself from a large tin of raisins and talking to George who had taken over the radio position which was working perfectly, he was listening out for 7VY, 15 Group HQ in Liverpool. An explosion, heard by Hollies who was still on the flight deck took place in the vicinity of the bomb bay. The aircraft lost power and dropped rapidly towards the sea, George stood up and opened the top escape hatch, the skipper looked round and at that moment the engines picked up, the skipper laughed and George shut the hatch. Then the aircraft seriously lost power, all four engines stopped firing at the same time and the aircraft dropped like a stone, Z was flying at 500 feet under low cloud. George opened the top escape hatch again and James shouted to Flight Sergeant Alfred Burton Craig RCAF, navigator to fetch the Mae Wests from the tail of the aircraft, he then pushed the control column forward to pick up speed and just off the water pulled back on the control column to stall her. 'Z' hit the sea tail first and then the nose went in. Craig had jumped into the bomb bay to make his way towards the tail, at the same instant Gordon looked between the two pilots and saw the sea coming up to meet them at a great speed, he realised that the navigator had no chance of reaching the Mae Wests and shouted for him to come back, Craig stood in the bomb bay looking up, seemingly not able to make up his mind who to listen to. Hollies also looked between the two pilots to see Archer frantically working the four ignition switches which were situated along side his right knee, up and down, in an attempt to get the engines to fire again, but they were dead. Hollies then laid flat on the flight deck.

As the aircraft hit the sea, George was thrown forward between the pilots seats, there was a heavy inrush of water, the nose section broke away and he was struggling to find his way out, he say in his own words 'I think I got out through a hole in the front perspex, losing a flying boot in the process, I was the last man out'. Gordon says 'We on the flight deck in the nose, managed to fight our way out through the broken perspex before she sank, to do so we had to wait until the cabin was almost filled with water, we were actually under water and the force of it coming in made it difficult to get out. Six of us got out, but Billy Clare and the first pilot drowned before we could inflate the dinghies. Owing to the swell and our being fully clothed, this took some time, none of us had our Mae Wests on'.

The Liberator carried two dinghies which could be released from inside the aircraft by a red painted handle above and to the left of the flight engineers control panel. Gordon made a grab for this handle but the aircraft hit the sea before he could reach it and he was thrown against the armour plate behind the pilot's seat knocking his head, he was stunned, he felt weights on top of him, which he says were probably the flight engineer and his control panel. It is possible that the flight engineer was also hit on the head by the panel; he was also thrown against the armour plate and was stunned. Suddenly the weights which were holding Gordon down left him and in his own words, 'Felt that he was drifting through cotton wool clouds, everything was very peaceful'. Then his face broke the surface of the sea and the full horror of the situation hit him. The first thing he saw was the flight engineers face. He seemed to be looking at him in a faraway fashion. He then vanished without a sound. He was not seen again. George also saw the flight engineer in the water some yards away from him, struggling to keep afloat, he came up went down and then disappeared. Sergeant Clare probably got out of the aircraft by way of the escape hatch above and behind the pilot's position which had been opened by George, he had managed to get onto the wing but was washed off in the heavy sea, he could not swim. The tail section containing the rear turret with Watson trapped in it, sank, he too was not seen again. The skipper had also managed to get onto the wing but he too had been washed off into the sea. James, a strong swimmer, was in the water close to Gordon and some distance away from George but a strong current was pulling then away from the aircraft. Archer, who was also close too George was struggling, he was wearing a collar and tie and they were restricting his breathing.

Z was now slowly sinking, the broken fuselage sticking up in the air, it had snapped off aft of the mid-upper turret which had lost its perspex cover. It is thought that the navigator was trapped in the bomb bay when the aircraft ditched.

Hollies was the only airman left on the aircraft. He had got out via the upper escape hatch and onto the fuselage but was afraid to let go and jump into the water as he too could not swim, he managed to reach and was standing in the mid-upper turret and as 'Z' got lower in the water he was forced to climb higher up the fuselage, in a last desperate attempt to escape the rising water held onto the R/T aerial with his teeth and made a grab for a handle which he managed to grasp. Immediately two dinghies fell out; one fully inflated the other not. They had dropped into the water alongside George, he found the air bottle on the under inflated dinghy and triggered it, up it came, upside down, George turned it over, got in and pulled Archer in after him.

By this time, James and Gordon were further away shouting for help.

George and Archer were trying to assemble the oars in the dinghy and shouted to them 'Swim to us'. Gordon pulled off his flying boots and battle dress blouse, as they were dragging him down and swam to the dinghy. Hollies was persuaded to let go of the handle and was pulled into the dinghy, as was Gordon. But James had disappeared.

The aircraft was carrying two anti-submarine bombs, so they paddled away to avoid a possible explosion and watched as Z sank into the Atlantic. They were depressed at the sight, as only bits and pieces were floating around where the aircraft had sunk. They took stock of the situation searching the dinghies, they found that there was no food, no water and no pyrotechnics, but one bar of chocolate was found in Georges battle dress pocket, two squares each, they did find a piece of string which they used to tie the dinghies together.

There was a heavy swell running and they all felt seasick, they lay back and those still wearing boots took then off to avoid damage to the dinghy and stored them in the other one. George had a sprained ankle and lacerated leg, while the others were alright but bruised. Archer was asked how far he thought they were from land but he did not seem to know for sure, but reckoned anything up to a few hundred miles. They rowed for the rest of the day in an easterly direction and rested best they could during the night, the sky was cloudy and it began to rain, it rained on and off all night, their teeth never stopped chattering. The next day the sky was clearer and around noon they were cheered by sunshine, two ships were sighted in the afternoon and aircraft heard, they shouted and waved but with no result. A seagull flew around them and settled on the water near to them, they tried to hit it with an oar but it was too quick for them and flew off. Gordon thought they must be close to land but the others said that seagulls could be found up to six hundred miles from land.

Early evening saw a ship close by, it seemed to be heading towards them; they could not believe their luck. They all stood up, Gordon brandishing an oar so they could be seen, the ship approached them bow on, it closed in, one of the seamen had a Lewis gun trained on them, following them around, the crew thinking they were Germans. The ship was a trawler, the *Glenagill* from Fleetwood, whose crew threw a line and picked up the four survivors. Heaven, hot cocoa, a plate of stew and a bunk to stretch out on and sleep. The next morning the four were transferred to a Naval vessel at the entrance to Lough Foyle, the *Bluebird*, a peace time motor yacht owned by Malcolm Campbell and loaned to the Royal Navy. They had a shower and food and were met at the dockside by the Squadron CO, Wing Commander Harrison and then on to the sick bay and later a few days at home on survivors leave.

When Z/120 crashed she was on course for Inistrahull, a light house close to the entrance of Lough Foyle and the turning point for Ballykelly, therefore close to the Irish coast. When the trawler picked them up they were 37 miles West South West of Tory Island and could see the coast of Donegal in the distance. The troopship, SS *Letitia* arrived unmolested in Halifax on 16 August. It was never discovered what ship sent the distress signal. [30]

A Coastal Command pilot, Squadron Leader R. P. Nehns, of North Harrow, Middlesex, had to ditch his Liberator which was badly shot up while attacking the first U-boat he had spotted on his second tour of operations. He had completed his first tour without his aircraft receiving so much as a bullet scratch. The Liberator was on fire when he tried to ditch. The aircraft struck the water heavily and Nelms was knocked unconscious. When he came to he was trapped in the aircraft beneath the Atlantic waves. For about thirty seconds he struggled desperately to get out of the aircraft and then realized what was holding him down - the safety straps.

'I pulled the pin from, my straps,' he recounted afterwards, 'pushed the wreckage aside, climbed out of the cockpit and bobbed up to the surface, to find the other members of the crew floating with the wreckage.'

The survivors recovered three one-man dinghies floating among the wreckage. These they tied together. They also salvaged a food pack, some flame floats and a stock of Very cartridges. For sixty hours the six survivors from the Liberator stuck together, helping one another through an ordeal of lashing rain and high-riding seas.

At the end of that time a searching Catalina spotted them and swooped down to the rescue.

'I don't know how long I was in the cockpit beneath the sea,' the Squadron Leader told the station Intelligence Officer later, 'but it seemed to be a long time and I was well down in the water.'

And that water happened to be well north of the Arctic Circle, in one of the most distant areas patrolled by Coastal Command aircraft. It was a miracle that the Catalina found the men clinging to the tied dinghies. There was a gale blowing at the time, whipping up a forty-foot swell on the sea.

When the war started, Terence M. Bulloch, a short, stocky, twenty-three year-old Ulsterman born in County Antrim on 19 February 1916 and educated at Campbell College, Belfast was a young pilot who had been commissioned as an Acting Pilot Officer on 25 January 1937. He proved himself an above average pilot on the Ansons he was flying. In May 1940 he changed to Hudsons and, on 206 Squadron, soon found himself with more excitement than patrols with Ansons could provide. Shipping off and around the Dutch coast were the favourite targets and Bulloch soon proved himself in this new pastime. 'It was an exhilarating business. You went in low - below 500 feet - to drop your bombs'. On several occasions when he scored a direct hit Bulloch found himself flying through the debris caused by his own bombs. It was on Hudsons, too, that Bulloch had his first taste of air-to-air combat, having several successful engagements with He 115 float planes. 'We did daylight raids dive-bombing Dutch harbours. The Hudson had five crew and was a good aircraft, although not easy to handle. Landing was the main difficulty. Some people tried to teach pilots to three-point them, which was fatal: they had a tail wheel and it would swing if you landed in a three-point position. So we used to come in on the main gear, with the tail up and then let it go down - then it didn't swing. Because if it swings, the undercarriage will come off and it will catch fire. That happened quite a few times, because we were not on runways, we were on grass fields with old flare pots. None of this fancy runway lighting!

'As far as weaponry went, nobody had heard of cannons; we had .303s, the pilot had two Brownings up front, we had a turret down the back with two and had two Vickers gas-operated guns out the side windows. We didn't carry very much - four 250lb- and six 25lb- incendiary bombs. We used to bomb the barge concentrations in the harbours at night. At this time, barge concentrations were building up in all the ports of Western Europe, in Germany and Holland, ready for the invasion. We used to go to Emden quite often at night. God knows what the results were. We used to bomb the harbours anyway. We were also doing a lot of shipping forays up in the North Sea. 16 Group, from Bircham Newton, used to escort convoys down the east coast. This was extremely dull: we would fly the length of the convoy and then turn round again. We would fly patterns. This was mainly on the Hudson, in the early days of the war. But on two occasions in August and September 1940 we encountered Heinkel 115 float planes off the Dutch coast and engaged them. I shot the first one down and we dropped a bomb close to the second. They both sank.

'Over the war years, the technology improved. It was scandalous; the early charges we used, Royal Navy 450-pounders. On one of the early attacks I did, in the late summer of 1941, one of them exploded on impact with the water. I was flying over at about eighty feet and it nearly blew my tail off. They had no ballistic qualities at all; they would just tumble over like an old oil drum. We didn't get any equipment. It was terrible - we didn't get the proper depth charges until the end of 1941 and beginning of 1942.'

When his first operational tour came to an end, Bulloch went for the usual 'rest period.' He was posted, at his own request, to the Atlantic Ferry Unit and sent to America. In America Bulloch had his first glimpse of the new B-17 Flying Fortress and after a rapid conversion course he was ready to ferry the first of these aircraft to Britain. Despite the fact that he was new to the aircraft and had never before crossed the Atlantic as pilot, Bulloch made the crossing in style. He broke all existing records by arriving in Scotland only eight hours and twenty minutes after taking off from Gander. 'We were at 23,000 feet, sucking oxygen out of a tube, quite primitive. We landed at Prestwick.'

Terry Bulloch was awarded the DFC and a Mention in Despatches. In August 1941 he joined 120 Squadron at Reykjavik, Iceland. Posted in at the same time was a young, tousle-haired Scotsman called 'Jock' McColl, a flight engineer. A friendship sprang up between 'the Bull' and McColl and it was not often after that that Bulloch would be found flying without McColl at the engineer's panel. Bulloch knew from the outset that antisubmarine warfare was a team effort which counted and was fortunate that his crew were invariably 'keen as mustard.' But keenest was undoubtedly the Captain himself - both in eagerness to get on with the job and in eyesight. One of his crew; when asked who spotted the U-boats in

Bulloch's aircraft replied: 'Oh, it's always Bull. When there are submarines around his eyes seem to stick out of his head.' But Bulloch also gave some thoughts to tactical questions. His keen eyesight had already enabled him to make several attacks on U-Boats, but he was not satisfied with the results. He blamed the text book method of attacking across the beam of a submarine. This meant that most of the eight depth charges would land nowhere near the target. Bulloch argued that, if the attack were to be made almost along the length of the target, all depth charges could get a chance of exploding near the submarine.

'We were supplied with Liberators, thanks to Churchill's intervention with Roosevelt' recalls Bulloch. 'The Liberator was the biggest aeroplane I'd ever flown up to that time. It had four Pratt and Whitney engines, great. The Mark I 'Lib' was actually built for the French, but that order was cancelled and pressure was put on the Americans to let us have them, because the U-boat campaign was becoming very critical. And we got them, but only nine. That's all the sods would let us have. And they were the early model, without self-sealing tanks. They only had two damn great tanks, holding 2,500 gallons and petrol used to slosh around, right in the main spar of the wing. It had 30-calibre guns; the Americans were so far behind. It had no turrets, nothing like that at all. At Prestwick it was modified; they put 20mm cannons down in the nose. Of course it would have been great against surface U-boats if they had given us any armour-piercing ammunition, but being Coastal Command, the Cinderella force, we never got any. We used to dive, drop depth charges, which we ran out of quite soon, because we only carried eight, fire our cannons and the stuff would bounce off, but at least it would make them go under water where they would have to slow down and the convoy would alter course. We used to succeed in doing that.

'Another problem was that the Liberator took quite a long runway; ours were never long enough. We used to fly them all over-laden otherwise they wouldn't carry anything. We had this Mark II ASV with aerials on the wings and what looked like a Christmas tree down the back. There were also side aerials and we used to carry eight crew. We'd fly sixteen- or seventeen-hour patrols. There wasn't much heating on the plane, but we'd cook meals on solid-fuel stoves and we had an Elsan chemical toilet, so we survived OK. We'd also smoke, though because the Liberator didn't have self-sealing tanks and there was always a petrol smell on the flight deck, we never knew when there would be a loud bang!

'We were tasked mainly with convoy escorts, but really, they weren't sure what to do with the Liberators. One time, we were detailed to go down to the Bay of Biscay to attack surface ships. It was not on, crazy. It was not the task that the thing was designed for: low-level, dropping a 550lb delayed-action bomb. That's where my rear-gunner got bits of shrapnel in his head and lost an eye, all because we weren't given a proper detail or task. We also used to do photographic reconnaissance at night; we'd fly over places like Stavanger and take photographs. We were looking for the Scharnhorst. The photo flash showed of course, which immediately exposed us, so they used to shoot hell out of us. We soon stopped that, thank God and then we started proper anti-submarine tasking and patterns. Each aeroplane was given a certain sector, because then they had good, reliable intelligence from the Enigma breakthrough. So we were sent out to where we would be useful, because they knew in essence where the submarine packs were. We never looked back after that.

'There was a standard procedure, but it was rather ancient. We were told that, if we saw a U-boat, we should go hell for leather at it and attack it at any angle. This invariably meant crossing its track at right angles, which was stupid, because you'd only get two depth charges near it. So I devised a system whereby, if you went in and out of cloud, you could stalk it and get into position and then either attack it up or down track at an angle of about twenty degrees. You had really to get within ten or twelve feet of its pressure hull to do any damage with depth charges. They used to go down to 25 feet; they were set hydrostatically by a fuse. So you had to get the U-boats either on the surface - which was difficult because if they spotted you they'd be down in sixty seconds - or just below it. If it was lower than 25 feet it would give them a bit of a shock, but do very little, if any, damage. I didn't work out my method properly until the end of 1941, when I started seeing quite a lot of U-boats. We used to figure it out. Mind you, I had a very good crew, well trained and they always kept a good look-out from the side and rear-gun positions (where a mirror-attachment camera was positioned underneath and activated when I pressed the tit to release the depth charges). The rear-gunner had a K24 hand-held camera as well, which was useful.'

It must be remembered that the pilot of a Liberator was not flying a fighter aircraft which responded delicately to control. A Liberator weighed about twenty-eight tons and it was stubborn to handle.

On 22 October 1941 Bulloch made 120 Squadron's first attack on a U-boat when he badly damaged U-203 with depth charges. In December during convoy escort for HG.76 when U-751 sank the escort carrier *Audacity*, U-71 was sighted on the surface and Flying Officer Bannister attacked with depth charges, forcing it to submerge, leaking oil. Bannister's Liberator was eventually relieved by Bulloch's aircraft and during his time on patrol he sighted three more U-boats but they all submerged before any attack could be made. By the second week in August 1942 Bulloch had sighted seven U-boats and attacked three of them. On 16 August in AM917 'F-Freddie' he seriously damaged U-89 commanded by Kapitänleutnant Dietrich Lohmann, which was on its second war cruise having left Brest for the US coast on 6 June. Two days' later Bulloch attacked and damaged U-653 commanded by Kapitänleutnant Gerhard Fieler, forcing the submarine away from Convoy SL.118. Depth Charges and cannon and machine-gun fire from the Liberator and a passing shot with two anti-submarine bombs failed to deliver the coup de grace.

On 12 October, while flying close escort to Convoy ONS.130 in AM929 'H-Harry', SSW of Iceland, one of Bulloch's crew sighted a U-boat eight miles to starboard. Bulloch closed on the submarine from out of the sun and lined up on the stern of the U-boat, which was later identified as U-597 commanded by 28-year old Korvettenkapitän Eberhard Bopst on it second war cruise, having left Brest on 16 September. Bulloch attacked along the length of the U-boat, dropping his six shallow-set depth-charges at 25 feet spacing. One exploded next to the stern, two either side of the submarine's hull and another next to its bow. Bulloch reported that the U-boat literally blew up, hurling a 'large oval chunk' of steel skyward that almost hit his rear gun turret. With its pressure hull ruptured in several places, U-597 sank with all 49 hands. Bulloch was awarded a bar to his DFC for this attack.

On 5 November, while operating with Convoy SC.107, Bulloch and his crew sighted a U-boat which dived before it could be attacked. They later found another U-boat, which Bulloch attacked with six depth-charges from bow to stern. It was either U-89, which Bulloch had attacked on 16 August or U-132 which was missing after 5 November 1942 with all 47 hands. Dietrich Lohmann was now on his third war cruise having left Brest on 4 October and was bound for the Mediterranean. U-89 disappeared, but a few minutes later, air bubbles came to the surface. Bulloch was credited with damaging U-89 and sinking U-132.[31] At 14:56 hours the crew found another U-boat, seen 25 miles from the convoy and this time Bulloch attacked with two depth-charges shortly after it submerged, but with no apparent success. On 1 December, Bulloch was awarded the DSO.

Bulloch's 'big day' was 8 December, piloting Liberator I AM921 and operating with Convoy HX.217, which had left Canadian waters and was being trailed by twenty-two U-boats in mid-Atlantic. With him went H. R. Thompson as second pilot and Flying Officer Mike Layton, as navigator. The flight engineer was of course, 'Jock' McColl. The crew was completed by Sergeants Turner, Clayton and Scoular, the gunners and wireless operators. 'We were operating out of Iceland' recalled Bulloch 'because from there we could get right down into the gap off Greenland, where the Germans had their submarine packs. This job was a convoy, 25 ships and five escort vessels, from Halifax to Liverpool. I spotted eight U-boats that day and attacked seven of them. I came down at about fifty feet - we had to, because we didn't have any bomb sights. I didn't worry about the sun: not in December, over the North Atlantic! I came in from the rear at an angle. The submarine looked very narrow; and as always it was just starting to submerge. I dropped off six depth charges right along the track of the U-boat. Then we saw a great patch of oil of about seven or eight hundred yards. I signalled a corvette that was near to investigate and he signalled back, 'You killed him; pieces of dead bodies seen'. Mind you, they were probably people from the conning tower - they'd left the poor buggers on top when they dived.

'Our second sub that day came within half an hour. It was ahead of the convoy, off to one side, several miles away. We did an attack on it, but it had spotted us and was submerging. We only had two depth charges left, so I dropped those, but it was no good. It gave them a fright, though. Then during the next five hours we spotted six more. They were bobbing up all over the place. At one point, I was trying to eat some steak and potatoes one of the air-gunners had prepared, with 'George', the automatic pilot, in charge. A U-boat popped up. The plate went spinning off my knee; it ruined my lunch, but we dived and fired our cannons, really had a go at them and made sure the U-boat didn't get within torpedo range of the convoy. When we got back, our ground crew knew from our signals about our successes, so we celebrated.'

In the space of five hours Bulloch had made eight sightings and seven attacks. He was credited with sinking U-611 commanded by 29-year old Kapitänleutnant Nikolaus von Jacobs, which sank with all 45 hands. [32] During all this, U-254 was crippled in a collision with U-221 during an attack on the convoy, which sailed happily on with the loss of only one vessel before reaching England. U-254 resurfaced but Kapitänleutnant Hans Gilardone the commander could not dive again. Four of the crew jumped overboard and were picked up by U-221 but U-254 remained on the surface and endured another attack by Terry Bulloch, who depth-charged U-254 and which sank with the loss of all 41 hands. Escorts sank another U-boat and other aircraft accounted for a third submarine. Air Marshal Sir Philip Joubert the C in C Coastal Command said that Bulloch and his crew had 'shown the greatest skill and determination in making attacks on each of the eight U-Boats sighted.'

Bulloch left 120 Squadron in December 1942. During his eighteen months on the squadron he had sighted no less than twenty-eight U-boats and had attacked sixteen of them. On 1 January he was awarded a bar to his DSO. Squadron Leader Terence 'Hawkeyes' M. Bulloch became the most highly decorated pilot in RAF Coastal Command, credited with sinking more U-boats than any other pilot. 'I reckon I sighted more than anybody else in the command during the whole war period: twenty-eight. Of these, I attacked nineteen. The others went under before I could get into position to do anything; if I'd tried, it would only have been a waste of my depth charges. They credited me with only four destroyed and a couple of those were marginal. We were under the Navy's control and they wouldn't give you the skin off a rice pudding.'

Operation 'Torch', the Anglo-American invasion of French North Africa in November 1942, placed an additional burden on Coastal Command. Patrols flown against U-boats in the Bay and the waters around Gibraltar were intensified and close escort provided for the convoys. The runway at Gibraltar was widened and at the same time extended 450 yards into the sea which made it possible for three more Coastal Squadrons - 210, 500 and 608 - to be sent out to join 202 and 233. After the first vessels had sailed, the Admiralty suddenly asked for air support for five more convoys, but Coastal Command aircraft were already fully committed so Joubert was allowed to borrow Halifaxes on 405 Squadron RCAF from Bomber Command and eight Liberators from the USAAF. Fortunately, several U-boats which might otherwise have played havoc with Operation 'Torch' were grouped well to the south-west, off West Africa. Though most of the fourteen invasion convoys crept along at no more than six or seven knots and some of them crossed the very mouth of the Bay, only two U-boats were seen to approach our line of passage. Both were sunk by Liberators on 224 Squadron. In the second case the depth-charges hit the vessel abaft the conning-tower, exploded on impact and seriously damaged the Liberator - especially in the elevators. 'Aircraft', runs the laconic entry in the squadron diary, 'went into steep incontrollable climb, almost stalling. Climb counteracted by combined efforts of both pilots. Rear-gunner saw elevators disintegrate and wreckage or debris flew up past the tail. Aircraft was extremely tail heavy and A/S bombs could not be jettisoned owing to damaged gear. One and a half hours' later flight-engineer managed to open bomb doors and jettison A/S bombs manually. All other loose heavy gear was also jettisoned. Flight back accomplished by both pilots continuously relieved, bracing hands and knees on control column and all crew in nose of aircraft. About one hour before landing control columns had to be tied forward with straps. W/T went u/s. Electrical equipment commenced to function with switches in 'off' position. Batteries were switched off in case of fire. Scilly Isles sighted about 1840 to starboard from 14,000 feet. Crew decided to chance crash-landing at Predannack. When over aerodrome, elevator control broke loose becoming u/s. Crash landed, Sergeant Rose suffered compound fracture of leg, rest of crew superficial scratches and cuts. Aircraft destroyed by fire'.

The U-boats to the south-west intercepted a lightly-escorted convoy from Sierra Leone. Other German submarines further out hastened to join in the slaughter and the unfortunate convoy became a veritable sacrifice for the success of the invasion. The Admiralty had reckoned that 'Torch' might suffer attack by seventy U-boats. On 2 November the first convoys came under air cover from Gibraltar and by 7 November, the eve of the landings, the Coastal aircraft on the Rock were putting up some 48 sorties a day, averaging nearly eight hours each. By then twenty-two U-boats were spotted by air patrols before the assaults were launched. Thirteen of these were successfully attacked and damaged while no Allied ship was lost. For many days the Gibraltar-based aircraft maintained this effort. Soon it became possible to bring out from home the second squadron, 179, to be equipped with the Leigh Light and the night patrols became as deadly as those flown by day. By mid-December the Coastal squadrons at Gibraltar had flown 8,656 hours on tasks connected with 'Torch'. In the course of these they had sighted 142 U-boats, attacked 83, damaged 23 and sunk three, apart from sharing a fourth' kill ' with an Albacore of the Fleet Air Arm. All this they had achieved at a cost of seventeen aircraft.

During the closing months of 1942 many U-boats began to 'fight back' when attacked from the air. 'Attacked a U-boat which was fully surfaced' records 311 (Czech) Squadron on 7 September; 'our aircraft dived to attack from a height of 1,200 feet. U-boat opened fire with cannon and machine gun and our aircraft was hit in the fuselage. Most members of crew injured. The Captain however, pressed the attack home and the six depth charges, dropped from seventy feet, straddled the conning tower. Our crew were unable to determine number each side of conning-tower owing to their injuries. Rear-gunner observed the U-boat lift bodily in depth charge explosions. Rear-gunner fired approximately 400 rounds and observed tracers hit the conning-tower. U-boat dived slowly and submerged one minute after depth charge attack. Owing to injuries to the crew the Captain left the scene of the attack at once, climbed to 500 feet and set course for base. Crash landed at St. Eval, owing to failure of hydraulics. Navigator seriously injured in both legs, front-gunner small finger of left hand shot away, wireless-operator splinter wounds in right arm, second pilot splinter wounds in leg'.

On 8 December a Liberator on 120 Squadron, joining convoy HX.217 far out in mid-Atlantic, found a 'Wolf-pack' in full cry. '0900 hours began escort', runs the entry in the Squadron diary: '0929 hours sighted and attacked one U -boat with six depth charges, straddling U-boat. Ten feet eruption of water seen, oil streak, numerous pieces yellow wood; many sea gulls collected on and over the oil patch. Aircraft informed Senior Naval Officer of attack and guided Corvette K.214 to oil patch. K.214 signalled 'You killed him' and that parts of dead bodies were seen'. In the remaining ten hours before this Liberator turned for home its crew spotted six more of the 'pack', but having already dropped their depth charges could attack only with cannon fire. In each case this drove the enemy below the surface and helped to save the convoy.

Meanwhile, two Hudson squadrons, 59 and 224, began converting to the Liberator but neither was operational until October 1942. Flight Lieutenant John Brooks, a flight engineer on Liberators, recalls converting 224 Squadron from two-engined Hudsons to the Liberator.

'Sixteen Liberator IIs and Vs were flown in between October and December 1942 from the USA to the Scottish Aviation works at Prestwick. All the necessary modifications to convert the high altitude bombers to anti-submarine aircraft were carried out. Defensive armament was largely stripped out and radar and British navigation equipment installed. (The stripping out of defensive armament was later abandoned as the enemy stepped up its fighter patrols in the Bay of Biscay in the defence of its U-boat force.) Crew training went remarkably smoothly but was hampered to some extent by the poor weather of the Western Isles and the unsuitability of the runways which were merely strips of tarmac laid on to the sandy soil of Tiree. The weight of the Liberators soon created a wave pattern at the touchdown points at the end of the runway and were temporarily filled in with wooden chips. The months of August and September were spent in type training exercises, circuits and landings, navigational and wireless exercises and air gunnery practice. On 25 August crews were formed and operational exercises carried out in co-operation with Royal Navy submarines and fighter aircraft. At the end of August the squadron moved to Beaulieu in the New Forest in Hampshire and became operational, flying convoy escorts and anti-submarine sweeps in the Bay of Biscay in October.'

In the meantime 120 Squadron continued to bear the brunt of anti-submarine duties in the Atlantic. Edward Bailey, a WOM/AIR, joined the pioneer RAF Liberator squadron in September 1942 at Nutts Corner. The Northern Ireland base was not without its problems as he recalls:

'The main Belfast to Londonderry railway line crossed one runway and railway signals were operated from flying control before we could take off. I was appointed to a crew under-going squadron training and spent a few months on ground and air training prior to becoming operational. Practice navigational flights were made to various positions over the Atlantic and sometimes we had to locate Rockall. There was also gunnery and bombing practice over Loch Neagh with 10lb smoke bombs. The flight engineer loaded these bombs while we were in flight and it was considered 'infra dig' for the pilot to open the bomb doors while the engineer was carrying out this task!

'We had about two Liberator Mark Is and the rest were Mark IIIs. The Mark I had no rear turret but had a 0.5 machine gun mounted in the tail protected by curved doors which could slide open for firing. Under the fuselage, just forward of the bomb bay, were mounted four cannon which we used when going into attack on the U-boats. Inside the aircraft we had a rudimentary cooking stove and a sleeping bunk just rear of the bomb bay which was very useful on the long seagoing patrols. At the time of my arrival the Liberator Mark Is were just going out of service and most operations were carried out by the Mark IIIs.'

Steps had been taken to help shorten the gap between American air patrols from Newfoundland and Nova Scotia and British air patrols from Iceland and Northern Ireland. In August 1942 Britain had asked the Royal Canadian Air Force if they could extend their anti-submarine and convoy protection sorties to 800 miles to help close part of the Atlantic gap but this was not possible as the first Canadian Liberators did not arrive until April 1943. In September 1942, 120 Squadron provided a detachment of Liberators in Iceland. The strategic value of this remote island in the North Atlantic had been recognized as far back as 1940 when British forces forestalled a German invasion and landed at Reykjavik. Liberators on 120 Squadron operated from an airfield on the south east edge of the capital. Edward Bailey recalls the procedure for a typical operation:

'The crew were called (often in the early hours) three hours before take-off and pilots, navigator and the 1st WOp or WOM went to the operations room for briefing. We then had a 'flying meal' (very good considering it was wartime) before loading the Liberator with parachutes, individual dinghies, Mae Wests and flying rations. In winter we sometimes had to help sweep snow off the main plane before we could take off. We always took off from Iceland using maximum boost. The runway was rather short and take-off with a full load and a cross wind could be difficult. Towards the end of 1943 we flew unladen to another airfield with a longer runway where we loaded up and took off.

'After becoming airborne, the crew who stayed on the flight deck for take-off got into their positions. The navigator went to his place in the nose. When the pilot had set course and adjusted the trim of the aircraft, one WOp/AG went to the rear turret and another went either to the radar or the nose to keep a lookout and the third took up a listening watch on the radio, ready to transmit messages if necessary. These three changed their positions every hour. Every half hour the weather report from Reykjavik was received. After about four hours of flying, fuel from the overload tanks in the bomb bay was transferred to the main wing tanks. On escort duties with convoys it was the Senior Naval Officer (SNO) who instructed the captain of the aircraft where he wished the search (often a square search) made. The length of time the Liberator stayed on patrol was generally left to the captain of the aircraft but normally it was about six to seven hours. As weather conditions in Iceland were extremely variable weather reports were vital. If the weather closed in over Iceland, the aircraft had to be diverted to Northern Ireland or the Hebrides.

'On this tour all navigation was carried out by dead reckoning which demanded great skill and hard work from the navigator - ours was very good. The navigator was the one member of the crew who had to work flat out for the whole length of the trip. Pilots could put the Liberator on 'George', the automatic pilot and although vigilance was essential from all members of the crew, a certain amount of relaxation was permitted. The navigator however had no chance to relax.'

Shipping losses in the Atlantic continued to mount and in October 1942 temporary relief was provided by the 330th and 409th Bomb Squadrons of the 93rd Bomb Group belonging to the Eighth Air Force. This Group had previously experienced anti-submarine duties in the Gulf of Mexico. On 25 October 1942 the 330th Squadron was transferred from its base at Alconbury to Holmsley South, Hampshire, while the 409th began operations from St Eval in Cornwall. That month 86 Squadron RAF began receiving Liberators and acting as a training unit for 160 Squadron until February 1943, when it received its own Liberators and in March began moving to Northern Ireland where it also flew anti-submarine patrols, 160 Squadron had already begun converting from Hudsons in August 1942 at Thorney Island with Liberators from 59 Squadron. By 24 October 1942 four crews were deemed fully operational and made eleven to twelve hour anti-submarine escorts for a convoy well out in the North Atlantic, landing back at St. Eval, Cornwall. From then the number of sorties by day and night built up rapidly and various actions took place in the Bay of Biscay and the Channel approaches, including at least three genuine U-boat attacks without radar, which was not then fitted.

Towards the end of 1942 Coastal Command was forced once more to diversify its operational strategy. The invasion of French North Africa placed considerable strain on the already overworked command which carried out photo-reconnaissance missions over French and Italian naval bases as well as the area where 'Operation Torch' would land. In addition, meteorological flights were flown far out over the Atlantic and a constant vigil maintained over German capital ships lurking in Norwegian fjords. Most important of all, the number of anti-submarine patrols in the Bay of Biscay and the waters around Gibraltar had to be stepped up to protect the convoys heading for North Africa. Coastal Command airfields in the West

Country were developed to meet the increase in operations. St Eval was converted to take seventy-two aircraft while Chivenor was organised for a peak compliment of eighty-eight aircraft. Coastal Command aircraft and the Liberators of the 93rd's 330th and 409th Squadrons, on detached duty with the RAF, were fully committed to Operation 'Torch', providing long range protection duties for the invasion fleet scouring the Bay of Biscay for up to twelve hours at a time searching for the elusive U-boats. Despite a handful of sightings, no attacks were made.

The Halifaxes on 405 Squadron and the eight Liberators from the Eighth Air Force helped provide excellent cover. The only two U-boats which were seen to approach their line of passage were sunk by two Liberators on 224 Squadron. They undoubtedly saved the operation from further trouble and on 2 November the first convoys came within reach of air cover provided from Gibraltar. German aircraft put in an appearance in November and two attacks were met by Liberators of the 93rd Bomb Group detachment. The most memorable clash occurred on 21 November when Major Ramsey D. Potts of the 330th was faced with an onslaught of five Junkers Ju 88s. Undaunted the B-24 gunners, aided by the Germans' cumbersome approach, dispatched two and damaged a third. In late November both squadrons, having provided excellent service in the Bay of Biscay, returned to Alconbury.

The training of RAF Liberator crews posed something of a problem. An environment free of interruption from enemy aircraft was needed and by the end of 1942 two large construction programmes by the Americans enabled 111 Operational Training Unit to start flying on the island of New Providence in the Bahamas. Oakes Field, the principal base, had a main East-West runway of 6,000 feet carved out of coral rocks and was used for operational training with a fleet of about forty B-25 Mitchell light bombers. Having successfully passed out of this phase of training, the aircrews moved to the other end of the island to the satellite station of Windsor Field which had 7,000 foot runways occupied by nearly thirty Liberators. Here the syllabus culminated in a very long flight over the sea almost to Bermuda and back searching for a small group of RN ships on anti-submarine exercises. Finally, the crews went to Canada and their ultimate destinations in UK or ACSEA Liberator squadrons. Besides RAF, the training intakes included batches of Czech, Canadian and Australian and New Zealand air force personnel. They came by way of the Canadian training organization and were joined by others who had already completed a tour of operations on other aircraft (mainly Hudsons) in the UK. In 1943 Coastal Command succeeded in training 1,233 crews for overseas commands and 630 for home commands. However good might be the work performed in the operational training units, the final hallmark of a successful and efficient crew was conferred by the battle itself. The old principle, an ounce of practice is worth a ton of theory, was demonstrated again and again.

Air crews started coming through to Coastal Command with regularity but aircraft like the badly needed Liberators were still in short supply. In late March 1943 59 Squadron returned to Thorney Island to re-equip with Liberators for the second time. Now it was the much-modified VLR (Very Long Range) Liberator V, stripped of much of its armour and armament but able to lift 2,000 gallons of fuel and still carry eight 250lb depth charges.

During the early part of 1943 and up to the middle of May 1943 the weight of the U-boat attacks was still to be felt in the North Atlantic. In this dreary waste of ocean Dönitz employed U-boats in large 'Groups' or 'Wolf Packs' against convoys. On 6 February 22-year old Squadron Leader Desmond J. Isted DFC on 120 Squadron whose home was at Reading, was flying X-X-Ray near SC 118, a large convoy of 61 ships. He was homed in on a U-boat after its signals were traced with HF/DF. It was U-465, which was commanded by 28-year old Kapitänleutnant Heinz Wolf. Isted's attack only damaged the boat but the presence of the Liberator overhead in the thinning cloud cover deterred other U-boats from making a close approach.[33]

Three days' later Squadron Leader R. C. Patrick DFC, a Canadian from Ontario, was leading a Fortress patrol on 206 Squadron when he sighted a U-boat six miles away. It was U-614 commanded by 26-year old Kapitänleutnant Wolfgang Sträter. The submarine was on its first war cruise having left Kiel on 9 January and on 7 February had sunk the 5,730-ton British tramp SS *Harmala* and damaged the 9,272-ton SS *Daghild*. The *Harmala*, which had fallen out of station, was loaded with ore and sank quickly. The watchers in the Fortress saw five Germans standing in the conning tower. 'They stood there and watched us just as though we were a friendly craft making a practice attack. Then down went our depth charges to straddle the U-boat just forward of the conning tower. In the explosion that followed the U-boat was lifted out of the water and slewed round thirty degrees and when things had quietened down a little there was not a sign of the hatless men. All we saw was the sub, fully four feet higher out of the sea than before the explosions. There was a terrific uprush of bubbles over a wide area and we saw that she had lost all forward way. Two or three minutes later, as my gunners raked her with cannon fire, she settled and sank.'[34]

Aircraft helped save ON (Outbound North) 166 from disaster in February 1943. From bases in Iceland, Ireland and the Western Isles flew Sunderlands, Liberators, Flying Fortresses and Catalinas, in the worst possible Atlantic weather to protect ships with vitally needed war cargoes. For five days, 21-25 February, the U-boat pack dogged the convoy, at times as near as five miles from the great concourse of ships, at others more than thirty miles distant. A running fight ensued over 1,100 miles with 21 U-boats, which sunk 14 ships of ON 166.[35] Coastal Command flew thousands of miles in less than four days. A single Liberator attacked three U-boats within four hours, depth-charging two of them and cannon-raking the third. Within twenty-four hours of the first German attack on a ship three U-boats had been attacked and a fourth sighted. In one patrol period of eight hours Liberators and Fortresses no less than five separate attacks and three additional sightings. On 21 February Squadron Leader Desmond

Isted DFC led a Liberator patrol that sighted two U-boats and attacked one of them. It was U-623, which was commanded by twenty-year old Oberleutnant zur see Hermann Schröder, who was from Hamburg.[36] Isted flew six miles to reach his target and swept down so low that he was or thirty feet above the underwater craft when his bombs slipped from their racks. 'The flight engineer, standing in the bomb-bay got the full effect of the blast from the explosion, which shook the plane. He actually heard the noise of explosion above the roar of our engines. It was certainly terrific and debris seemed to be falling on the water for several seconds afterwards. A large black object, probably the bottom of the U-boat, leaped out of the water and then slowly sank. The crew were convinced it was a kill, for when we left the spot there was an ever-increasing patch of oil and a two foot length of bright yellow timber was floating in the middle of it. The inside of a U-boat is painted yellow. Seagulls hovered, vulture-like, overhead.' U-623 sank 540 miles north of the Azores and was lost with all 46 hands.[37]

Footnotes

24   On 17 January 1941 the first Liberator for the RAF made its maiden flight. In August deliveries to the RAF of 139 Liberators on an original French contract began and by December that year 65 had been delivered to Britain. Many were delivered without turrets and these began operations as transports while the armed version became the Liberator II. The Liberator I was the designation applied to LB-30Bs which were modified and armed for use with RAF Coastal Command. The forward bomb bay was sealed off and a gun pack consisting of four 20mm cannon was mounted underneath. The majority of the Mark I 'Sticklebacks' were equipped with early ASV radar antennae on the nose, under the wings and on the top of the rear fuselage. Other LB-30Bs flew as transports while LB-30As also flew with RAF Transport Command and the Return Ferry Service. All Liberators up to and including the Liberator Mark III (B-24D) were supplied under direct British contracts.
25   By the end of the war Liberators equipped a dozen Coastal Command squadrons – Nos. 53, 59, 86, 120, 200, 206, 220, 224, 233, 301, 502 and 547 - at one time or another.
26   These were later supplemented by squadrons of Liberator IIIs, which were used for general maritime duties far out in the Atlantic. The Liberator Mark IIIA and subsequent versions were supplied under Lend-Lease and handed over to the RAF by the USAAF. A later series B-24D, used in RAF service, was designated the Liberator Mark V, equipped with additional fuel tanks in wing bays and centimetric ASV radar either in a retractable radome in the ventral position aft of the bomb bays or in the 'Dumbo' or 'chin' position. B-24Ds were supplied to the RCAF in September 1943 and twelve others went to the RAAF in 1944. The RCAF Liberators were similar to the RAF Mark II. Deliveries of the 'Dumbo' version were also made to the RCAF. In November 1943 deliveries of the B.VI and GR.VI Liberators began. These versions were Convair-built B-24H and J with American turrets except for the tail turret which was by Boulton Paul. The GR.VI anti-submarine aircraft later incorporated a radome containing centimetric radar in place of the ball turret. The B VI was used by RAF squadrons overseas and was also used by the RCAF for training while in the Atlantic and Bay of Biscay. By the end of the war over 1,800 Mark VIs and VIIIs had been used by the RAF, RCAF and RAAF, the greatest number of all models. In the Middle East the Liberator Mark VI was used mainly against enemy shipping in the Mediterranean. Beginning in July 1944 36 Mark VIIIs were delivered to the RAF in that theatre, each equipped with centimetric radar designed for PFF operations against ground targets. By the end of the war almost 2,500 Liberators of one sort or another had been delivered to the RAF, RCAF and the RAAF of which 1,694 were supplied by Consolidated alone.

27   Sixteen B-17Cs and thirty B-17Es.

28 One, FK185, was used as a test-bed for an experimental 40mm cannon in the nose intended for use against U-boats on the surface.

29   Most were used by Coastal Command, although during 1944-1945, some served on two RCM squadrons in 100 Group.

30   Thanks are due to Bill Clare's son Peter for this story. W. C. Gordon. F. N. Hollies and P. F. George survived the war. Archer was killed in May 1943, having been shot down over the Bay of Biscay.

31   U-89 was sunk on 11 December 1943 by a Swordfish on 811 Squadron FAA from HMS *Biter* and depth charged by the destroyer HMS *Broadway* and the frigate HMS *Lagan* escorting Convoy HX.237 450 miles north of the Azores and was lost with all 48 hands. *U-Boat Fact File* by Peter Sharpe (Midland Publishing Ltd 1998).

32   *U-Boat Fact File* by Peter Sharpe (Midland Publishing Ltd 1998) attributes the kill to a Catalina piloted by Lieutenant L. L. Davis of USN squadron VP-84 south of Iceland.

33   *The Real Cruel Sea: The Merchant Navy in the Battle of the Atlantic, 1939-1943 by* Richard Woodman (John Murray 2004). U-465 was damaged again on 10 April 1943 by a Catalina of 210 Squadron. A Sunderland of 461 Squadron RAAF finally sank the boat on 2 May 1943 west of St. Nazaire. *U-Boat Fact File 1935-1945* by Peter Sharpe (Midland 1998).

34   U-614 was damaged in the attack.

35   *U-Boat Fact File 1935-1945* by Peter Sharpe (Midland 1998).

36   *U-Boat Fact File 1935-1945* by Peter Sharpe (Midland 1998).

37   *U-Boat Fact File 1935-1945* by Peter Sharpe (Midland 1998).

Chapter 3

Convoy Escort

'... *Have you ever prayed for death? Have you ever longed for a swift, merciful release from it all in the shape of a quick bullet in the brain?*
I longed for it many times after my ship was torpedoed in the Atlantic.
Is your hair white? Mine is like the driven snow. And it's not through age or infirmity. It is the result of a sequence of events that marked the patrol in the summer of 1943 of the U-123.
In May of that year I was master of the 4,566-ton British steamer SS Holmbury and was congratulating myself on my immunity from enemy attack. My steamer was heavily laden with Argentine foodstuffs - tinned meats, linseed and hides - and we were on our way from Buenos Aires to the West African port of Freetown.
At that time the approaches to Freetown were a top priority target for Hitler's U-boats and for three days and nights I had been almost continuously on the bridge, scanning those sinister waters for the tell-tale 'feather' a periscope always leaves.
Then, without warning, on 5 May, came the crash of a torpedo exploding in the stokehold. It was closely followed by another plump into No. 1 hold.
One minute my ship had been a whole living unit. The next she was a shambles of twisted metal, hissing steam, flames and the pungent smell of cordite.
The ship was sinking fairly rapidly and above the deafening hiss of escaping steam I gave the order to the crew to abandon her. With only one boat left serviceable this was quickly done.
I jumped to the nearest raft and, prompted by seaman's instinct, looked over the side. All was clear, except that out of the corner of my eye I saw the long greyish-white body of a shark.
Then, with a snort of air bubbles, the submarine surfaced.
The conning-tower hatch opened, the gun's crew filed swiftly along the watery fore-deck and I found the muzzle of a 3·9 gun looking my way.
Their intentions were obvious. They were going to shell the ship. I was faced with the alternative of shark's teeth or Nazi shells. I lived a lifetime in those few moments of indecision. Suddenly I made my mind up. I chose the shark.
In a matter of seconds I had released the raft, pulled it alongside and clambered on board. I paddled toward the lifeboat. Willing hands helped me into it and I made a check-up on the crew. All were present except two firemen who had been killed by the first torpedo.
The submarine now began to approach us and in clipped and faultless English a voice from the conning-tower loud-hailer ordered us alongside.

Quickly I told my men to keep their heads down and to agree with me in saying that the Captain had been killed.

From the conning-tower the Commander, Count von Schroeter, scrutinized us with an alert and youthful eye.

He spoke in cultured tones: 'I want the Captain, please.'...

No reply. One by one he asked every man in the boat if he knew of the whereabouts of the Captain. The reply was always the same. The Captain was dead.

After a while he said to me: 'You are chief-officer. Please come on my submarine.' I obeyed. I had no option.

I told the crew the course to set to make the coast, ninety miles to the eastward, told them to notify the ship's owners and my wife of what had happened, waved them bon voyage and they were off - leaving me with a decided lump in my throat.

No sooner were they out of the line of fire than the U-boat's gun opened up. She put twenty-six shells into the Holmbury and hastened her sinking.

The Commander ordered me below and subjected me to a routine interrogation. At first he seemed annoyed.

'Why did you order your men to keep down in the boat? Were you afraid I was going to machine-gun you?'

I nodded and his voice became almost guttural with rage. He drew himself up to his full height and beat his chest. 'Damned lying British propaganda,' he snarled. 'I am a German naval officer; I do not do things like that.'

After searching me, he gave me a change of clothes, cigarettes and a glass of brandy, which I certainly needed.

Space was limited, so I was given a hammock in the bow torpedo-room. Then I set about acquainting myself with my new surroundings.

The crew were quite friendly and all very young. The Commander himself was only twenty-five and most of the others were between nineteen and twenty-one.

On the third day after my capture I confessed that I was the Captain of the Holmbury, The Commander wagged his finger, gave me a wicked grin and said: 'Do you think I did not know? I always pick the man who looks the most worried.'

Von Schröter then made a little speech to his crew that stamped him as a humane gentleman in spite of the Nazi eagle that decorated his cap. 'This prisoner,' he said, 'is the Captain of a ship, so please me by treating him with the respect his position commands.'

The submarine used to lie on the surface all night charging her batteries and on the fourth night after my capture she was doing just that.

I was in the conning-tower assisting the second officer in the navigation, a task I undertook in the hope of learning something of value that I could tell the Admiralty later. There were four look-our men in the conning-tower and one of them pointed and handed his binoculars to the second officer. He looked and then pressed two electric bells. In a second the Commander was in the conning-tower and the rest of the crew at battle stations. I managed to get a glance through the binoculars and there, under the tropical moon, was a grey-painted armed merchantman heading north. Obviously a convoy straggler.

The Commander turned to me and said: 'We are going to submerge to conning-tower depth and stalk that ship until the moon goes down. It will not be pleasant for you to witness the misfortunes of your countrymen, so please go below.'
I went and seconds later I heard the diesels throb. The sub was closing in for the kill. The diesels stopped. The four young torpedo-men were at battle stations. I saw them load the tubes. Suddenly came the Commander's voice. Five crisp words in German and then, 'Fire!'
A button was pressed, there was a hiss of compressed air and the bow of the boat lifted as four tons of death sped on its way. Sixty-five seconds passed and then came two great muffled rumbling explosions. Another thirty seconds and then the Commander's voice sharp with triumph: 'Schiff gesunken'. She [the 6,244 ton SS Kanbe] had gone down like a stone.
For the German Navy it was another triumph. For U-123 another scalp and for two score of my countrymen a watery grave somewhere in the Atlantic.
Then we were off again to run into an experience that still haunts my dreams. We were just west of the Azores, motoring along on the surface when an RAF Sunderland dived slap-bang on to us out of a cloudy sky.
There was a clang of alarm bells and in sixty seconds we were 180 feet below the sea - trying to dodge a hail of cannon-shells and the first of the depth-charges. We levelled off at 280 feet and down came two more depth-charges. For thirty minutes the attack went on and little did those RAF men know that the most frightened person aboard the submarine they were out to destroy was one of their own countrymen.
After four hours' lying low, Von Schroter decided to surface.
As we came up I saw the blood drain from his face as he scanned the horizon.
'Dive to one hundred metres - British destroyer!' he shouted. Down we went again and - horror of horrors - this time the vessel could not be kept on an even keel. We seemed to be slithering fast toward the bed of the ocean.
At 260 feet we hovered almost vertically and then down came the depth-charges. I felt the horror of being trapped in a tomb underseas.
The crashes around us were like hammer-blows on a sardine tin. Electric bulbs went out and still we were stuck almost vertically.
Desperately the U-boat crew fought to level their ship. Then we were all ordered forward and slowly we began to get on an even keel. Then the engines started, we began to creep away from the attack.
But that destroyer seemed to have second sight. Down came another salvo of depth-charges - another and yet another.
We were deeper than the crew had ever been before. Breathing became difficult. And more and more depth-charges came down.
Six hours passed. Then twelve and still we lay below the ocean.
The air was almost solid but our hopes were rising: the last salvo of depth-charges had been far away.
Then came a new salvo much nearer and this time I felt the angel of death at my throat. Noises drummed in my ears. The nose of one of the crew was bleeding. For the next few hours our lives hung in the balance. I felt I was being strangled. I tried to speak, but no words came.
It was twenty-eight hours before Von Schröter gave the order to surface and

those first breaths of fresh air were nectar itself.
I was alive, but when I looked into a mirror the shock of my image nearly
stopped my heart.
Before that submarine submerged I was a vigorous dark-haired man of thirty-
nine. Now my hair was grey. I swear that there was a grey tinge, too, in the hair
of von Schröter himself.
Three weeks later the patrol was over and we were entering the French port of
Lorient and the famous submarine pens there.
As we lined up on deck Von Schröter beckoned to me. 'Have you anything to ask
of me before you go into captivity?' he said.
I said I would like a large bottle of German beer and at once my request was
granted. Ten minutes later I was escorted down the gangway while a German
brass band sarcastically played:
'We'll be hanging out our washing on the Siegfried Line.'
As I passed the conning-tower Von Schröter beckoned to me again.
'I had photographs taken of the sinking of your ship. You shall have them one
year after the war has ended.'
I thanked him and went away to two years of captivity. Those were years that
turned my grey hair into white...'

**U-boat captive J. B. Lawson, quoted in *70 True Stories of the Second
World War* (Odhams Press Ltd). U-123 was a Type IXB of 1,051 tons
commanded by Oberleutnant zur see Horst von Schröter, who was born
in Bieberstein on 10 June 1919. It was in its 10th war cruise, having left
Lorient on 13 March 1943. On 19 August 1944 it was blown up at
Lorient as unseaworthy. von Schröter was awarded the Knight's Cross
on 1 June 1944. He took command of the U-2506 that August and
continued in command of this submarine until the end of the war.**

'The U-boat war' said Mr. Churchill at one point 'is a war of groping and
drowning, of ambuscade and stratagem, of science and seamanship.' This
was never more true than during 16 to 20 March 1943 when U-boat hunting
in 'Wolf Packs' successfully attacked two convoys, HX.229 and the
eastbound Slow Convoy 122, composed of fifty merchant ships, which
sailed from New York with a Canadian local escort on 5 March. Four days'
later, a feeder convoy of fourteen ships from Halifax, Nova Scotia,
including a rescue ship joined the convoy, swelling the convoy to fifty laden
merchant vessels; five bound for Iceland and forty-five for the British Isles.
On 8 March the fast convoy Halifax 229 left New York. It consisted of forty
merchant ships plus a local escort group of five vessels. Two merchant ships
aborted, leaving thirty-eight, one of which eventually reached Northern
Ireland on her own. On 15 March Slow 122 sailing along at about seven
knots, ran into a furious gale and the two smallest ships in the convoy fell
behind; one of which left the convoy and reached Iceland safely and the
other after she developed leaks in a coal bin that could not be stopped was
sunk by a corvette after her crew were taken off.[38]
At dawn on the 16th in heavy weather, U-91 picked up convoy Halifax

229. Other U-boats were summoned to the scene and by the evening most of the pack were present and able to make a determined assault. The first ship sunk was the *Elin K* with a full cargo of wheat and manganese ore, which was picked off by U-603 commanded by 26-year old pipe-smoking Oberleutnant zur see Hans-Joachim Bertelsmann who fired four torpedoes at the 5,214-ton Norwegian vessel.[39] On March 16 and 17 eight U-boats attacked Halifax 229 in the mistaken belief that it was Slow Convoy 122, which was about 100 miles ahead of HX.229 which was following approximately the same route. Twenty-eight year old Kapitänleutnant Manfred Kinzel commanding U-338 found Slow Convoy 122 on 16/17 March. He sank four ships with five torpedoes; *Kingsbury, King Gruffydd*, which was carrying iron ore, 500 tons of tobacco and 493 tons of high explosives; the 7,886-ton Dutch vessel *Alderamin* and the old 4,071-ton Panamanian freighter *Granville* loaded with military stores for Iceland and also carrying 500 bags of mail for the American garrison there.[40] The SC.122 rescue ship *Zamalek*, screened by the corvette HMS *Saxifrage*, fell out to pick up survivors.[41] Kinzel also damaged *Fort Cedar Lake* before damage caused in a depth-charge attack by Fortress 'F' on 206 Squadron flown by Pilot Officer Leslie G. Clark and from surface escorts forced him to abort on the 19th. The attack by the Fortress killed one crewman and badly wounded three other men. On 22 March U-338 was limping back to port when Halifax BB314 on 58 Squadron piloted by Flying Officer L. McCullock spotted her. Kinzel decided to stay on the surface and fight. His gunners shot the Halifax down on its approach to attack. The only survivor on the crew was the flight engineer, Sergeant J. Taylor, who was picked up by the U-boat and taken to St Nazaire.[42]

Dawn on the 17th found the commodore in charge of HX.229 very anxious. The U-boat pack was obviously increasing in strength and to counter it only the surface escorts were available. At 0200 hours his fears were justified. By then the convoy was reaching a point at which it could be given air cover from extreme range. Five ships in Convoy HX.229 were torpedoed in quick succession, some so swiftly that the flames which engulfed the whole of their after-part barely had time to take hold before they were quenched with a savage, indescribably cruel hissing roar. U-91, commanded by 27-year old Kapitänleutnant Heinz Walkerling, who was on his third patrol, sank the old 6,366-ton American freighter *Harry Luckenbach* which went down in four minutes. Walkerling then sought out hulks damaged and abandoned by other U-boats to administer the Fangschuss (finishing-off shot). He quickly sank the 8,174-ton Royal Mail passenger-cargo-liner *Nariva* (which had been damaged by U-600) loaded with 5,600 tons of frozen meat loaded in the Rio de la Plata and the 6,125-ton American freighter *Irénée Du Pont*, which had also been damaged by U-600.[43] The newly-built 7,176-ton American Liberty ship *James Oglethorpe* loaded with her first cargo of steel, cotton and foodstuffs in her holds and aircraft, tractors and trucks on her decks, which had been damaged by U-758, attempted to make St. John's but never arrived. The abandoned 7,196-ton American Liberty ship *William Eustis*, loaded with 7,400 tons of sugar, which had been damaged by four torpedoes fired from U-435 did not sink, even after being depth-charged by HMS *Volunteer*.

U-758 commanded by 26-year old Kapitänleutnant Helmut Manseck sank the 6,813-ton Dutchman *Zaanland*. U-600 commanded by 24-year old Kapitänleutnant Bernhard Zurmühlen disposed of the thirty-year old 12,156-ton British whale factory ship-cum-tanker *Southern Princess*, which was loaded with 10,000 tons of low grade fuel oil below decks and carried two railway locomotives and several invasion barges on the flat whale-flensing deck above the main deck. A torpedo hit on the starboard side under the bridge and the explosion ignited the gas in the top of the rearmost cargo tank and the oil in the holds soon caught fire. A brilliant orange flash split the sky, died down and flared up again. She burned for a long time reddening the water, finally becoming a flickering oily pyre.

Hans-Achim von Rosenberg-Gruszczynski commanding U-384 torpedoed the 7,252-ton British Liberty ship *Coracero* loaded with frozen Argentinean meat; U-631 commanded by 25-year old Oberleutnant zur see Jürgen Krüger sank the 5,158-ton freighter and Dutch prize *Terkoelei* taken in Sourabaya.[44] U-665 commanded by 32-year old Oberleutnant zur see Hans-Jürgen Haupt, which was on its first and only war cruise, sank the 7,134-ton British freighter *Fort Cedar Lake* damaged earlier by U-338. Damage from air and surface escorts forced Haupt to abort and on 22 March a Whitley on 10 OTU[45] flown by Sergeant J. A. Marsden found U-665 with ASV-IV radar and sank the submarine west of Nantes. The U-boat was lost with all 46 hands.

HX.229 had been allocated three Liberators as cover during the day but there was a Force 7 wind blowing across the runways in Iceland and the two Liberators on 120 Squadron detailed to take off in the early morning were unable to take off. Aldergrove in Northern Ireland had detailed two Liberators for each convoy. Flying Officer Chas Hammond on 86 Squadron was detailed to provide SC.122's pre-dusk patrol but failed to find the slow convoy after a four-hour search. (Hammond finally landed in Northern Ireland on two engines having been in the air for twenty hours and thirty minutes). Flying Officer S. E. Esler, a red-haired Northern Irishman on 120 Squadron, was allocated to cover HX.229 in Liberator 'L'. He and his crew were veterans and had already made seven attacks on U-boats on their previous 31 operational sorties. Flight Sergeant T. J. Kempton, Esler's navigator flying in the nose of the Liberator noticed that 'the convoy consisted of far fewer ships than our briefing had indicated'. For two hours Esler's crew saw no U-boat activity but at 1705 hours two U-boats were spotted on the surface ten miles distant. Esler was able to approach out of the sun and got to within 3,000 yards of one of the submarines before it dived. He dropped five depth-charges in a line ahead of the swirl and the bows and conning tower of the U-boat surged up and then sank again beneath the surface. It was U-221 commanded by 27-year old Oberleutnant zur see Hans Trojer. One man was injured but the submarine was undamaged. Three more U-boats were next sighted and two of these dived as the Liberator ran in but U-608, commanded by 26-year old

Kapitänleutnant Rolf Struckmeier, stayed on thesurface and opened fire, which was returned by Esler's gunners. Another U-boat was then sighted almost immediately but all Esler could do was attack with machine gun fire. His patrol time was almost up and all the Irishman could do was signal 'Six hearses [Coastal Command code for a U-boat] in sight bearing 180 degrees 25 miles. I go.'[46]

It was not until 1655 hours that Liberator 'J for Johnnie' on 86 Squadron piloted by Flying Officer Cyril W. Burcher RAAF was able to reach HX.229. 'J for Johnnie' was able to provide escort for four hours. 'Its advent' records the Senior Naval Officer was 'a very welcome sight'. Burcher, who was from Sydney and his crew, which had a RAAF navigator - Flight Sergeant Douglas Paine and Sergeant John Lloyd RNZAF as second pilot - had a record probably unsurpassed in the U-boat war. At one time this crew achieved the distinction of attacking at least one U-boat on every sortie - in one period five in four sorties. Burcher later received the DFC after ten submarine attacks, including one 'kill' and a share in the destruction of another.[47] Burcher discovered a U-boat - it was U-439 commanded by Oberleutnant zur see Helmut von Tippelskirch. Burcher's depth-charges did no material damage but dissuaded U-439 from approaching the convoy.[48] Burcher then attacked two more U-boats with depth charges and one with machine-gun fire, forcing them down. One of them was U-338 commanded by Kapitänleutnant Manfred Kinzel. Although he had no more depth-charges Burcher offered to remain with the convoy as long as his fuel allowed and he continued to patrol ahead until 0915. Seven hours later, with insufficient fuel to land at Aldergrove he landed at the Fleet Air Arm airfield at Eglington near Londonderry. The Liberator had been in the air for eighteen hours and twenty minutes.[49]

Night drew on the U-boats maintained their attack and a storm of 'near hurricane' fury sprang up, visibility fell to two miles and the escorting aircraft failed to find the convoy. Taking advantage of the bad weather, the U-boats renewed their attack and sank two ships in the afternoon, the U-221 sinking the 7,191-ton American Liberty ship *Walter Q. Gresham* and the 8,293-ton fast British refrigerator ship *Canadian Star*, which usually sailed alone but was ordered into convoy because her 4-inch gun was broken. Thirty of her 87 passengers and crew perished in the sinking. [50] The storm of 'near hurricane' fury had struck Slow Convoy 122 and the thirteen pursuing U-boats. After daylight, when Liberators appeared over SC.122, they drove the U-boats off and under. The two convoys were now about 250 to 300 miles west of Iceland. U-305, commanded by 27-year old Kapitänleutnant Rudolf Bahr had earlier been prevented from attacking SC.122 ten miles short of the convoy by Flight Sergeant W. 'Smokey' Stoves piloting a 120 Squadron Liberator. Stoves had continued to patrol the convoy for the next two hours at a range of ten miles and forced U-305 to dive twice more. Bahr however, would not be shaken off on what was his boat's first patrol. He kept the convoy in sight all afternoon before he attacked and damaged the 8,789-ton British cargo liner *Port Auckland* loaded with 8,000 tons of frozen meat and 1,000 tons of general. Later he sank the 4,256-ton *Zouave* loaded with iron ore from Pepel and finished off the stricken *Port Auckland* with a single torpedo.[51]

Three Liberators from Northern Ireland and two from Iceland covered Convoy HX.229 from 1038 hours until 2038 hours. They made six sightings of U-boats and carried out four attacks, scoring no kills but their presence certainly prevented further assaults upon the battered convoy. Squadron Leader Desmond Isted on 120 Squadron attacked U-610 commanded by Kapitänleutnant Walter von Freyberg-Eisenberg-Allmendingen. At least one of his depth-charges exploded right over the U-boat damaging both periscopes, both compasses, a compressor and many instruments and fuses. The damage took five hours to repair, after which the submarine never came into contact with the convoy again. The second U-boat contact was by Flying Officer R. Goodfellow's crew, which was unusual in that it was the only occasion that radar was used during the passage of the two convoys but the submarine dived before an attack run could be made.[52]

Five Liberators on 120 Squadron provided cover for Slow Convoy 122 for a period of ten hours or more. These made four attacks but got no kills. Flying Officer J. K. Moffatt put in a good attack on Bahr's U-305 with four depth-charges but nothing was found. Pilot Officer A. W. Fraser RAAF made two attacks using up all his depth-charges before flying right over a fully surfaced U-boat but could only make it dive.[53] Flying Officer R. T. F. Turner flying at 600 feet just under the cloud base sighted a U-boat three miles in the distance. Twice Turner lined up to attack but each time the submarine - it was U-642 commanded by Kapitänleutnant Herbert Brünning - crash-dived. The Liberator was nearly at the end of its patrol so depth-charges were dropped more in hope than expectation. No damage was caused but Brünning was forced to remain below for the next hour.[54]

Night passed uneventfully, but in the early hours of 19 March, while it was yet dark, another ship was sunk when U-527 commanded by 27-year old Kapitänleutnant Herbert Uhlig got two hits and seriously disabled the 5,848-ton American freighter *Matthew Luckenbach*, which was finished off by U-523, commanded by 25-year old Kapitänleutnant Werner Pietzsch, with one torpedo.[55]

On 19 March the commodore could breathe more easily. His sorely harassed charges were now well within range of Coastal Command. During the day the largest air umbrella yet was mounted to protect a North Atlantic convoy. Three Liberators on 86 and 120 Squadrons and four Fortresses on 206 and 220 Squadrons at Benbecula covered the ships for twelve hours and further sorties were flown by five Sunderlands that had taken off from Castle Archdale on Loch Erne in Northern Ireland at dawn. Although neutral, the Irish Republic had permitted the flying-boats to fly through a narrow corridor up the valley of the River Erne in County Donegal and out over Bundoran to the Atlantic. This greatly extended their range and endurance.[56] These aircraft carried out six attacks on U-boats. Six hundred miles south-east of Greenland, Fortress FK208/B on 220 Squadron flown by Pilot Officer Leslie G. Clark dropped through a snow squall to find and sink U-384 on the surface with four depth-charges. von Rosenberg-

(with 'Dumbo' radome) on 86 Squadron and two other Liberators at Aldergrove, Northern Ireland near Belfast in March 1943. FL933 later operated on 224 Squadron as XB-K. On 4 March 1943 FL952 was being piloted by Flying Officer R. H. Coy and was shot down by return fire from U-844 during his attack on the submarine (which sank 360 miles SW of Iceland). GR.V FL984/S on 59 Squadron was also shot down. (IWM)

With a gaping hole torn in its hull in a rescue attempt at sea this 461 Squadron RAAF Sunderland flying boat was flown back to Wales by Flying Officer Gordon. O. Singleton RAAF on 29 May 1943 and brought down to land safely on the airfield at Angle near St. Ann's Head in Pembrokeshire. Inset: Two dinghy journeys out to the Sunderland were made with the injured men.

Wing Commander (later Air Vice Marshal CB DSO DFC) Ronald B. Thomson DSO, CO, 206 Squadron in June 1943. On 11 June Thomson, was piloting Fortress FA704 'R for Robert' on an anti-submarine patrol and sank U-417. During its run-in to attack 'R for Robert' had been hit in the nose, wings, bomb bay, cockpit and rear turret and three of its four engines and Thomson was forced to ditch. He and his crew were picked up after three days adrift by a Catalina flown by Squadron Leader J.A. Holmes DFC on 190 Squadron.

Flight Lieutenant Kenneth Owen 'Kayo' Moore a Canadian pilot on 224 Squadron laid claim to sinking two U-Boats in a single sortie on 8 June 1944.

Squadron Leader Terence 'Hawkeyes' M. Bulloch became the most highly decorated pilot in RAF Coastal Command, credited with sinking more U-boats than any other pilot. Here he is pictured by the side of LR.V BZ721/R (B-24D 42-40300) on 224 Squadron, which he was flying when he sank U-514 in the Bay of Biscay on 8 July 1943.

Liberator GR.V BZ877 2:Q on 224 Squadron was fitted with rocket projectile sponsons but these were deleted by a wartime censor. On 2 January 1944 this aircraft was piloted by Flight Lieutenant H J. Rayner who sank U-867, which the day before had been attacked on the surface near Bergen by a Mosquito with cannon and machine gun fire and depth charges. BZ877 was allocated to 86 Squadron on 28 September 1944 and served with 22 MU before being SOC in 1947.

Above and below: the superb Leigh Light invented by Squadron Leader Humphrey de Verde Leigh an administration officer at Coastal Command HQ in 1940 which later proved very effective in detecting the enemy U-boats.

Liberator GR.V 'K' on convoy patrol. The 'Dumbo' radome in the nose housed American SCR-517 ASV radar.

U-189 a Type IXC under attack by Liberator III FL923 on 120 Squadron at Reykjavík, Iceland flown by Flying Officer J. K. Moffatt DFC on 23 April 1943. Kapitänleutnant Helmut Kurrer and crew had left Kristiansand twenty days' earlier. The action began when two U-boats were sighted about 450 miles SW of Iceland and Moffatt dived on the nearest boat and dropped four depth charges. U-189 opened fire before they exploded. Moffatt circled and dropped two more DCs. The U-boat began to sink, leaving many crew in the water.

Liberator GR.VI KG865 ZZ-K on 120 Squadron with a Leigh Light fitted below the starboard wing airborne for Lagens in the Azores on 18 April 1945.

Liberator GR. III being loaded up with depth charges, flame and smoke floats and sea markers etc, on 26 February 1944. (IWM)

The *Arandora Star* of the Blue Star Line, which in May 1940 was converted into a troopship and was sunk on 2 July. It was torpedoed 75 miles west of the Bloody Foreland, County Donegal by the U-47 under the command of Günther Prien, who on 14 October 1939 had entered Scapa Flow and sunk the *Royal Oak*.

Above: The *City of Benares*, which departed Liverpool on 13 September 1940 with 199 passengers, o whom 90 were evacuee children, bound for Montreal and Quebec and was torpedoed on the night of Tuesday, 17 September 1940 with the loss of 77 of the evacuee children. On 29 September a Sunderland on 10 Squadron RAAF captained by Squadron Leader W. H. Garing sighted one lifeboat containing six children, two nurses and thirty-eight Lascar seamen. The survivors were picked up by a destroyer and landed at Greenock.

Below: On 3 November 1940 a Sunderland gave protection when the survivors from the *Laurentic*, which had gone to the aid of a sinking ship and was sunk by the U-99 off the Bloody Foreland, County Donegal were picked up. Three torpedoes sent her quickly to the bottom with the loss of 49 lives.

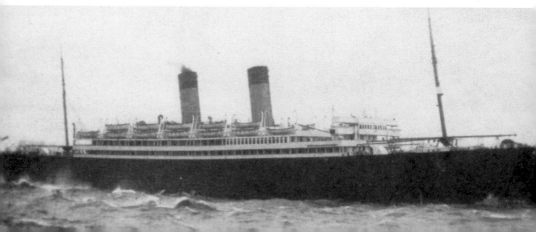

The second *Empress of Britain*, the largest ship ever to be built for the Canadian passenger service across the Atlantic, on fire and listing on 26 October 1940 after being hit by high explosive and incendiary bombs from a long-range German bomber. A Sunderland helped naval units to pick up survivors. Two days' later she was finished off by torpedoes from a U-boat. She was the largest British merchant ship lost in the Second World War.

Crew of Fortress II FA706 'S-Sugar' which claimed the first U-boat sinking from the Azores. L-R: Flight Sergeant J. B. Fitzpatrick; Sergeant F. D. Galloway; Pilot officer J. B. Brodie; Flight Lieutenant R. P. Drummond (skipper); Flight Lieutenant G. A. Grundy; Flying Officer R. D. Thompson; Flight Sergeant F. L. Fitzgibbon and Sergeant L. S. G. Baker. (IWM)

Fortress IIA 'W' on 220 Squadron. In November 1942, 220 Squadron operated from Ballykelly, Northern Ireland and a Met flight detachment operated from St. Eval. During the month Flight Lieutenant Wright depth-charged a U-boat for the squadron's first attack on a U-boat.

Fortresses on Terceira airfield in the Azores in December 1943.

Beaufighter TF.X LZ414 carrying a torpedo. Trials with Beaufighters carrying torpedoes began in 1942.

On 1 March 1944 Beaufighters on 143 Squadron escorted by Spitfires attacked enemy shipping off the Dutch coast and off Texel they found the merchant ship MV *Maasburg,* which was disabled in the first wave of attacks and sunk in a second attack with torpedoes.

Beaufighters on 143 Squadron of the North Coates Wing attacking a German convoy on 22 June 1943.

A Consolidated Catalina on patrol.

blister gunner behind his .50 inch Browning machine gun in a Catalina amphibian.

At 0719 hours on 24 May 1944 a Catalina V flown from Sullom Voe in the Shetlands by Captain C. W. L. Maxwell, a South African serving on 210 Squadron RAF, attacked U-476, a Type VIIC, at about 300 miles North of the Faeroes. This boat was commanded by Oberleutnant zur see Otto Niethmann and had left Bergen on 20 May. U-990 commanded by Kapitänleutnant Hubert Nordheimer rescued twenty-one Germans including Niethmann - ten from a raft and eleven from the wrecked hulk - and then sank the abandoned U-476 with a torpedo. Thirty-four other men perished. Next day U-990 was attacked by Liberator GR.V FL984/S on 59 Squadron piloted by Squadron Leader B. A. Sisson 120 miles NW of Trondheim. The U-boat and its escort returned fire but the 37mm flak gun failed and Sisson dropped six depth charges, which sank the boat. The escort rescued fifty-two Germans, including Niethmann and Nordheimer.

Three inch RPs (Rocket Projectiles) fitted with 25lb armour-piercing heads on the starboard underwing rack on a Beaufighter.

Strike Wing Beaufighters crossing over their shipping targets on 24 July 1944. (IWM)

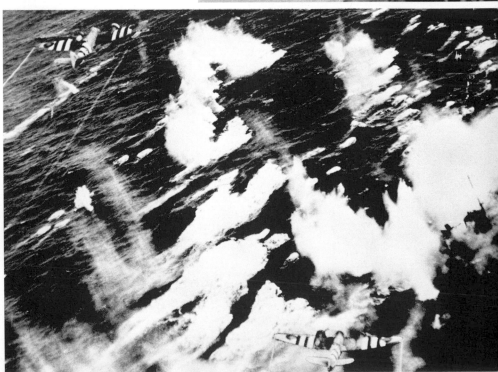

Gruszczynski and all 46 hands were lost. Flying Officer Bill Knowles flying Fortress 'M' on 220 Squadron also attacked a submarine. It was U-666 commanded by Kapitänleutnant Herbert Engel who earlier that same day had torpedoed and severely damaged the 5,234-ton Greek tramp *Carras*, loaded with wheat, which was then sunk by U-333 commanded by Oberleutnant zur see Werner Schwarff.[57] U-666 was slow to dive and Knowles' close straddle of four depth-charges brought firstly oil and then the submarine itself to the surface. U-666 lay there motionless; its decks awash. Knowles was too close to attack again and Engel managed to dive again while the Fortress was circling to make a second attack run. Knowles made his second depth-charge attack just as the U-boat disappeared and more oil came to the surface after this. Engel's boat had suffered severe damage and he was forced to abort to France.

Two of the five Sunderlands caught U-boats on the surface. Flight Lieutenant G. A. Church and crew on 228 Squadron carried out a depth-charge attack on a U-boat well astern of SC.122 but no damage was caused to the submarine. Flight Lieutenant Clare Bradley and crew on a 423 Squadron RCAF Sunderland saved the *Empire Morn* 'from almost certain destruction' at the hands of Manfred Kinzel who was working U-338 into a position to torpedo the straggling 7,000-ton cargo ship which had developed boiler trouble.

Bradley sighted a periscope five miles behind SC.122 during the mid-morning hours, but it was too far off to enable him to deliver an attack. Later U-338 was sighted again, this time barely six miles from the *Empire Morn*. Bradley flew over the cargo ship to warn her of the nearby U-boat and then flew back, found the submarine on the surface and intended to attack with six depth-charges but four hung up and only two were released. U-338 was forced to dive. Bradley remained in the area for some time and finally was able to drop his four remaining depth-charges, one by one for 'scare effect' before turning for home.[58] In the words of the Senior Naval Officer in charge of the convoy's escort, 'These aircraft were a tremendous asset to the escort in preventing day shadowers'. Unfortunately, not being equipped on any large scale with Leigh Lights, the aircraft of Coastal Command were not able to be of assistance during the hours of darkness, though at that time of the year in those latitudes it was possible to remain with the convoy until 0200 hours. Flying Officer 'Red' Esler remained above the convoy for those extra two hours. A fast moving shape was sighted by the navigator Flight Sergeant T. J. Kempton in the nose of the Liberator and only when they were nearly on the vessel was it positively identified as a U-boat. It was U-590 commanded by Korvettenkapitän Heinrich Müller-Edzards whose 33rd birthday had been on 18 March. As Esler went into the attack the bomb doors were still opening. The pilot's press-button release was only operative with bomb doors fully open and the release mechanism failed to work. The rear gunner fired five long bursts which scored hits around the conning tower but the submarine dived by the time Esler could attack with depth-charges. Finally, Esler set course for Aldergrove having flown for 36 out of the past seventy hours, having sighted eight U-boats and making five attacks.[59]

On 20 March the presence of the U-boats was still manifest, but by then the air escort had been increased and three Fortresses covered the convoy continuously for nearly thirteen hours while ten Sunderlands carried out a sweep close by to cover not only convoy SC.122 but also HX.229, which, composed of faster vessels, was closing on it from astern. In this sweep 'T for Toc' on 201 Squadron found a U-boat on the surface and claimed to have sunk her. 'Z for Zebra' on the same squadron damaged a second. In the meantime convoy HX.229 was drawing near on a converging course. There were in it forty ships steaming in eleven columns. In all twenty-two ships were sunk in Convoy HX.229 and SC.122. 'This is so far the best result obtained in a convoy battle' noted the German Admiralty in its War Diary.

On 25 March Flight Lieutenant William 'Bill' Roxburgh, a Glaswegian, was skipper of Fortress FK195/L on 206 Squadron at Benbecula, flying yet another monotonous 'water-watching' patrol, escorting Convoy RU.67 80 miles SSE of Iceland when his 'moment' came.

'We'd been stooging around for hours when, as we emerged from a cloud, someone shouted over the intercom, 'Look-out'. He was so excited he couldn't say another word. Less than two miles away was a U-boat, a peach of a target. [It was U-469, commanded by 25-year old Oberleutnant zur see Emil Claussen on its first war cruise having left Kiel on 16 March]. I was too high and too close to make an orthodox attack and I knew if I circled down he'd crash-dive before I could get there, so, as seconds counted, I thought I might as well crack right in. I pushed everything forward and down we went, touching 270mph! Everyone in the aircraft became momentarily unstuck, but our drill stood us in good stead and as the crew picked themselves up from the floor they scrambled to their action stations. Flight Sergeant Eley the front-gunner, who had been standing beside me, reached his turret and cordite fumes blew in my face when he opened at point-blank range and pumped fire into the side of the sub. We could see his bullets slapping off the metal. Away went the depth charges and as I pulled out of the dive with all my strength and then banked around, I saw our target submerging with a pronounced list to port and making very little way. A little while later it popped up again, bows first, at a very steep angle and with a rolling motion. By then I'd got into position for the more usual pattern of attack and when it made its second appearance I flew in again - but it disappeared, rather shakily this time, before we got over it. However, we dropped our DCs on the spot and results were soon apparent. There was a terrific underwater explosion and bits of wood, cylindrical objects, a huge piece of wood that looked like the top of a long table, a bundle that looked like clothes, all 'jack-in-the-boxed' to the surface, accompanied by a quantity of heavy oil which, when we left it, was over a thousand yards long.'

Roxburgh's victim disappeared with all 49 hands. Only forty-eight hours later, skippered this time by Flying Officer A. C. I. Samuel of Sutton Coldfield the same lucky Fortress found and attacked another U-boat while escorting Convoy RU.67 180 miles SSE of Iceland. It was U-169 commanded by 25-year old Oberleutnant zur see Hermann Bauer, which was on its first war cruise having left Kristiansund on 18 March. There were about ten men in the conning tower as Samuel swept down to barely a hundred feet to deliver the cargo of depth charges. U-169 sank under a spreading patch of oil a hundred yards wide. 'Fizzing like a dose of Eno's' was the description supplied by one of the crew at base. The submarine was lost with all 54 hands.

In May no less than 41 U-boats were claimed sunk. Of these, 28 were lost around mid-Atlantic convoys - six being put down in attacking convoy ONS.5 on the night of the 5th/6th. Between the 19 and 21 May convoy SC.130 went through a very large pack of U-boats without loss, Coastal Command aircraft obtaining thirty sightings, one, 'P for Peter' of the indefatigable 120 Squadron, making eight in one sortie. British and American auxiliary aircraft carriers were also well to the fore. As a result of these combined efforts the average of merchant vessel tonnage sunk for every U-boat lost fell swiftly from 40,000 to 6,000 tons. Well might the German Admiralty ruefully record that 'the losses in May reached an impossible height'. The German War Diary reported that 35 five per cent of the losses occurred when U-boats were approaching the operational area and all were caused by aircraft. Within the operational area itself, the total losses were 26 per cent, ten per cent being attributed directly to the air and thirteen per cent to a combination of attack by aircraft and surface vessel. When in close contact with the convoy, the losses rose to 38 per cent, of which 22 per cent were caused by the escort vessels, ten per cent by aircraft and six per cent by a combined operation. The German Admiralty records said: 'The Royal Air Force played an important part in causing such high losses. This is to be attributed to the increased use of land-based aircraft and aircraft carriers combined with the possibility of surprise through radar location by day and night.'

On 28 May 1943 the destruction of U-304 360 miles south-east of Greenland by a Liberator, 'E for Edward' on 120 Squadron, provides a typical example of the skill acquired by experience. The aircraft, piloted by Flying Officer D. C. Fleming-Williams, was due to protect convoy HX.240 crossing the Atlantic from the United States of America to Britain. On his way to meet it he flew through unexpected and very bad weather for about four hours and had just emerged when he sighted a submarine five miles away at the very limit of his visibility. There was a 35-knot wind blowing, the sea was very rough and covered with white caps and it was the irregularity in their pattern which first excited the pilot's attention. His practised eye had not deceived him. The flurry of foam in the midst of the wind-lashed sea was caused by a submarine fully surfaced. Fleming-Williams immediately turned away so 'as to give the submarine commander the feeling that I had not seen him'. U-304, which was on its first war cruise, having left Kiel on 27 April, was commanded by 29-year old Oberleutnant zur see Heinz Koch. Fleming-Williams made for a cloud and taking cover in it emerged much closer to the U-boat. Koch began to dive, but Fleming-Williams, bringing his Liberator down to 100 feet, dropped four depth charges. They fell along the port side of the U-boat, which was immediately hidden by vast sheets of spray. These dissipating, 'I saw a big cylindrical object which I took to be a torpedo tube that had come adrift '. The depth charges had been accurately placed, due allowance having been made for the strong wind on the starboard quarter. U-304 was lost with all 46 hands.

In July 1943 Squadron Leader Terry Bulloch was temporarily attached to 224 Squadron at St Eval in Cornwall, testing rockets. Bulloch, 'Jock' McColl and Flying Officer Colin V. T. Campbell, a gunnery officer who had much to do with the development of the rockets and who had been given permission to fly operationally with Bulloch, arrived at St. Eval on 4 July. Bulloch was told that the best effects would be obtained with a dive of twenty degrees, the rockets being re¬leased at a range of 500 yards from the target. A convenient wreck off Selsey Bill had been earmarked for practice and Bulloch soon made his first rocket runs. He soon found out that he had been given no easy task. Speed built up rapidly in the diving attack and he had to pull out at about fifty feet above the sea. It required considerable skill to do this without damaging the aircraft by too sudden a pull-out. It was not long, however, before Bulloch was getting consistently good scores on the much riddled wreck.

'The rockets' he recalled 'were solid-shot, 25lb, very primitive' recalled Bulloch. 'They were under sponsons, little bits of metal bolted on just outside and below your window. There were four either side and they were fired electrically. You used to get into a 20-degree dive in a Liberator, from 2,000 feet, with cruise power on. I devised this system: you would dive down, fire the first two at 600 feet, two at 400 feet and a stick of four at about 200 feet. Then you would pull the thing out. You had to get the trim absolutely right, or else you'd damage the wing. At the bottom of your dive, the aeroplane's nose was up in the air, but you were still sinking. It was great fun, I loved it. The rockets were very accurate. You could see them go into the water. They had ballistic qualities, believe it or not, under water.'

On 5 July Terry Bulloch and his crew made their first operational patrol with rockets. There were no sightings. But Bulloch was not depressed. Bad weather held them back until the eighth when they made their second patrol out towards the Bay of Biscay; a good hunting ground for submarines. Terry Bulloch and his crew on BZ721 'R-Robert' took off on patrol at 0853 hours. While on patrol off Cape Finisterre, Colin Campbell was looking at some Spanish fishing vessels through his binoculars when he spotted a U-boat right in among them. It was U-514, commanded by 28-year old Kapitänleutnant Hans Jürgen Auffermann, which was on its fourth war cruise from Lorient bound for South Africa. Bulloch went into the attack and at 800 feet loosed off two rockets and a second salvo at 600 feet and four more at 500 feet from 500 yards. As the Liberator flew over, the front, rear and port-beam guns raked the U-boat along its length. 'One of my rockets went right through the pressure hull of the U-514 and straight out the other side. To make sure of it, I turned back quickly and dropped eight depth charges in a straddle and followed that up with 'Wandering Annie', an acoustic mine and down he went to the ruddy bottom. We were tickled pink with that one. It was the first time that I'd fired that method in earnest and of course you couldn't miss.'

Bulloch believed that it would have been sensible to equip more squadrons with rockets but a 311 Czech Squadron Liberator was damaged during practice and they were abandoned.

Valuable anti-submarine aircraft had been lost during 'Operation Torch' when control of RAF Gibraltar was temporarily transferred from Coastal Command to the Air Officer Commanding in French North Africa. It was not until 8 October 1943, when an air base was established in the Azores as the result of an agreement between Great Britain and Portugal that the Gibraltar squadrons were returned. 1944 a somewhat curious US Navy PB4Y-l marking occurred due to diplomatic reasons when US Navy PB4Y-1s based in the Azores were forced to display RAF roundels as well as the American star and bar insignia.

Edward Bailey's crew on 120 Squadron in Iceland had become operational in January 1943 and had commenced anti-U-boat patrols in the North Atlantic: 'The longest trip we made was sixteen and a half hours although some crews flew trips of eighteen hours duration. On 5 April 1943, when escorting convoy HX.231, we sighted and attacked our first U-boat [U-635 commanded by Oberleutnant zur see Heinz Eckelmann, 440 miles southwest of Iceland]. It was sighted by the captain [Flying Officer Gordon L. Hatherley] from his 1st pilot's position. The normal flying height while on patrol was about 1,000 feet depending on the height of the cloud base and attacks were generally made at about fifty feet. Though evasive action was taken during the run in, it was important that just before the release of the depth charges, flight was straight and level. On this occasion we dropped a stick of four depth charges close to the U-boat and the result was a probable kill [U-635 was lost with all 47 hands]. An automatic camera, located under the rear portion of the fuselage and a hand-held camera, operated by the fear gunner, were used to provide evidence. Before and during the attacks the WOp transmitted a sighting report and an attack report to base and held down the Morse key so that ground stations could take a fix on the plane's position.

'On 14 May 1943 we attacked another U-boat while on convoy escort and five days later we attacked two more U-boats. This latter operation lasted fifteen hours. As the U-boats stayed on the surface and fired a 37mm gun from this position in the stern of the conning tower, there was always a strong possibility of being shot down. In 1943 a 0.5 inch machine gun was mounted in the perspex nose compartment of the Liberator to upset the U-boat gun crews. We were lucky but at least two Liberators were believed to have been brought down while making such attacks. The chances of surviving in a dinghy (assuming one made a successful ditching) in the North Atlantic were considered very slim.'

In May 1943 53 Squadron replaced its ageing Whitleys with Liberators and for the following sixteen months flew patrols from Northern Ireland over the Channel and the Bay of Biscay before moving to Iceland in September 1944. During May 1943 they were joined in Northern Ireland at Aldergrove by 59 Squadron. Their Liberators carried the then top secret Mark 24 American acoustic torpedoes which revolutionized the task of killing U-boats. The Mark 24 was popularly known as 'FIDO' or 'Wandering Annie' although it was a criminal offence even to discuss it. It entered service in May 1943 and was found to be a most effective weapon against U-boats which had just dived. Liberator FK229/B flown by Flight Lieutenant John Wright DFC on 86 Squadron badly damaged U-456 with the device on the night of 12/13 May 1943.

During June 1943 224 Squadron Liberators were also given more 'teeth'. Extra waist guns and gunners were carried during the squadron's anti-U-boat sweeps in the Bay of Biscay. The squadron was now based at St. Eval and one of its advantages was that the officers were billeted at the Watergate Bay Hotel and the NCOs at two hotels at Porth Bay near Newquay, Cornwall. From June onwards 224 Squadron hunted the U-boat packs in the Bay supplemented by ever-increasing numbers of Liberators on 59 Squadron and others. John Branagan, a Liberator WOp-air gunner on his second tour of operations, recalls a memorable operation on 59 Squadron at Aldergrove:

'On 29 July we took off at 0350 hours for a special escort for a large convoy heading for Britain, When we arrived one ship was on fire and ships were being attacked by a Focke-Wulf 200 using high level bombing technique. The Senior Naval Officer of the convoy instructed us by radio to attack the enemy aircraft, which now numbered seven! To climb we had to lose weight. We dared not jettison our lethal cargo or we would have sunk almost half the convoy so we flew on about thirty miles and jettisoned our bomb load in the sea. We then broadcast a coded signal to our headquarters and headed back to the convoy.

'We got on the tail of a Focke-Wulf which was going into attack but the gunners on the ships let all hell loose. They fired at the Focke-Wulf 200 and ourselves but caused the enemy aircraft to swerve just as he was dropping his bombs. His missed his target altogether and to our amazement all seven Condors broke off the action and scurried for home. They may have intercepted our radio message calling for reinforcements on the emergency air attack code. It was probably just as well for them because at first light the following day eight Liberators on 59 Squadron arrived to protect the convoy. Our total flying time on this mission was fifteen hours thirty-five minutes.'

U-boat operations were not always centred on the Bay of Biscay and mid-Atlantic. Not so well known are the anti U-boat operations carried out from North West Africa. Peter Lee on 490 Squadron RNZAF recalled: 'To patrol the Atlantic sea lanes off the west coast of Africa, West Africa Command had four Sunderland squadrons, 95 at Bathurst, 204 and 490 at Freetown and 270 at Lagos. During my tour - in the last nine months of the war - there were few U -boats in the area except the odd one in transit from Japan with a special cargo. Our biggest hazard was the weather.

'Coming back from an eight or ten-hour patrol in the early evening, huge tropical storms were often encountered. These would form off the mountains and extend for 300 or 400 miles out from the coast. The mass could rise to 40,000 feet above sea level. Approaching this barrier in darkness was a pretty unnerving experience with the constant flashes of lightning along the line of the front. To reach base we could only go under the storm where there was usually only a few hundred feet between the sea and the base of the clouds. The trouble was that once there, the pressure readings dropped away and the altimeter reading might be several hundred feet out. In pitch-darkness it needed extra vigilance to see you didn't fly into the sea. On the other hand, if you were too high the vicious up-currents and down-currents would take the boat up and down like a yo-yo; it was impossible to fly straight and level. A French Sunderland crew from Dakar tried to penetrate too high one night and before they knew what was happening they found themselves upside down at 14,000 feet. They managed to get out of it - a bit shaken, no doubt. The weather also affected reliability. Maintenance was difficult with all the boats moored out on the river. It was either pissing down with rain or scorching hot. Our crew came back four times with one engine stopped. Sometimes the weight of rain was so heavy it was impossible to get enough lift to take off even though the mid-upper turret was removed and the fuel loads reduced to save weight.'

In August 1943 200 Squadron at Bathurst in the Gambia, began exchanging its Hudsons for Liberators. On 11 August Liberator BZ832 'D-Dog' on 200 Squadron at Bathurst (now Banjuil) in Gambia, was on anti-submarine patrol off the coast of West Africa. Its pilot, 29-year old Flying Officer Lloyd Allan Trigg RNZAF, sighted U-468 about 240 miles south-west of Dakar. The submarine, commanded by 25-year old Oberleutnant zur see Clemens Schamong, was returning to La Pallice after a war cruise in the Atlantic. Trigg, the son of a farmer, was born at Houhoram, North Auckland and educated at Whangarei Boys' High School. Since boyhood he had been deeply interested in flying, was married and the father of two sons and had joined the RNZAF on 15 June 1941. A fellow pilot once said that Trigg 'seldom spoke, but had a fantastic determination. He hated the Germans and his sole interest was getting the war won so that he could return to his family.'[60]

As soon as he saw U-468 Trigg immediately went into the attack. The submarine was on the surface and prepared to defend herself with anti-aircraft guns: shells from two of her 20mm cannons hit the Liberator in the centre section and the Liberator was on fire in several places when it arrived in a position to attack. Trigg could have broken off, but as he flew over the vessel at just 50 feet, he ordered a stick of six shallow-set depth-charges to be released. In a near-perfect straddle two exploded just six feet from the U-boat's hull and caused chlorine gas and panic below decks. Within twenty minutes U-468 was sinking beneath the waves with the loss of 42 hands. However, the stricken 'D-Dog' perished with her, a victim of the submarine's anti-aircraft fire and Trigg and his gallant crew died. About twenty German sailors managed to climb to safety, but several of them were killed by sharks and barracuda and soon only Schamong, his 1st Lieutenant, Leutnant zur see Alfons Heimannsberg and five others were left. They all clambered into one of the Liberator's dinghies which had floated clear after being released by the impact of the plane hitting the sea and were located the following day by a Sunderland on 204 Squadron which dropped another raft and directed the corvette HMS *Clarkia* to the rescue. Later, Schamong's and Heimannsberg's evidence and outspoken admiration for the gallant attack was taken into account and Trigg was posthumously awarded the Victoria Cross, on 2 November 1943.[61]

September 1943 began with two Liberator losses on the 2nd, both on 224 Squadron. Flying Officer J. V. Gibson took off at dawn and he and his eight crew on FL959/G were killed. They were probably shot down by a Ju 88 in the Bay. Ju 88s were responsible for the loss of Liberator FL938/P flown by Flying Officer G. H. 'Charlie' Wharram on a later patrol. [see Chapter One] Wharram and Sergeant E. A. 'Pat' Moloney were killed. Sergeant R. J. 'Jack' Foss the second pilot, took over the controls, but with one engine out, a second on fire and the remaining two both cutting out, he had no choice but to ditch. The crew got into their dinghy without further mishap, but their ordeal had only just begun. As if the experience of suffering an attack by the Ju 88s and then ditching in the Bay of Biscay was not harrowing enough, Sergeant W. W. 'Maurice', W. Op/AG Dilks and the surviving members of the Liberator crew, caught sight of what they thought was a ship's mast in the distance and realised that the mast was the periscope of a U-boat which surfaced nearby. The crew manned the machine guns and turned on the dinghy. At this point the survivors thought the end was near. The Germans began arguing and then one of the guns began firing, the shells circling the dinghy. After a few minutes, the crew re-entered the U-boat, which then submerged and left the area. The men in the dinghy could only assume that the U-boat was on an outward journey and did not want passengers and that the crew were in disagreement regarding the fate of the dinghy. They were next seen on the 6th by a Sunderland and that night two Catalinas flew around and overhead looking for them with Leigh Lights but failed to pick them up in their beams. The next day Canadian Flying Officer J. C. 'Jack' Miller died.

A Sunderland found them on the 8th and dropped supplies but the men were too weak to haul them into their rubber craft. Finally on the 9th - a week after being shot down - a Catalina directed HMS *Wild Goose* to them but it was too late for Pilot Officer W. R. Collins and Sergeant D. H. 'Dave' Bareham, the flight engineer, both of whom died on the *Wild Goose* before reaching Liverpool where Foss, Pilot Officer J. R. 'Jack' Wilcox, Pilot Officer Johnstone and 'Maurice' Dilks, were put ashore and taken to RAF Hospital West Kirby. On the 22nd September, Dilks wrote this letter to a friend from his hospital bed:

Dear Dennis,

I suppose you gave me up after we'd been missing for two or three days. The same as we did when poor old Willie Smith and his crew went down... Well, from now on, you'd better regard me as the proverbial bad penny - I always turn up. In short, we were attacked by four Ju 88s just north of the Spanish Coast. After three quarters of an hour, Charlie Wherram and Pat Maloney were dead - Charlie was killed by the first shell that entered the kite. Pat got his in the rear turret... a 30 foot flame was coming from No. 3 engine, No. 2 was u/s and the other two missing badly. The intercom, both turrets and the hydraulics for the flaps were all jammed. The undercart was up, the ailerons and elevators weren't responding.

All of us were wounded. We'd got one of them before our turrets went, which is some consolation. But we were in a pretty bad way. We made an attempt at ditching. The kite broke up as soon as we touched down and although we all managed to get out - six crew and one passenger - we only got one (two-man) dinghy and no emergency equipment out of the back. We all piled in and spent the next seven days like that - the worst of my life. We were wearing tropical kit by the way.

By the time the Navy picked us up, Jimmy Miller and Jack Wilcox had gone. Next day Dave Bareham, then Bill Collins passed away. Jack Foss and our passenger (Flying Officer Johnstone) and yours truly gradually picked up under the wonderful treatment the Navy gave us. Three days before we docked we were up and hobbling about.

We're getting along fine now, although we're still terribly weak, of course and I suppose we'll have a long spell of convalescence after the hospital has finished with us...

Cheerio Pal. Be seeing you. Maurice.[62]

In September 1943 120 Squadron had ceased flying anti-submarine patrols between their base in Iceland, the Westmanear Islands and The Faeroes and reverted to convoy protection patrols in the North Atlantic just south of Cape Farewell. On 30 September 1943 they were joined by a detachment of 59 Squadron Liberators. John Branagan on 59 Squadron recalls. 'We landed at Reykjavik but the runway was too short for the Liberator VIII. We almost hit a hospital at the end of the runway. After that experience we were transferred to Meeks Field, Keflavik and became the first RAF aircraft to operate there. It was rather primitive but the Americans were very friendly and sociable, no doubt encouraged by our supplies of whisky and spirits. The American authorities had decreed that because Iceland was a 'dry' country at that time, all Americans stationed there should be 'dry' also!'

By the middle of September a number of U-boats had been able to elude Allied patrols and a pack of about fifteen, armed with acoustic torpedoes, was in the North Atlantic lying in wait for a prey. Their opportunity arrived when two Allied convoys, Outbound North 202 and Outbound North (Slow).18, amounting in all to 68 ships, were about 90 miles from each other moving on a converging course. They were 650 miles outward bound from England and still under the protection of the Liberators on 120 Squadron in Iceland and the Newfoundland-based 10 Squadron RCAF, which had begun operations from Gander on 10 May. Late on the 19th U-341 was bombed by Liberator 586/A flown by Flight Lieutenant R. F. Fisher on 10 Squadron RCAF near Convoy ONS.18, 330 miles SSW of Iceland. Fisher and two other Canadian pilots on 10 Squadron had escorted Prime Minister Winston Churchill and party returning from the 'Quadrant' meetings on the battlecruiser *Renown* and were on the way home to Canada.[63] U-341, which was commanded by 26-year old Oberleutnant zur see Dietrich Epp, who had left La Pallice on its second war cruise on 31 August, was lost with all 50 hands.[64]

U-boat attacks on both convoys began at dawn on 20 September when the frigate HMS *Lagan*, one of the escorting vessels, was torpedoed and lost her stem, including her propellers and rudder. Twenty-nine crew were killed and one was missing. She was ultimately towed to the United Kingdom. The next victims were two merchant vessels and thereafter the attacks developed on a considerable scale. U-338 commanded by Kapitänleutnant Manfred Kinzel was bombed by Liberator 'X-X Ray' on 120 Squadron and then depth charged by HMCS *Drumheller* 450 miles ESE of Greenland and lost with all 52 hands. About noon, ON.202 and ON.18 were instructed by Western Approaches to join company so that their escorts might act in concert. This was only finally accomplished by darkness but by then the Canadian *St. Croix* had been sunk, by U-305 with the loss of 66 of 147 men and the corvette HMS *Polyanthus*, had been sunk by U-952. Fourteen hours' later the frigate HMS *Itchen* rescued 81 survivors from the *St. Croix* and one man from the *Polyanthus*.

The night of 20/21 September passed quickly and there was thick fog the next day which prevented any serious attack. By that evening there were indications that the U-boats were again massing. They began their attacks at 2100 hours and continued them until 0600 hours on 22 September but without any effective result. U-377 was hit by a Liberator on 10 Squadron RCAF. Two of the crew were killed and the 25-year old commander, Korvettenkapitän Gerhard Kluth and several crewmen were wounded. The next day, too, was foggy until the evening, when, on the weather clearing, Liberators on 10 Squadron RCAF appeared from Newfoundland. The crew of one of them, 'L for Love' spotted a U-boat on the surface about sunset and at once went into the attack. The German gunners offered fierce resistance, put a bullet in the crank-case of one engine and with another 'parted the hair above the navigator's left eye'. The Liberator's depth charges were accurately dropped, but the U-boat still remained on the surface. 'L for Love' signalled for help, but none could be given, for the surface escort was fully engaged and the only other aircraft in the neighbourhood replied from forty miles away, 'Have a U-boat of my own'. This aircraft, 'X for X-Ray', had just dropped four depth charges on it and was about to drop four more. Having done so, it then engaged the U-boat with machine-gun fire but without definite results. The battle continued through 23 and 24 September. In all, six merchant ships and three escorting ships were sunk, four of them by acoustic torpedoes.

The Germans' next attempt to regain the initiative took place in the first fortnight of October within easy reach of Iceland. The result was disaster. By now some Liberators became very formidable indeed. They were fitted with rockets to carry out attacks on U-boats which stayed on the surface to fight it out. Some were also fitted with long range tanks in the forward bomb bays giving a total endurance of nineteen hours. Some Mark Vs were also equipped with eight million candle power Leigh Lights mounted under the outer starboard wing and others fitted with sonar buoys and modified to carry ninety anti-tank bombs converted for use against U-boats.

On the night of 4/5 October Flight Lieutenant W. J. F. McEwen piloting Liberator FK236 'X for X-Ray' on 120 Squadron attacked U-389 on the surface 140 miles south-east of Angmagssalik, Iceland with rockets and depth-charges. U-389 was commanded by Kapitänleutnant Siegfried Heilmann and was on its first war cruise, having left Trondheim on 18 September. U-389 'split open like a pea pod' wrote flight engineer Robert Fallon. The air crew vaunted 'nine to eleven' Germans in the water. McEwen dropped three one-man inflatable dinghies and two emergency kits containing food and medicine and so on but nothing further was heard from U-389 [65] which was lost with all 50 crew. [66]

Sea going Swordfish and land-based aircraft sank another three U-boats on 8 October.[67] A Liberator on 86 Squadron from Northern Ireland piloted by Flight Lieutenant John Wright DFC, who had badly damaged U-456 on 12/13 May, attacked U-419 commanded by 25-year old Kapitänleutnant Dietrich Giersberg while escorting Convoy SC.143 450 miles SSW of Iceland. U-419 was lost with 48 hands. After the submarine sank fifteen survivors were seen in the water but only the commander, who suffered a broken leg, was rescued when the destroyer HMS *Orwell* arrived later. Alerted by Wright, another Liberator on 86 Squadron - FL954 'Z-Zebra' - piloted by Flying Officer Cyril W. Burcher RAAF, as well as Liberator III FK223/T on 120 Squadron from Meeks Field flown by Flying Officer Dennis C. L. Webber DFC found the U-643 commanded by 26-year old Kapitänleutnant Hans-Harald Speidel, which was on its first war cruise having left Bergen on 14 September. Burcher dropped four shallow-set depth charges on U-643 but saw no firm evidence of a kill. Later, in two attacks, Webber dropped eight depth charges. Returning to the scene, Burcher dropped two more depth charges. These four depth-charge attacks together with machine gun fire destroyed U-643.[68]

John Luker, 2nd pilot on Flying Officer Dennis Webber's crew recalled later: 'This was our first op after leave in the UK. In daylight we flew either at 5,000 feet or cloud base (if lower). At 56° 18'N; 26° 30'W our radar operator (using the earlier limited-range ASV radar) reported a contact dead ahead at ten miles. We the pilots saw it almost simultaneously. 'Action Stations!' Our skipper pulled into cloud in the hope of making an undetected approach, but when we came out of it and roared in to attack we had insufficient time to get down to a proper height to drop our depth charges, so we did a tight turn to make another run. I remember seeing lots of tracer whizzing underneath us and heavier flak bursting in black puffs above us - fortunately we weren't hit. We had one .50 calibre gun firing forward and four .303 inch Brownings in the rear turret and all were used during the attacks.

Second time round we arrived to attack from the bows because the armament of UBs was reported to be more deadly to the rear. However the UB easily out-turned us and our attack was more or less broadside on. We pressed home the attack in face of heavy fire and dropped one stick of four 250lb DCs from about 50 feet. I don't know what the effect of this attack was - we didn't wait to find out but came in again to drop our second stick of four DCs from about 30 feet; a perfect stick which entered the water and exploded as we banked away (wing span 110 feet!) after the attack. As we passed over the U-boat on attack three I stuck my head into the blister in my side window and noted that guns and gunners seemed to have disappeared.

'The U-boat stopped dead on the surface - we had no more DCs - and we were amazed to see all the crew tumble out on to the deck and conning tower wearing life-jackets and carrying dinghies. Another Lib [Burcher] joined us but we had thoughts of the homing destroyers catching a live U-boat and no more attacks were undertaken.'

'Boy, this is it!' was the excited cry of Sergeant John Lloyd the second pilot on 'Z-Zebra' when he spotted the U-643. Cyril Burcher looked to where the second pilot pointed and saw the 740-ton U-boat surfaced and making perhaps ten knots. 'Three or four men were attempting to man the heavy guns fore and aft and another was trying to bring a smaller gun in the conning-tower to bear on us. We flew along the track of the U-boat to release our depth charges and passed over it at about thirty feet but none of us saw the guns fired, although they were trained on our aircraft. As we passed over the conning tower an officer jumped almost head first into the hatchway, followed by other members of the crew, who closed it after them. By the time we turned to make a second attack only twenty feet of the sub was above the water. The bombs fell just ahead of the swirl caused by the conning tower and soon after the explosion we were heartened see an ever-increasing patch of oil and a black object which looked like a body. The U-boat went down so quickly that at least one of the crew must have been left behind.'

'Suspecting a ruse' continues John Luke. 'We kept a careful eye on the U-boat whilst awaiting arrival of the destroyers. Once the weather threatened to close in and we made low-level runs to drop smoke floats to mark its position. The U-boat crew thought we were attacking again and I saw their fists clenched and raised in anger. We replied suitably. Eventually the destroyers picked up the survivors but not before the crew had scuttled the U-boat. One minute it was there on the surface - the next it was gone without trace, except, of course, for the crew in their dinghies and life-jackets - they were lucky to survive. My log book suggests 15 survivors including the captain [Speidel] were rescued but we were not really sure of the number.[69] We were also told later that photos showed the aerials of radar, not known previously to be carried by U-boats, though I cannot confirm this. Certainly the U-boat was ready for us when we came out of cloud - perhaps they simply heard us. Once the survivors had been rescued we had reached the PLE - Prudent Limit of Endurance - and turned for home. We never saw the convoy (SC143) we were to have escorted. Now we were diverted to Ballykelly because of bad weather at Reykjavik and landed triumphantly after 15 hours 50 minutes. Dennis Webber received an immediate award of the DFC, while the crew received a congratulatory telegram from the C-in-C Western Approaches sent to AOC Iceland.

Then on the 16th and 17th October came the climax when a host of aircraft and escort ships were directed to cover convoys ON.206 and ON (Slow) 20. On the 16th three U-boats were sunk, all by Liberators on 86 and 59 Squadrons and on the 17th, three more - one by the Liberators and two by the Navy. On the 16th 25-year old Günther Möller commanding U-844, which was on its first war cruise since leaving Bergen ten days' earlier was ordered to approach and attack Convoy ON.206 and he surfaced with U-964 and U-470. These three boats then shot down an 86 Squadron Liberator piloted by Flying Officer R. H. Coy on 86 Squadron. Flying into heavy flak, another Liberator (FL952) on the same squadron flown by Flight Lieutenant Eric A. Bland toggled four depth charges, but none released. Tenaciously circling U-844 out of flak range on two engines, Bland radioed for help. Liberator FL984/S flown by Flying Officer W. J. Thomas on 59 Squadron from Northern Ireland had received Bland's message and he arrived and carried out two attacks on U-844, dropping eight depth charges. The flak from U-844 knocked out Thomas's starboard inboard engine. Between Thomas's attacks, Bland boldly ran in, but again his depth charges failed to release and flak from the U-boat knocked out both his port engines and damaged the port side of the fuselage and he had to ditch. HMS *Pink*, a corvette, rescued Bland and four others, but two airmen perished. *Pink* left the convoy and took the airmen to Halifax. Nothing more was ever heard from U-844, which was lost with all 53 hands. Bland was awarded the DSO.

Five hundred miles ESE of Cape Farewell another Liberator on 86 Squadron - FK241 'Y-Yorker - piloted by Flying Officer George D. Gamble BEM, found and attacked U-964 commanded by 27-year old Oberleutnant zur see Emmo Hummerjohann. Flying into intense flak, Gamble dropped four depth charges and then hauled out of flak range and called for a surface escort. This attempt at a coordinated attack could not be carried out, so Gamble attacked U-964 a second time, dropping three depth charges. One hit close and destroyed the boat. Gamble reported thirty-five German survivors in the water, but the surface escorts rescued none. U-231, commanded by Kapitänleutnant Wolfgang Wenzel, came up and found four of the survivors, but one died during the rescue. Gamble was awarded the DFC.

On 17 October 1943 while escorting convoys ON.206 (Outbound North 206) and Outbound North (Slow) 20, Sunderland JM712 on 422 Squadron RCAF from Castle Archdale captained by Flight Lieutenant Paul T. Sargent obtained two radar blips at five miles' range. The aircraft was in a rain squall at the time, but after emerging from rain cloud and using binoculars, two fully-surfaced U-boats were seen sailing at 16 knots five miles ahead. They were 740-tonners with a 37mm gun forward and two 20mm on the lower bandstand and two 20mm on the upper bandstand abaft the conning tower. There were also several machine-guns on the bridge. The position was about 20 miles south of the convoy and the sea was rough, with a north-westerly wind of 35 knots.

Flying in to attack taking evasive action by undulating, Sargent picked out the U-bat to port. It was U-470 commanded by 26-year old Korvettenkapitän Günter Paul Grave which opened fire at 2,000 yards with every gun that would bear. The Sunderland's evasive action and the good shooting of Flight Lieutenant Woodward the Group Gunnery Officer manning the forward -5-inch Browning and Flight Sergeant Needham in the front turret, who cleared the enemy's decks, enabled the Sunderland to escape damage on its first run. The attack was made from the enemy's port beam at 50 feet but the stick undershot the target by 30 feet. The Sunderland then did a tight turn to port at a range of half a mile and came in at 100 feet for a second attack. On this run no evasive action was taken and the aircraft was heavily shelled by both U-boats. The R/T was shot away and the front turret recuperator destroyed, the automatic pilot was blown out of the aircraft, the W/T destroyed and the radar damaged; the control quadrant was hit and the throttle and pitch controls shot away, the wing dinghy was blown out, the mid-upper turret and the hull generally riddled. Woodward's head was blown off and Needham was killed also. Flying Officer Chesley Steves, navigator, had a leg completely blown away by an explosive shell. Despite this, he insisted on giving a DR position to the second pilot, Flying Officer A. R. B. Bellis before collapsing and dying within a few minutes.

In spite of this heavy and accurate shooting Sargent carried on and from 50 feet released two depth charges across the U-boat's beam. The third failed to release. The U-boat was straddled, lifted noticeably and disappeared without seeming to dive in the normal way. The second U-boat remained on the surface during throughout the action. After the action Sargent radioed an SOS and steered the crippled aircraft toward ON20, reported the attack to HMS *Drury* in the 4th Escort Group by Aldis lamp, informing the frigate that he was going to ditch. This was achieved at 100 knots into wind touching down at 75 knots on top of the swell about 100 yards ahead of the escort before the nose buried and the hull disintegrated with the whole tail assembly breaking off. The survivors were in the water for 15 minutes. Sargent became entangled in the wreckage and went down with Steves, Woodward and Needham. Bellis was wounded in the shoulder and lost consciousness, it being thought that he had been thrown through the pilot's window. Despite a 20 foot swell; Robert Leitch of Glasgow, a rating on HMS *Drury*, swam to Bellis, untangled him from the wreckage and swam with him back to the ship. Two others of the Sunderland crew - Rutherford and Mesney found themselves under the aircraft. Rutherford had concussion and lacerations; Mesney an arm temporarily paralysed and a leg fractured in four places. They escaped from the Sunderland when the tail section broke off. Sargent was awarded a posthumous DFC and two of the seven surviving air crew received DFCs also.

'Z-Zebra' and 'E-Edward', two Liberators on 120 Squadron piloted by

Flight Lieutenant Harold F. Kerrigan RCAF and Flight Lieutenant Barry E. Peck respectively, had heard radio transmissions from a ditching aircraft and came up and found U-470 some 380 miles south-west of Ireland. Kerrigan attacked first, dropping four depth charges while incurring flak damage. Nonetheless, he attacked a second time and dropped four more charges, one of which fell 'very close' to the stem of U-470. Peck then carried out an attack into the face of 'a hail of flak,' dropping six depth charges ahead of the boat. On a second run into another 'hail of flak,' Peck dropped two depth charges that closely straddled the boat and blew it 'clear of the water,' Peck wrote. In between Peck's first and second attacks, a Liberator on 59 Squadron piloted by Pilot Officer Wesley G. Loney, attacked U-470, dropping four depth charges. These and those of Kerrigan and Peck destroyed U-470, which sank stern first. Peck notified the destroyer Duncan of this kill, reporting 'fifteen to twenty survivors' in the water. He then homed the destroyer to the scene. Owing to the presence of other U-boats, Duncan declined to mount a major rescue effort, Peck wrote. Instead, Duncan cruised through the German survivors at 'moderate speed' with grapple nets streamed. Two crewmen on U-470 caught a net and saved themselves. Forty-six Germans perished. Credit for the kill was divided among Kerrigan, Peck and Loney.[70]

Next day two aircraft returning from convoy escort to Iceland found U-540 commanded by 29-year old Kapitänleutnant Lorenz Kasch. Flight Lieutenant Eric Knowles on 59 Squadron flying Liberator 'D-Dog' attacked first, dropping eight depth charges in two runs. Warrant Officer Bryan Turnbull RNZAF piloting Liberator AM929 'H-Harry' on 120 Squadron (who had previously damaged U-135 and U-762) attacked next, also dropping eight depth charges in two runs. Turnbull recalled that both of his salvos closely straddled the boat and broke it in half and that Knowles radioed 'You got him, good show!' credit for the kill was divided between Knowles and Turnbull; the New Zealander receiving the DFC. Although Turnbull notified the surface escorts that he could see 'about thirty' German survivors in the water, none was rescued. The U-540, which sailed from a fuel stop in Bergen, Norway, on 4 October, had served only fourteen days in the Atlantic force.[71]

John Branagan on Eric Knowles' crew recalls.

'On 17 October we sighted a U-boat and destroyed it. It was one of a large concentration reported in the vicinity of a big Atlantic convoy somewhere south of Greenland. Having heard that U-boats were fighting it out on the surface and that one Liberator had been shot down we remained very alert. Towards the end of our patrol we spotted a U-boat on the surface travelling at about eight knots. It immediately opened fire with everything it had. I was just changing over from the radar to the radio and the bomb doors were open when I saw tracer shells passing under the wings. We dived down to attack I ordered our young flight engineer, who was standing on the flight deck wondering what to do, to man the 0.5 inch beam gun and be careful not to shoot our tail off because there was no restrictor gear. Then I resumed my position on the radio ready to broadcast if necessary. The second pilot handed me a message in code which read 'I am attacking enemy submarine on surface' and went on to state the time and our position. My Morse was not exactly perfect because of the noise of the guns and the swerving of the aircraft. Reception from our Iceland base was bad and I failed to contact them. Here is where professional operators at other headquarters showed their merit. First of all 15 Group at Liverpool acknowledged, closely followed by St John's, Newfoundland and strange as it might seem, Gibraltar! I finally managed to contact Iceland via Liverpool.

'Once more we circled the U-boat and dropped our second salvo of charges. The German crew scrambled out through the conning tower and abandoned ship. Seconds later it exploded and broke in half, leaving about thirty survivors in the sea. I broadcast again to Iceland to signal the result of our engagement with the enemy. We landed back at Keflavik after being in the air for sixteen hours forty five minutes.'

Before the month was out the Allies claimed seven more U-boats in the North Atlantic. On the 20th U-378 was sunk by Avengers from the USS *Core*. Next day U-271 was attacked by an unidentified aircraft and was so badly damaged that it was forced to abort with one crewman dead and others wounded.[72]

The next two U-boats that were lost were sunk by Liberators. On the 23rd U-274 commanded by 24-year old Kapitänleutnant Günther Jordan was sunk 420 miles SSW Iceland by Liberator AM929/Z on 224 Squadron flown by Squadron Leader Edward Jacques 'Billy' Wicht DSO DFC who was a Swiss national serving in the RAF. He attacked with eight rockets, gave the alarm and dropped a smoke float. The destroyer HMS *Duncan* accompanied by another destroyer, HMS *Vidette* raced to the float trailed by slower corvettes. Wicht meanwhile, drive the U-274 under with gunfire and dropped two depth-charges. Upon gaining sonar contact *Duncan* twice attacked the submarine with 'Hedgehog' and *Vidette* carried out a depth-charge run. These attacks destroyed U-274 which was lost with all hands and the kill was shared with Wicht's Liberator crew.[73] U-420 was sunk 480 miles ENE of St John's on the 26th by Liberator 'A-Apple' flown by Flight Lieutenant R. M. Aldwinkle on 10 Squadron RCAF. That same day U-91 commanded by Kapitänleutnant Heinz Hungershausen, which was looking for a U-boat tanker for fuel was damaged by an attack probably carried out by a Liberator on 10 Squadron RCAF. Two days' later U-220 was sunk by two Avenger aircraft from the USS *Block Island*. On 29 October U-282 was sunk by *Duncan*, *Vidette* and *Sunflower*. On the night of 30/31 October U-584 was sunk by Avengers from the USS *Card*.

Hugh Fisher on 224 Squadron recalled: 'Sixteen-hour sorties to patrol over the Bay were laid on in November 1943; the longest I did was just coming up to 18 hours. As we were called four hours before take-off and when we got back didn't have a priority for transport, it was at least another three hours before we finally got to bed. This made rather a long day. The Liberator was a noisy aircraft and it was the noise that tired you as much as anything. We may have been young but sometimes, being awake for 24 hours, you did feel a little the worse for wear. It was always a struggle to keep awake during the final hours of the flight. We WOp/AGs used to swap round positions every couple of hours but even so, with the very bright sunlight, it used to make your eyes tingle and you would have given anything to drop off. However much you tried to remain alert the act of continually scanning sea or sky had a mesmerizing effect and the efficiency of your observation declined. That was when you could miss seeing a surface vessel or be jumped by Ju 88s.'

'In November 1943' recalls John Luker 'we were gradually re-equipped with Mk.V Liberators, equipped with Leigh Lights and H$_2$S radar and converted to a night squadron for Leigh Light patrols. Conversion was done on the squadron to keep us operational and we were the first crew trained on 120. It was a dodgy business in winter, Icelandic weather, getting down to 50 feet at night to home onto a moored buoy - we had no radar altimeters. We did our first op on 12 December - with heavier aircraft our flights were now about 12 hour endurance. In the early ops we had some odd experiences until the radar operators were sufficiently well practised at 'reading' contacts. Once, in gathering dusk, we homed on to a contact only to see - just in time - the Ile de France looming up in front of us - no one had told us she would be in our patrol area. We homed on squalls and birds and God-knows-what but saw no more U-boats from Iceland. As a crew we flew our last (29th) op at the end of January 1944.'

During November four attacks were made on U-boats but all that was observed after the depth charges had been dropped was whitish steamy smoke at the head of a long wake of bubbles. No submarines were sunk by Coastal Command that month. But north west of the Orkneys on 25 November, alerted by Sunderland 'G' on 330 Norwegian Squadron the frigate HMS *Ascension* depth-charged U-322, commanded by 24-year old Oberleutnant zur see Gerhard Wysk, on its first war cruise, having left Kristiansund on 15 November bound for the English Channel to patrol off Cherbourg. All 52 hands were lost. Other aircraft were trying to make it as difficult as possible for German ships to make use of the seas within range of Great Britain. To operate the blockade, surface vessels and submarines of the Royal Navy were helped by Anti-submarine aircraft of 19 Group operating from Plymouth. Their targets were for the most part fast ships carrying rare and urgently needed commodities, such as rubber, tin, vegetable oil and wolfram from the Far East to the Biscay ports. By the summer of 1943 this traffic had been brought to a standstill.

One of the squadrons allotted the task of intercepting blockade runners was 311 (Czechoslovak) Squadron at Aldergrove, Northern Ireland. During the summer of 1943 this unit had converted from Wellingtons to Liberators and in December distinguished itself with a particularly gallant attack. A little before ten o'clock on the morning of 27 December, Sunderland 'T for Tare' on 201 Squadron sighted the German blockade runner *Alsterufer*, a vessel of 2,729 tons, which left Kobe in Japan on 4 October loaded with essential war supplies, coming from the South Atlantic and making for Bordeaux with a somewhat disgruntled crew on board. They had hoped to reach that port in time to celebrate Christmas, but had not been able to do so and their commander, Captain Piatek, imbued with a caution natural in the circumstances, would not allow even one of the 6,000 bottles of beer aboard to be opened for fear of entering the 'danger zone' 'with a tipsy crew'. The moment Piatek realised that he was being shadowed he broke wireless silence and called for help. All that morning he was under attack from Sunderlands 'Q for Queen' on 422 Squadron RCAF and 'U for Uncle' on 201 Squadron. The *Alsterufer* defended herself stoutly and with some success. Although the bombs of the Sunderlands fell very close none of them hit the ship, which steamed ahead undamaged. As the day wore on the situation on the bridge grew very tense. The Luftwaffe and German Admiralty had promised aid in the form of aircraft and destroyers, but a further signal that the destroyers would not arrive until the following morning damped the spirits of captain and crew who were not to know that the cruisers HMS *Glasgow* and *Enterprise* had put the destroyers to flight. The promised aircraft were equally elusive and by four o'clock in the afternoon none had appeared. The Chief Petty Officer Telegraphist said afterwards that he could have wept with rage at the failure of the Luftwaffe to provide the promised help. The Luftwaffe and the Kriegsmarine failed to bring relief and at 1607 hours the mortal blow fell. It was struck by Liberator 'H for How' on 311 (Czech) Squadron from Beaulieu in Hampshire flown by Pilot Officer Dolezal, who roared in at low level raking the ship with all its machine guns while resolutely facing fierce anti-aircraft fire and small mines fired into the air which descended on parachutes. Four pairs of rockets were fired and one 250 and one 500lb bomb released from only 600 feet. Five of the rockets struck home and caused a fire in the afterpart of the *Alsterufer* and both bombs struck her decks opening up the hold and killing two ratings on the mess-deck, who were inexplicably playing chess at the time to soothe their shattered nerves. The *Alsterufer* began to burn fiercely and was presently abandoned. She did not sink for four hours and her end was hastened by two Liberators on 86 Squadron. Seventy-four survivors, drifting about in boats or rafts, were picked up and brought in as prisoners and many were loud in their praise of the Czech Liberator, which they said had flown 'unperturbed through the heaviest barrage' and whose pilot was obviously, as the master of the *Alsterufer* put it, ' a cunning old fox'.[74]

A few days before the *Alsterufer* met her end, the *Pietro Orseolo* of 6,344 tons was severely damaged by Beaufighters on 254 Squadron when anchored off the Brittany coast south-west of Concarneau. The *Osorno* of 6,951 tons was attacked on Christmas Eve and Christmas Day and was later found beached at Le Verdon at the mouth of the Gironde.

During the closing months of 1943, 120 Squadron had been heavily involved in several U-boat engagements. Edward Bailey's crew attacked them on six occasions during convoy escort duties. In January 1944 120 Squadron continued anti-submarine sweeps operating from Iceland. The following month Bailey and his fellow crew members completed their tour of operations and went on 'rest' leave as instructors at training units. In

March 1944, 120 Squadron was replaced in Iceland by 86 Squadron and returned to Northern Ireland to fly patrols from there until the end of the war. In February 1945 Edward Bailey joined 86 Squadron to begin his second tour of operations:

'This squadron was now equipped with the Liberator Mark VI and VIII. The Boulton Paul turret had been replaced by American turrets in the nose and tail and each contained two 0.5 machine guns. The wireless operator's position was now over the bomb bay and the radar operator's on the flight deck. Single 0.5 machine guns were mounted in each of the beam positions although great care still had to be taken not to shoot one's tail off because there was still no interrupter gear. There were now two navigators in the crew and the aircraft was fitted with various electronic navigational aids'.

From May 1 to D-Day, 6 June 1944 aircraft of 15 Group and 18 Group hit twelve U-boats in Norwegian waters, sinking seven and damaging five. It will be remembered that during May Sunderlands attacked and sunk three U-boats in the area. On 17 May off Trondheim, Catalina 'C' on 333 Norwegian piloted by Harald E. Hartmann, hit the U-668 commanded by 28-year old Wolfgang von Eickstedt whose gunners shot back and riddled the Catalina, killing one crewman. U-668 aborted to Trondheim for repairs. Hartmann limped back to base and landed the Catalina safely. In the early hours of 18 May 120 miles north-west of Stadtlandet, Catalina 'S' on 210 Squadron piloted by Flying Officer B. Bastable DFC sank U-241 commanded by 23-year old Oberleutnant zur see Arno Werr. Bastable saw 'many survivors' in the water, but all 51 hands were lost.

On 24 May off Namsos another Catalina on 210 Squadron, piloted by a South African, Captain F. W. L. Maxwell, fatally damaged U-476 commanded by 24-year old Oberleutnant zur see Otto Niethmann. U-990 commanded by Kapitänleutnant Hubert Nordheimer, rescued twenty-one Germans including Niethmann - ten from a raft and eleven from the wrecked hulk - and then sank the abandoned U-476 with a torpedo. Thirty-four other men perished. Next day Liberator GR.V FL984/S on 59 Squadron piloted by Squadron Leader B. A. Sisson attacked U-990 120 miles NW of Trondheim. Nordheimer and his escort returned fire but the 37mm flak gun failed and Sisson dropped six depth charges, which sank the boat. The escort rescued fifty-two Germans, including Niethmann and Nordheimer. That same day an unidentified aircraft hit U-276 while the commander, 30-year old Kapitänleutnant Rolf Borchers was attempting to assist in the rescue of survivors from the sinking U-746. This submarine suffered three casualties and such severe damage that it was later retired from front-line service.

On 27 May off Trondheim, a Liberator on 59 Squadron flown by Flight Lieutenant V. E. Camacho, a lawyer serving in the RCAF, sank U-292 with six depth charges and it was lost with all 51 hands. In the early hours of 3 June 150 miles north-west of Stadtlandet Flight Lieutenant R. E. MacBride piloting Canso 9816/T on 162 Squadron RCAF braved heavy flak and sank U-477 commanded by 23-year old Oberleutnant zur see Karl-Joachim Jenssen with four depth charges. MacBride circled the site for four hours, reported 'at least five' survivors in the water, but there were no survivors from all 51 hands.

Footnotes

38 *Hitler's U-boat War: The Hunted, 1942-1945* by Clay Blair (Random House 1998).

39 On 1 March 1944 580 miles north of the Azores, U-603 was depth-charged by the US destroyer *Bronstein* and lost with all 51 hands. *U-boat Fact File* by Peter Sharpe (Midland Publishing Ltd 1998).

40 Several bags of this mail were later picked up by U-603. *Convoy: The Battle for Convoys SC.122 and HX.229* by Martin Middlebrook (Penguin 1976).

41 *Hitler's U-boat War: The Hunted, 1942-1945* by Clay Blair (Random House 1998). On 20 September while 450 miles ESE of Greenland, U-338 was attacked by Liberator X on 120 Squadron and then depth-charged by HMCS *Drumheller*. *U-boat Fact File* by Peter Sharpe (Midland Publishing Ltd 1998).

42 *U-boat Fact File* by Peter Sharpe (Midland Publishing Ltd 1998) and *Handley Page Halifax: From Hell to Victory and Beyond* by K. A. Merrick (Chevron Publishing 2009).

43 U-91 was depth charged by frigates HMS *Affleck*, HMS *Gould*, HMS *Gore* and HMS *Garlies* on 25 February 1944 630 miles north of the Azores. Sixteen of the crew were rescued by the Royal Navy. Thirty-six hands died. *U-boat Fact File* by Peter Sharpe (Midland Publishing Ltd 1998).

44 *The Real Cruel Sea: The Merchant Navy in the Battle of the Atlantic, 1939-1943* by Richard Woodman (John Murray 2004).

45 Originally, the kill was credited to a Wellington and was changed to a Whitley in a post-war reassessment by the Admiralty. *Hitler's U-boat War: The Hunted, 1942-1945* by Clay Blair (Random House 1998).

46 *Convoy: The Battle for Convoys SC.122 and HX.229* by Martin Middlebrook (Penguin 1976).

47 On the night of 5/6 April U-632 was depth-charged by the frigate HMS *Tay* escorting Convoy HX.231 400 miles south-west of Iceland and bombed the next day by Burcher flying Liberator FL930 'R for Robert' 440 miles south-west of Iceland. U-632 was lost with all 48 hands.

48 *The Real Cruel Sea: The Merchant Navy in the Battle of the Atlantic, 1939-1943* by Richard Woodman (John Murray 2004). The 26-year old U-boat commander was killed on 4 May 1943 when U-439 collided with U-659 during a convoy attack, 180 miles west of Cape Finisterre and was lost with all 40 hands. U-659 was lost with 44 hands. *U-boat Fact File* by Peter Sharpe (Midland Publishing Ltd 1998).

49 *Convoy: The Battle for Convoys SC.122 and HX.229* by Martin Middlebrook (Penguin 1976).

50 It will be remembered that U-221 was attacked on 27 September by Halifax HR932/B flown by Flight Lieutenant Eric L Hartley DFC 420 miles south-west of Cape Clear and sunk with the loss of all 50 hands. The Halifax was shot down by U-221's gunners and crashed nearby. *Hitler's U-boat War: The Hunted, 1942-1945* by Clay Blair (Random House 1998) and *U-boat Fact File* by Peter Sharpe (Midland Publishing Ltd 1998).

51 Also, U-663 commanded by Kapitänleutnant Heinrich Schmid probably sank the British freighter *Clarissa Radcliffe*, which, on the second day out, was one of three ships in SC.122 that became 'stragglers' when the Slow Convoy ran into a gale. *Hitler's U-boat War: The Hunted, 1942-1945* by Clay Blair (Random House 1998). U-663, it will be remembered, was sunk on 7 May 1943 by a Sunderland on 10 Squadron RAAF. U-305 was depth-charged by RN destroyer HMS *Wanderer* and the frigate HMS *Glenarm* 420 miles WSW of Cape Clear on 17 January 1944 and lost with all 51 hands. *U-boat Fact File* by Peter Sharpe (Midland Publishing Ltd 1998).

52 *Convoy: The Battle for Convoys SC.122 and HX.229* by Martin Middlebrook (Penguin 1976).

53 Pilot Officer (later Flight Lieutenant) A. W. Fraser RAAF was killed at Odiham on 4 July 1944.

54 *Convoy: The Battle for Convoys SC.122 and HX.229* by Martin Middlebrook (Penguin 1976).

55 On 23 July 1943 U-527 was attacked with depth charges by an Avenger flown by Lieutenant R L Stearns of VC-9 from the USS *Bogue* south of the Azores. Forty crewmen were killed and 13

seamen were rescued from the sea and taken prisoner by USS *Clemson*. On 25 August 1943 U-523 was depth-charged to the surface by the destroyer HMS *Wanderer* and corvette HMS *Wallflower* west of Vigo. Abandoned by its crew of whom 17 were killed and 37 rescued and taken prisoner. *U-boat Fact File* by Peter Sharpe (Midland Publishing Ltd 1998). The telegraphist on U-523 told his interrogators that 'The Commanding Officer' [25-year old Werner Pietzsch] was continually on my tail telling me to report immediately the slightest contact. His nerves communicated themselves to the entire crew. We had had a shake-up before. As we left our base we were impressed by the sight of another U-boat arriving in a practically sinking condition after aircraft attack...'

56 *Convoy: The Battle for Convoys SC.122 and HX.229* by Martin Middlebrook (Penguin 1976).

57 On 31 July 1944 U-333 was attacked with 'Squid' by the sloop HMS *Starling* and the frigate HMS *Loch Killin* 50 miles WSW of the Scillies and lost with all 45 hands. *U-boat Fact File* by Peter Sharpe (Midland Publishing Ltd 1998). 'Squid' was a triple mortar which fired depth charges in a triangular pattern ahead of the escort ship much like 'Hedgehog' but coupled with advanced asdic equipment which gave precise depth of a submarine. This allowed the bombs to be fused to explode at the same depth as their quarry. The sinking of the U-333 was the first success with the new weapon.

58 *Convoy: The Battle for Convoys SC.122 and HX.229* by Martin Middlebrook (Penguin 1976).

59 *Convoy: The Battle for Convoys SC.122 and HX.229* by Martin Middlebrook (Penguin 1976). 'Red' Esler became a test pilot after the war and was killed near Blackbushe on 30 September 1949 flying the Avro 707 one-third scale prototype of the Vulcan bomber.

60 *Quoted in For Valour: The Air VCs* by Chaz Bowyer (William Kimber & Co).

61 Trigg's award of the DFC was gazetted on 16 June 1943, news of which did not reach 200 Squadron until shortly after his death. The Victoria Cross was awarded to Trigg's widow by the Governor General of New Zealand, Sir Cyril Newall, on 28 May 1944. In May 1998, Trigg's VC was sold at auction by Spinks of London for £120,000, the equal highest price ever realised for a VC at that time. The medals were purchased on behalf of the Michael Ashcroft Trust, the holding institution for Lord Ashcroft's VC Collection. The VC is now on display at the Lord Ashcroft Gallery at the Imperial War Museum.

62 In recognition of Sergeant Dilks' bravery and his efforts to prolong the other crewmember's lives, he was awarded the DFM. Quoted in Ordinary People: True Accounts from wartime ex-aircrew, edited by Cyril Thompson.

63 *Hitler's U-boat War: The Hunted, 1942-1945* by Clay Blair (Random House 1998).

64 *U-Boat Fact File* by Peter Sharpe (Midland Publishing Ltd 1998).

65 *Hitler's U-boat War: The Hunted, 1942-1945* by Clay Blair (Random House 1998) and *U-boat Fact File* by Peter Sharpe (Midland Publishing Ltd 1998.

66 On 4 October Commander C. L. Westerhofen USN piloting Ventura B on VB-128 newly-arrived in Iceland severely damaged U-305 and sank U-279 which was lost with all 48 hands. U-336 commanded by 28-year old Kapitänleutnant Hans Hunger, which sailed from Brest on 14 September, was sunk that morning south-west of Iceland by Hudson FK764/F on 269 Squadron piloted by Flight Sergeant Gordon C. Allsop DFM. He attacked into flak, firing eight rockets in salvoes of two, two and four. These hit and fatally holed the submarine. Allsop saw momentarily 'about 15' Germans in the heavy oil slick but by the time he came around for a second pass, they had disappeared. Hudson 'S-for Sugar' on 269 Squadron piloted by H. M. Smith hit and damaged the U-731 commanded by 24-year old Kapitänleutnant Werner Techand, wounding him and five other crewmen. It will be remembered that on the 8th Sunderland 'J for Johnnie' on 423 Squadron RCAF sank U-610 while on convoy escort 480 miles SSW of Iceland. *Hitler's U-boat War: The Hunted, 1942-1945* by Clay Blair (Random House 1998) and *U-boat Fact File* by Peter Sharpe (Midland Publishing Ltd 1998 and *Handley Page Halifax: From Hell to Victory and Beyond* by K. A. Merrick (Chevron Publishing 2009).

67 Flying Officer Alfred H. Russell DFC on 423 Squadron RCAF flying Sunderland DD863 'J-Johnnie' on convoy escort 480 miles SSW of Iceland sank U-610. U-539 was attacked by a Liberator that dropped two depth charges causing heavy damage that resulted in the submarine having to abort to France. U-762 was hit by a Liberator on 120 Squadron piloted by Warrant Officer Bryan W. Turnbull DFC CGM RNZAF who on 8 February 1943 had damaged U-135 while escorting Convoy SC.118. U-762 was sunk on 8 February 1944 by three Royal Navy sloops.

68 *Hitler's U-boat War: The Hunted, 1942-1945* by Clay Blair (Random House 1998).

69 U-643 was lost with 30 hands; 21 surviving crewmen including Speidel were picked up by the destroyers HMS *Musketeer, Orwell* and *Oribi*. On *Orwell*, Ian Weddeburn recalled that Speidel bitterly claimed that machine gun bullets from one of the Liberators had hit German survivors in the water but John Luker totally refuted any such suggestion. *Search, Find and Kill* by Norman Franks.

70 *Hitler's U-boat War: The Hunted, 1942-1945* by Clay Blair (Random House 1998).

71 The corvette HMS Sunflower attacked and sank U-631 which was lost with all hands. The frigate HMS *Byard* found and sank U-841, commanded by 26-year old Kapitänleutnant Werner Bender. Byard rescued 27 survivors from U-841.

72 U-271 was sunk on 20 January by Liberator E of VP-103 flown by Lieutenant C. A. Enloo 210 miles west of Blacksod Bay, Limerick and lost with all 51 hands. *U-boat Fact File* by Peter Sharpe (Midland Publishing Ltd 1998).

73 *Hitler's U-boat War: The Hunted, 1942-1945* by Clay Blair (Random House 1998).

74 311 Squadron operated Leigh Light Liberators during the closing months of the war and in June 1945 transferred to Trooping Command.

Chapter 4

Battle of the South-Western Approaches

On 19 July 1588 the Spanish Armada set out to invade England, but after it crossed the Bay of Biscay 'the feathers of the Spaniards were plucked one by one,' and the English, who always blame Parliament for their defeats and thank the Almighty for their victories, cast a medal with the motto, 'God blew and they were scattered.' The Spaniards described their pompous fleet as the 'most fortunate Armada,' but this was before Howard of Effingham, stationed in Plymouth, sent out the English ships to destroy them. Three hundred and fifty-six years later, on 6 June 1944 another armada, of U-boats and German shipping, tried to move over the same waters, with a different purpose. The U-boats aimed at destroying the invasion fleet of the Allied Forces landing in Europe. The Germans failed because of the destructive attacks by aircraft of Coastal Command and ships of the Royal Navy... This task of sinking U-boats and German shipping by aircraft was called the Battle of the South-Western Approaches and was also conducted from Plymouth, by 19 Group of Coastal Command, near where Effingham planned his attack upon the Spaniards three and a half centuries before... Drake's drum was heard again in the moment of England's peril, but it was silenced and one month after the invasion of Europe began the Air Officer Commanding was able to announce that not a life had been lost or a pound of equipment sunk through the action of an enemy U-boat.
Hector Bolitho, Task For Coastal Command

A dismal Royal Air Force bus carried its passengers from the quiet beach over the Cornish hills to St. Eval, where 224 Squadron of Coastal Command flying Liberators would help to shield the invasion forces from attacks by the fleet of German U-boats lurking in the Bay of Biscay, waiting for D-Day. Hector Bolitho was to travel from aerodrome to aerodrome in South-West England and describe the combats between heavy aircraft and U-boats, also the attacks by fighter aircraft on German fighters and enemy shipping off the French coast. During the past five years he had learned a great deal of the heart of the RAF and for one and a half of those years he had been with Coastal Command. His work was to write of the attacks on U-boats and sorties against enemy shipping off the Norwegian, Belgian, Dutch and French coasts; the chief tasks of the Command. He therefore knew the spirit with which the aircrews went into this phase of the European War. The bus chugged up the sun-baked hill to the aerodrome, past the horde of

Liberators which were waiting to patrol the entrance to the Channel the moment that D-Day came. In the camp cinema four thousand personnel stood 'packed tight as asparagus' were told something of the plans for the invasion as far as it concerned Coastal Command.

'Watergate', the 224 Squadron mess, was, according to Bolitho, 'a stark, ugly edifice, its foundations almost lapped by the high tides: 'a requisitioned hotel by the sea where old ladies took the air and clergymen sipped a cautious glass of sherry in the days of peace. Trees are unable to survive the Atlantic storms on this coast, so the officers' mess was surrounded by barren earth and hungry fields. There were clumps of stingy tamarisk, a few yellow irises in the stream and dusty purple veronica on the edges of the cliffs. It was mournful country when the storms came but when the sun arrived in great splendour the sand and the cliffs are ablaze with light.' The mess was 'full of arguments' on the night of 4 June, which Bolitho liked.

'Mike Ensor, who was from a placid farm in the South Island of New Zealand, said that he did not like civilization as he finds it in the old world. He wishes to return to the innocent hills and the silence of New Zealand. If the war had not come he might still be sitting on a five-bar gate on his father's New Zealand sheep farm. If the war had not come he might still be sitting on a five-bar gate on his father's New Zealand sheep farm.' His terrific experiences had aged him. 'He looks more than twenty-two' observed Bolitho. 'Mike' is a tiger for work, yet capable of ridiculous boyishness. His pleasures are as fierce as his labour. It has all made him a little intolerant of fools, self contained and mentally secretive, with a wise sense of cold justice which many a man in his fifties has missed. He still plods along the road, shoulders bent, like a sheep farmer climbing the hills. His decisions now come in instinctive flashes, fortified by experience, so they are usually right. He is stern, ruthless and free of vanity. He has the assurance of leadership and the respect of the squadron, especially of his crew.

'Nobody said much about the invasion. Nobody said much about anything because 'Butch' Pugh was there and his voice is always triumphant. He said, 'This is what I have been waiting for all these four and a half years. And it will be just my luck to be in hospital with tonsillitis or something when the day comes. If I am I'll jump out of bed and fight in my underpants.' 'Butch' was round as a tub and his voice could pierce three floors of solid Victorian brickwork.'

The aircrews on 224 Squadron were an astonishing company. 'Forty-four of them were Canadians, thirty-three Australians and eight New Zealanders. One was an American, one who helped to build up the reputation of the squadron was a Swiss ['Billy' Wicht], one was a Chilean and one a Brazilian. One of the NCOs was a Chinese who was born in Australia. One hundred and thirty-seven were Britons.

'Benny Benson, 5 feet 6 inches high, came from the mining district of Chile and he grew up with the fixed wish to fly. He is English, with flashes of Latin temper. He looks so young that one imagines him swinging a bundle of school books rather than flying a heavy Liberator over the conning tower of a U-boat. When he is not flying he works at advanced mathematics, until evening comes. Then we see him walking down the stairs, his trousers immaculately pressed, his buttons glittering and his cap over one eye. Then he jumps on a bus and goes into Newquay with romance twinkling in his eyes. He was only fifteen when war came and he was afraid that the Germans would collapse before he could join in the battle. One day, a few weeks after his eighteenth birthday, he was walking in the park with his mother when a servant ran over to him and said that his father wished to speak to him on the telephone.

There was a ship leaving for an unknown destination in North America at five o'clock that afternoon and there was a cabin booked for Benny to sail. Benny hurried to the ship, with enough money to take him to Canada from any port the ship happened to stop at. But he found that the ship was short of crew so he worked as mess boy and was paid $100 for the trip. His first duty was to empty the wireless operator's waste-paper basket, full to the top with thousands of minute pieces of yellow paper; secret documents torn into fragments. Benny did not know much about wind direction at that time and he emptied the basket over the wrong side of the ship. The thousands of scraps of yellow paper blew back and covered the deck. 'I hid for an hour after that,' Benny told me. He learned his first war lesson crossing the Caribbean which was then a prosperous hunting ground for U-boats. Many ships had been sunk in the Caribbean and off Miami. Benny emptied the garbage over the side, to the horror of the first mate, who told him that floating vegetable peelings might give away their position to the enemy. Benny landed in Canada and eleven days later he was in the Royal Canadian Air Force.

Eric 'Batch' Batchelor, for whom the invasion meant no more than a change of scene, was a six-foot-three British Columbian who knew as well as any of them what the German fighters based on the Brest Peninsula could do. Last September he was flying his Liberator home from the Bay when he was attacked by six Ju 88s for over an hour, with a break of only ten minutes when he was able to escape into clouds. He was decorated for his 'masterly evasive tactics' against the six fighters, but he had admitted to me, 'I was frightened all the time. An hour and ten minutes is too long to be frightened. It was like having your stomach filled with butterflies.'

'Lofty' Lord, the only member of the mess who did not smile with pleasure when he was told that he had been awarded a DFC, is an old hand and he has had every rank from AC2 to Flying Officer, nine in all. He is very suspicious of the written word and has usually been amiable but canny when I talk to him. Except for bicycle rides over the hills in search of a harmless pint in the evening, he seems to think of nothing but his job. The citation for his DFC mentioned his 'experience and influence' and his 'magnificent record' of operational flying since the war began. I think his calm reception of the decoration hides a secret delight, but he would not show it for the world. He was a gunner in a fighter Blenheim squadron in Iraq when war was declared and was sent off to Amirya in the desert to fly sorties in defence of Alexandria Harbour. Lofty shot down one Savoia 79 [75] and damaged another at the time when the Italians were trying to bomb our fleet: when the *Warspite* and *Ajax* were on the way through the Mediterranean. In September 1940, when five Savoia 79s were bombing Mersa Matruh, Lofty shot down one of them and on the day when the Italians sent over fifteen Savoia 79s to bomb Sidi Barrani, his squadron provided part of the defence force of two Blenheims, two Hurricanes and nine Gladiators, which was waiting for them. It ended in a running battle during which Lofty's aircraft chased five of the Savoias and shot down one of them.

Then he went with the first RAF squadron to Greece, in November 1940. They took nine fighters and six bombers across the Mediterranean to patrol over Athens and for what Lofty calls, 'looking for trouble' flights over the Greek Islands and near the Greek and Italian front lines. On one of these trips he finished off an Italian flying-boat. He took part in covering the fleet for six days and-nights during the evacuation from Greece and just before the fall of Crete went back to Egypt to join a medium bomber (South African) squadron, He did twenty-two raids with the South Africans over the Bardia and Tobruk areas and on the last raid his Maryland was separated from the formation and chased by two Messerschmitt 109s. After a good run the Messerschmitts caught them up. Lofty was on the bottom guns, without the protection of armour plating and a cannon shell which hit the aircraft exploded twelve inches from his face. A piece went into his left shoulder and another through his jaw, severing an artery. He was dazed and bleeding at the mouth.

The Messerschmitt went on attacking until its ammunition was exhausted. Lofty was hit again, the bullet passing through his right leg, but he managed to remain conscious. When the intercom was broken and the air gunner tried to repair it, Lofty was unable to speak because of the wound in his mouth, but he wrote instructions on a piece of paper. Then followed hospital, blood transfusion and England. In May 1943 he joined 224 Squadron and has since flown on thirty-two sorties with them. On one trip his aircraft met four Junkers in the Bay and nipped into cloud before they could attack. On a brilliant summer evening, two more appeared, but again Lofty's aircraft got away. After the attack on six German destroyers by the Glasgow and Enterprise, his aircraft shadowed two of the destroyers. He has taken part in two attacks on U-boats since joining the squadron and on the last occasion a shell exploded in the navigator's compartment preventing the crew from dropping their depth charges.'

On 5 June Hector Bolitho wrote that 'I suppose that we can say the Battle of the South-Western Approaches has begun. On 26 May a U-boat stopped the Portuguese liner Serpa Pinto in mid-ocean and ordered the passengers, mostly refugees into lifeboats where they kept them for nine hours. Three people, including a sixteen months' old baby, lost their live during the transfer to the boats and two American passengers were kidnapped by the U-boat captain.'[76] The Navy and the RAF have naturally been trying to kill the German ever since and last night one of our aircraft attacked a U-boat which may be the one. Johnny Posnett came up to my room this afternoon and told me that he took off about seven o'clock last night in a thirty-knot wind and a haze and while they were in the outer Bay, about 3 o'clock in the morning, the radar contacted a possible U-boat. Johnny Posnett said:

'It was still hazy, but there was a moon and a few stars. We decided that we had enough petrol left to investigate, so we homed on the U-boat, got ready to attack and switched on the Leigh light when we were a mile away. Then the flak came up, good and strong and tracer from all directions. My navigator, R. E. Smith, had seen what he thought was the U-boat, but when we flew in we realized it was a shadow. We decided to do a second attack, up moon, so we came in again. Smithy saw a colossal wake and the long low hull of the U-boat. The Hun captain must have been an: old hand because he showed remarkably good seamanship. He was going round in small circles, doing everything he knew to avoid us. The flak was pretty terrible but we were not hit once. We flew off and when we were a mile away the U-boat ceased firing at us. But when we were two miles away we must have made a perfect silhouette against the moon for he opened up with his heavy stuff. Again we got away without a scratch.'

Johnny looked at his watch and said, 'Well. I must be going. My wife is having a baby today and I am catching the eight o'clock train to go up to London to see her.'

A telegram came before he went to say that it was a boy.

[Next morning] 'Perry Allen walked past my door while I was shaving. 'Well, it's begun,' he said.[77] 'Butch' Pugh put his head out of his door and asked, 'What's begun?' and Perry said 'The bloody invasion.'

Somebody along, the passage yelled, 'Well, I can swim forty miles, what of it?' and Perry answered, 'Yes and put your foot on a bloody land mine just as you step on the beach.'

'Butch' said, 'Well, I'm ready when the call comes for me to get mowing.'

'Mowing?' I asked.

Yes, get the old reaper out. You know, Death,' he answered. 'Butch' is round as a tub and his voice can pierce three floors of solid Victorian brickwork.

We went downstairs and listened to the voice over the radio.

'In a moment you will hear the Supreme Commander, Allied Expeditionary Force, General Dwight D. Eisenhower' and then the comfortable, friendly American voice that does not seem to be very belligerent, 'A landing was made this morning on the coast of France.'

Then followed the astonishing figures; thousands of ships, thousands of aircraft, thousands of men in them. I thought of the lonely pilot who flew back to England during the evacuation from Dunkirk, to fill the bullet holes in his aircraft with chewing gum and return to fight again.

'Later, I went up to the aerodrome at St. Eval early in the evening. On the edge of the aerodrome is a church with a graceful tower which one can see far out in the Bristol Channel... The old sundial over the south porch has a melancholy inscription, 'We shall all die.'

'Through the window of the duty-crew room I could see the tower of the church which lies where the aerodrome melts back into the fields. It was about a minute to eight in the evening and I sat with the airmen, waiting for the news. Outside I could hear the clatter of airmen's boots on the mesh of the steel runway. Flight Sergeant Lee was drawing with a ruler and the others were bending over the fire. Big Ben began to sound eight o'clock and the flight sergeant looked up and said, 'Sounds bloody mournful, like when the King died.' One of the airmen said, 'Sounds more like the abdication to me.'

'When the voice announced that 31,000 Allied airmen had been over enemy territory that day, everybody in the hut said, 'Phew,' but there was no other comment as we listened. It is strange how parochial we can become over our own little corner of the war. On this quiet edge of Cornwall it is not easy to visualize the terrifying pattern of the Channel and I soon turned from the bewildering statistics to think only of the four aircraft outside and of the crews who are to fly them to-night.

'Perry Allen and his crew were taking off a little after nine o'clock and 'Batch,' Bob Rayner and Buchan-Hepburn were to follow at intervals during the night. I went up to see the Liberators, immense and white, waiting before the church. One imagines that aircraft become slightly human when they have flown many times and that they are conscious of their mission, as ships must be when they have sailed the seas. There were drops of oil on the lips of the guns, the Leigh lights were waiting to be switched on to their prey and the fish-like bellies of the aircraft seemed to be stained by salt air, rather than the dry air that blows over the land.

'Perry Allen and his crew came up, Perry on his motor bicycle. He inspected the aircraft, touching it intimately now and then; and he watched tile astonishing collection of trippers' baggage being pushed up through the bomb bay. Perry waved his American Air Lines' bag at me as he climbed in and waved once from the cockpit as he taxied away. He was born under the protection of Gemini and as he had said when we were walking over the perimeter track: 'This is a lucky day for us Geminis.'

'Then 'Batch' and his crew arrived and I saw them take off. Rayner and Buchan-Hepburn followed, after I had walked back among the silent buildings and hangars. I waited at the bus station with Sidney Drake, who was an architect before he came into the RAF. While we waited I took out a piece of paper and we sketched our notion of the perfect small house. Then back to the mess by the sea in time to hear the midnight news with Mike. We found three inches of sherry in the bottom of a bottle and drank it while we were listening.

'Next morning I went up to the aerodrome early to see the Liberators come home. The grey clouds were edged with pink sugar floss, but they cleared and 'Batch's' aircraft appeared from down the coast. Bob Rayner landed an hour or so afterwards, but Perry Allen and Buchan-Hepburn did not come back.' In all Coastal Command reported the loss of three Liberators and a Wellington on the night of 6/7 June.[78]

'Batch' sat on the edge of the cliff with me after breakfast and told me his story. There had been more than twenty sightings of U-boats during the night, so it is obvious that they are moving out, hoping to attack the convoys in the Channel, as was expected.

Perry Allen and Buchan-Hepburn had been patrolling areas stretching from the French coast into the Atlantic and 'Batch' had covered the area between La Pallice and Ushant. He said that after he took off he flew over an endless chain of ships, coming from the north and rounding Land's End to join the frightening armada in the Channel. 'They went in two's' he said, 'like couples walking up an aisle.' He flew over the Scilly Isles and then down into the Bay of Biscay towards Ile d'Yeu, south of St. Nazaire. As he was flying at 250 feet over a tip of island, in lavish moonlight, his navigator, Ed Annis, saw the shadow of what they thought was a U-boat, lying close to the shore. When they were three hundred yards away they realized that it was a line of jagged rocks with waves breaking over them. They were still flying at 250 feet when a searchlight from the cliffs picked them up; then two from the island, fixing the aircraft in a cone of light which must have been alarming at that height. At the same time the island sent up myriads of flares. 'All colours,' 'Batch' said. 'A real picture display. And there was heavy ack-ack firing at us. Each of the flares broke into about one hundred and fifty dots of coloured light so that the sky was brilliant. We supposed that the Ile d'Yeu was trying to warn a U-boat or night fighters on the mainland that we were near.

'We stooged west and began picking up numerous French fishing boats. They were about twenty miles out and I don't suppose they even knew that the invasion had begun. We turned on the Leigh light to see what the first ones were, flying low so that we saw the shadow of their sails on the water. There were so many that we dared not waste our batteries so we passed on. We came to what we supposed was our twentieth fishing boat, a little bored by them then and we flew down to investigate. When we were half a mile away Ed Annis saw a wake and realized that it wasn't just another fishing boat after all. He switched on the light and exposed a U-boat on the surface, on our starboard bow and just outside our turning radius. If only we had switched on the light a mile away we would have been able to drop our depth charges. We were disappointed, but the U-boat was also taken by surprise and the Germans did not fire at us as we passed over them. But there was fire from about half a mile to the west and we realized that there must be two of them. We kept on our course for a few minutes so that we could turn and attack and this time we homed on the second U-boat. They must have known that we were coming because they did everything they could to evade us; but they were canny enough not to open fire and thus give away their exact position. The sea was very rough and there was a twenty-knot wind. We lost contact and did not get it again until we were too late to drop the depth charges. We crossed over and Ed Annis could see the terrifying long wake of the U-boat ... three times its length.

'Both of them opened fire on us with tracer and I simply don't understand how they missed us. Jack Greenfield, who was in the bomb bay, said afterwards that the noise of the tracer coming up at him was like the crackling of very dry sticks on a fire. Our starboard side gunner opened up on one of the U-boats, but the gun jammed. The fire, coming from both sides, was a pretty terrifying experience and Jerry Jervis, who was standing between the starboard and the port beam guns, said that he saw a bullet pass right through the aircraft. I suppose he saw two of them, one on either side, at the same moment.

'The U-boats had had enough of us then and submerged. We flew away to try to tempt them on to the surface again but they weren't having any.

'A little time before this, McMurtrie, one of the wireless operators, leaned over and told me that he had picked up a signal sent by Buchan-Hepburn to base saying that he had sighted a U-boat and was attacking it. I knew that he was a very capable captain and silently wished him luck, but nothing more was heard from him and base kept calling him all night. There was no answer so I was afraid that he had bought it.'

'Batch' turned for home then and flew back to the Cornish coast under a bright blue sky, with the moon still shining and pale stars. He crossed the entrance to the Channel but there were no signs of the invading forces which were still crossing the water. He saw only a few other Liberators which were taking their part in the patrols. The entire system of patrols is so punctual that the pilots call it 'the bus service,' and even when an aircraft attacks a U-boat it is expected to resume its place in the continuity when the attack is ended.

'When 'Batch' finished his story we went back to the mess and telephoned to see if there was any news of Perry Allen and Buchan-Hepburn but none had come. This means the loss of twenty trained men from the squadron in one day. It has cast gloom over all of us, although the aircrews do their best not to show it.

'Later, news came from Predannack of an attack on a U-boat early this morning by a Wellington and a Liberator, which was probably the one flown by Perry Allen. About twelve minutes past two that morning a Wellington of 179 Squadron was about three miles north-west of Ushant when the second pilot saw a U-boat. I drove over to Predannack and the pilot, W. J. Hill, told me the story.

'My second pilot called out, 'There's something on the water down there;' and I said, 'Poppycock.' But he was right and we were almost over it. We were too close to attack so we turned and came in a second time. At that moment a Liberator with a Leigh Light flew in and fired at the U-boat. It was in my way so I had to pass over and try again. There was plenty of flak coming up at us and my front and rear guns returned the fire. When we flew in again the U-boat had disappeared and there was nothing but an oil patch to show where it had been. I looked up the moon path and sure enough there was another U-boat sitting pretty. Then we saw the Liberator running in again to attack the second U-boat. They were both silhouetted against the moon, about 500 yards away, with a fierce gun duel going on between them. Then I saw still another lot of red sparks coming up and realized that there was a third U-boat joining in. I flew in just forward of the beam, withholding my fire. Then we opened up and caught him completely with his pants down. We could even see the Germans working their guns against the Liberator. We dropped our six depth charges amidships and the spray obscured the U-boat but the wake led right into the centre of the disturbance. We dropped a marker and flew off to resume our patrol. When we were about ten miles away the rear gunner said that he could see a terrific fire on the water where we had dropped our marker. I suppose it was Perry Allen's Liberator, shot down and burning on the sea.'[79]

In the late evening of D-Day eight U-boats were ordered to proceed at top speed on the surface and patrol the area between the Lizard and Harland Point. Almost immediately their escort left and all seven submarines came under air attack. Four were damaged and forced to return to port. No less than 36 U-boats tried to block the Neptune armada heading for Normandy and within the first 96 hours RAF aircraft claimed five U-boat sinkings and five forced to abort.[80] The Leigh Light-equipped Wellington and/or a Liberator and perhaps other aircraft as well hit the U-415, newly commanded by 24-year old Oberleutnant zur see Herbert Werner. At a briefing he and fourteen other U-boat captains had been informed that their directive was to 'attack and sink the invasion fleet with the final objective of destroying enemy ships by ramming'. Werner wrote:

'Was suicide the purpose for which we had been trained so long? Was this futile gesture the greatest glory and satisfaction we were permitted to take down with us to our wet graves? Werner described the air attacks in his book Iron Coffins:

'00.30: Radar impulses chirped all around the horizon, their volumes shifting rapidly from feeble moans to high-pitched screams. The Tommies were obviously flying at various distances around our absurd procession. They must have thought we had lost our minds. Sometimes I could hear aircraft engines at fairly close range, but could not spot a plane. The hands of my watch crept slowly ahead while the British waited for reinforcement; our eyes sharpened and our hearts beat heavy under our breasts.

'01.12: The battle began. Our leading boats were suddenly attacked. Tracers spurted in various directions and then the sound of gunfire hit our ears. Fountains reached into the sky.

'01.17: One of the enemy aeroplanes caught fire. It flashed comet-like towards the head of our file, crossed over one of the boats, dropped four bombs and then plunged into the ocean. The bombs knocked out Sachse's U-413. With helm jammed hard-a-port, the boat swerved out of the column. She lost speed rapidly and sank below surface.'

U-415's 37mm flak gun crew then claimed a Liberator shot down.

'Open fire!' I screamed. Five barrels, all that we had available, blazed away at the Liberator as it dropped four depth charges ahead of U-256 and roared past us. Four giant water columns leaped skywards behind the riddled aircraft as it tried to escape our fire. But some shells from our 37mm gun hit the plane broadside. It exploded in mid-air and then plunged into the sea.'

Of the eight U-boats that had sailed out together, only U-415 and two others limped back to Brest with several wounded and severe battle damage. Werner dry-docked U-415 for emergency repairs and went to a hospital to have a slight head wound dressed.[81]

On 8 June at about half past two in the morning, a Halifax on 502 Squadron piloted by Flying Officer J. Spurgeon found U-413 which opened fire at about one mile. Spurgeon flew in five times before he could track right over the conning tower. Four 600 lb anti-submarine depth charges were dropped and they were heard to explode and the rear-gunner saw a large plume close to the conning tower. On this fifth run the aircraft was hit badly and the port inner engine was put out of action. The Halifax was unmanageable for a few moments but Spurgeon regained control and turned, close enough to see that U-413 was low in the water. The U-boat gunners made one last attempt with their guns but the fire was wild and inaccurate. The damaged submarine aborted to Brest for repairs.[82]

At St. Eval at five o'clock in the morning, while he was in a deep sleep, Hector Bolitho was awakened by 'Butch' Pugh and Mike Ensor who opened his door and switched on the light. They had just arrived back from patrol. 'Butch' said, 'Come on you lazy so-and-so. Get up and get out that bloody typewriter of yours. 'Kayo' Moore has just made history.'

Flight Lieutenant Kenneth Owen 'Kayo' Moore, a Canadian pilot on 224 Squadron and his crew - seven Canadians, an Englishman, Scotsman and a Welshman – had laid claim to sinking two U-boats in a single sortie. Bolitho could not sleep and an hour or so afterwards the mess woke up to such excitement that the gloom of the previous day's losses was forgotten. After an early breakfast he found an oil truck going up the hill so he jumped on and arrived at the aerodrome in time to meet 'Kayo' Moore walking out of the canteen with his crew. 'His face, which might be described as rugged Canadian, incapable of false expression, was good to see. He was white with exhaustion but as excited as a child. 'You've made history' was all that anyone seemed able to say. All the four thousand men and women on the station seemed to catch the spirit of victory and I have seldom seen so much jaunty walking or heard such whistling. Even the Group Captain; usually cool and self-controlled, was rushing about with the photographs of the attacks in his hand. I travelled back to the beach in the van with Kayo Moore, but he was too tired to talk. When we arrived at the mess he went off to sleep. About three hours later I saw him carrying plates of fish and chips to the other members of his crew still in their beds.'

'Kayo' Moore and his crew had taken off in 'G-George' at 2214 hours on 7 June on a anti-submarine sweep - part of Operation Cork designed to seal off the western end of the English Channel from any U-boat attempting to attack the Allied invasion fleet off Normandy. On every operational sortie they carried a crew mascot, 'Warrant Officer Dinty', a stuffed panda bear, rigged out in mini-Warrant Officer's uniform and wearing an observer's half-wing brevet. By the time Moore had begun his designated 'beat' the first of a total of 42 U-boats were beginning to penetrate the Cork patrols' zone and at 0211 hours on 8 June Moore's radar operator reported a contact, dead ahead at twelve miles. The night was bright moonlight, with near-perfect visibility, so Moore decided not to use his Leigh Light. At three miles a U-boat was sighted on the surface. It was believed to be U-629 commanded by 27-year old Oberleutnant Hans-Helmuth Bugs which was on its third war cruise, from Brest. Initially, the claim for U-629, which was lost with all 51 hands, was credited to Moore but later it was awarded to Flight Lieutenant John William Carmichael, pilot of Liberator 'L' on 53 Squadron who sunk the submarine in the early hours of 7 June. The Admiralty later credited Kayo Moore's crew with the sinking of U-441.

Hector Bolitho saw Carmichael after he arrived home that morning with evidence of a kill.

'I went up to the camp early and found him, still in his flying kit and looking very tired. But he wouldn't go to bed. He was waiting for the photographs of his attack to be developed. Carmichael told us that he had seen what he supposed were two U-boats making for the Channel about 5.15 this morning. He flew in to attack the nearest one. He said that he had them at his mercy as they had no time to fire back. He dropped his depth charges but could not see any results. He flew in again and this time he was fired on from three different points. He realized then that there must be three U-boats instead of two, all steaming towards the invasion area: He realized also that they were going to stay on the surface and fight back, so he went in again, flying into the moon.

Carmichael managed to evade the flak until he opened up with his own front gun. The flak was silenced, but not before one engine of the Liberator had been hit and a cannon shell had exploded in the bomb bay while the navigator was preparing to release the depth charges. The navigator saw the blinding flash but was able to release the depth charges and to photograph the U-boat as they passed over it. The rear gunner squirted his bullets at four Germans in the conning tower. A light automatic weapon opened fire at the Liberator but it was silenced and the gunner was seen crumpling on the deck. The gun went on firing, out of control. The U-boat was obliterated by the plumes of water, but soon after eighty feet of the bow was seen in the air at a steep angle. The U-boat sank slowly and the oil left behind burst into flames.

The Liberator was damaged by the cannon shell and one engine was useless, so Carmichael set course for base. He told me that it was the first U-boat he had ever seen and he has done 600 hours of operational flying. This gives some idea of the monotony of the patrols, of the patience of the crews, staring into nothingness for the target that so seldom appears. But their reward is coming.

Carmichael it appears had damaged the U-963 commanded by 30-year old Oberleutnant zur see Karl Boddenberg who was forced to return to Brest for emergency repairs. An hour after attacking U-963 Carmichael hit and damaged the U-256 commanded by 29-year old Kapitänleutnant Wilhelm Brauel, which had been converted into a flak ship following repairs after being badly damaged in air attacks.[83] Brauel was forced to limp into Brest and U-256 was later decommissioned.

In the evening Bolitho sat with 'Kayo' Moore and Alec 'Al' Gibb, his front gunner and between them they told him their story:

Gibb: It was a wizard night; a calm sea and a full moon that just laid a white path down the water. Our patrol was between the Scillies and Ushant.

The first thing we saw sixty miles out from Brest were fishing vessels, still unaware that the invasion had begun. About 2.15 in the morning we contacted a U-boat, between us and the moon. It was a perfect silhouette, as if it were painted on white paper. We could see the conning tower quite clearly.

Moore: 'I could make out the conning tower perfectly. As we approached at 40 feet height we could see the U-boat's crew had been taken by surprise. About eight German sailors on deck, apparently in utter confusion, were running like hell to man their guns. The U-boat commander however, made no attempt to crash-dive and those manning the guns waited for us to close the range. Al Gibb opened fire when we were within 1,000 yards and scored repeated hits on the conning tower and deck. Simultaneously the Germans opened fire on us. I took evasive action while Gibb continued to blaze away and then tracked over the conning tower. The flak had been silenced during the last yards and from about fifty feet as we released our six depth charges in a perfect straddle, three on either side. I saw one of the crew in the 'bandstand' double up and fall overboard into the water.

Gibb: 'I could see four or five of the crew in the conning tower and some more of them running along the deck to the guns. Then, as one of the guns opened up, I saw one guy grab his stomach and fall.'

Moore: 'The U-boat seemed to jump into the air and explode, splitting wide open. The rear gunner, Flight Sergeant Webber, saw the plumes and he squealed with delight. 'Oh God, we've blown her clean out of the water.' I made a steep turn. We ran in and passed over the spot once more and saw the heaving waters and distinct patches of black oil in the dark green sea; distinct as ink remains when you pour it slowly into a glass of water. In the oil patches were darker spots. I suppose they were bodies. We sent a message back to base, 'definite kill,' and then we went on with our patrol.'

Gibb: It was then that you said, 'Now let's get another one.'

Moore: Yes and we did.'

'Kayo' Moore and the crew of 'G-George' continued their patrol 'beat', having still six depth charges and a homing torpedo in the bomb bay.

Moore: 'As we resumed patrol over the Channel the wireless operator, Warrant Officer Mike Werbiski was busy at the wireless set sending out a flash report to advise Coastal Command HQ that we had just made an attack. Almost immediately Warrant Officer MacDowell, the Scottish navigator, who at the time was adjusting the bomb sight, shouted a warning that he could see another U-boat ahead, travelling fairly slowly. It was a small U-boat [U-373 commanded by 26-year old Kapitänleutnant Detlef von Lehsten, which was on its twelfth war cruise, also out of Brest] and remained fully surfaced, making no attempt to avoid a fight. We got another contact so we lost height again and I made a weave to port to put the second U-boat on our starboard side. As we closed to attack Al Gibb opened up from the front turret and we met heavy flak, which came up in the shape of a coloured fan.

Gibb: It was an absolute duplicate of the first attack. The U-boat was dead up moon, slightly to port, so we did a slight turn and opened fire on him at about one mile. His return fire was heavy and there was a perfect fan of tracer from the conning tower. As we passed over the depth charges straddled a line ten feet behind the conning tower. Four fell on one side and two on the other.

Moore: It was another perfect straddle according to my rear gunner. We did a quick turn to port and flew in again to see what had happened. The U-boat was slowing down and coming to rest with a list to starboard. There was a heavy trail of oil behind him and he was down by the stern, but we had no right to think that we had killed him. Our hopes slackened because we had no depth charges left. We were just going to send a message to base, hoping someone might come to finish the job when the mid-upper gunner, Warrant Officer Griese, shouted 'She's going down. It's just like a Hollywood picture.' As we circled I saw the bow of the U-boat rise 25 feet out of the water at an angle of 75 degrees, sliding slowly back into the sea. We all felt much better then. There was a good deal of smacking on the back and screaming of delight. We did another turn to port and for the first time we switched on our Leigh light. Both attacks had been made without it. The light revealed three dinghies, shining yellow against the dark water, with the Germans in them, floating among the debris and oil. It had all happened so quickly that Werbiski, did not realize what was going on. He had been busy sending a full report of the first attack back to base and he thought we were kidding him.'

U-373 was lost with six hands. Forty-seven survivors including von Lehsten (who claimed that they had shot the Liberator down) were rescued by a French fishing smack.

'Moore's achievement made us realize the patience and devotion that have been poured into the art of U-boat hunting.' On 224 Squadron 'the evening' recalled Hector Bolitho 'was mostly celebration. We went up to the NCO's mess where, with dart boards, pretty wives and a good-hearted barman, the crew were toasted into a pleasant fog of tipsiness. Out of it all I realized the crew spirit that thrives in the Command. Peevish cynics imagine that phrases like esprit de corps, morale and team spirit are lecturers' clichés but they are not. This bond between the ten members of a Liberator crew is one of the silent strengths of Coastal Command, easy to comprehend when one realizes what the ten men share as they fly; boredom, disappointment and hope, for twelve or more long hours over the sea, with death as their near companion. It is an unspoken bond in which rank has no place or importance.

'But this is a solemn estimate of something which expresses itself in laughter. We drank too much, laughed and talked too much. All that the sergeant who had seen the first attack could say to me as he poured a sly double whisky into my glass when I wasn't looking was, 'It was a bloody miracle. A bloody miracle. It was like something you read about but never dare hope to see.'

'During the morning Kayo Moore told the story in the officers' mess. Others who were sleeping after their patrol came down in their pyjamas and crept silently in to hear him. At the end he said, 'Well, there must have been nearly one hundred Huns who bought it. That squares things for Perry Allen and Buchan-Hepburn.' Then he slid to the floor on his knees and made faces at Mike Ensor's dog, 'Liberator' to make him bark. The Border terrier with the aloofness of a cat and an irritating habit of treating me as if I were an interloper had chewed a hole in the leg of Ketcheson's trousers. But he was so exhausted after his patrol that he did not notice it.'

Moore received an immediate DSO, while DFCs were awarded to Warrant Officer Johnston McDowell, one of the navigators and Warrant Officer Peter Foster, the WOp/AG. Sergeant John Hamer, the flight engineer, received a DFM.

On 9 June, west of Scillies, Liberator 'F' on 120 Squadron piloted by Flight Lieutenant Alfred Kenneth Sherwood was thought to have sunk the U-740, which was lost with its 27-year old commander, Kapitänleutnant Günther Stark and all 50 other hands. Not all air attacks went well. Johnny Posnett on 224 Squadron returned with another disappointment. Just before midnight, while he was flying about twenty-five miles from the French Coast, he contacted a U-boat. He flew in but before he could drop the depth charges the U-boat opened fire on the Liberator, wrecking one engine and causing damage in the bomb bay. Hector Bolitho recalled that his story revealed what he had been trying to write about the bond between the members of a crew flying 'these big aircraft'; why they stick together like a bunch of burrs in your hand. It is partly because, in a moment of crisis, any one of them might become the saviour of all the others and of the aircraft. In this case it was the engineer, Keith Bettany, a quiet little Welshman, who comes from the Rhondda Valley. He was sitting under the flight deck, getting the marine marker ready, when the flak began pouring up from the U-boat. I saw him after the aircraft came back and he said, 'While I was sitting there two cannon shells exploded in the bomb bay. It shook me up quite a bit and I thought of my mother and father, as one does at a time like that. I dropped the marine marker and then waited for the depth charges to fall, but they didn't and I realized that something had been hit. It was actually the electric circuit, broken by the cannon fire.

'At that moment I looked down at the sea through the open bomb doors. There was a little light remaining from the sun, which had set and the Leigh Light was still shining on the water. I could see the U-boat two hundred feet below me and the flak coming up towards me. I tried to close the bomb doors, but two of them jammed. I looked around to see what damage had been done and found a depth charge hanging down, with its nose through the bomb door. I pulled the lever and the depth charge fell and I was then able to close that one door, but the other one was still open. We still hoped to prang the U-boat so the navigator tried to release one of the depth charges, to see if they would fall. It failed, so we set course for base.'

'This was the modest version of a very gallant story. What Bettany had done was this. The oil pressure in No. 4 engine began to fall and the crew realized for the first time that it had been hit and that they would have to make their way home on three engines. Bettany feathered the damaged engine and the aircraft began to lose height. He went back to the bomb bay to release the depth charges, by hand. For twenty minutes he stood on the twelve-inch wide cat walk which was covered with hydraulic oil. The sea sped past below him and a howling gale was blowing up his legs. He hung on to the bomb rack with one hand and released the depth charges with the other. As each one fell he could feel the aircraft leap to gain height. As the last one was released they reached 700 feet and flew back to base. I asked Bettany what he did when the twenty awful minutes were over and he answered, 'Oh, I closed the bomb doors and went back between the two pilots and stayed there until we got home.'

Four days' later when U-270 was attacked by a Liberator on 53 Squadron the submarine shot the aircraft down. Earlier the U-boat's gunners had destroyed a Fortress on 206 Squadron. A Leigh-Light Wellington on 172 Squadron flown by L. Harris hit U-270 and caused so much damage that the commander, Kapitänleutnant Paul-Friedrich Otto, was forced to abort to Lorient. The nine U-boats that sailed from Brest and 19 more that left Biscay ports after 6 June sank no Allied ships. Eighteen U-boats were recalled to Lorient, St. Nazaire and La Pallice to be kept in readiness for an Allied invasion of Brittany.

On the night of 14/15 June John Carmichael on 224 Squadron was 'half-excited and half-depressed'. His brother had escaped from a prison camp in Germany and had telegraphed to say that he was on his way to Cornwall. Carmichael was on operations that night so he would not see him until he returned in the morning. A signal was received while Carmichael was flying, announcing his promotion to Squadron Leader and the award of a DFC. When Hector Bolitho went down to breakfast at Watergate the miserable news came through that he had not returned. Carmichael had attacked a U-boat but was shot down by return fire. There were no survivors. They might have been shot down by U-415 commanded by 24-year old Oberleutnant zur see Herbert Wagner whose gunners claimed a Leigh-Light equipped Wellington and another aircraft 'possibly a Liberator'. U-415 also limped back to Brest with several wounded men and severe battle damage.

Two weeks after D-Day Flight Lieutenant Gilbert G. Potier was on his third operational Liberator patrol on 53 Squadron when he contacted a U-boat, at night, three miles away; too close for him to get down from 500 feet and home accurately. Potier was from Huguenot stock and was qualified as a chartered accountant in 1936. He was 24 when the war began and was just going into the comfortable little niche of chartered accountancy when he went to see Dawn Patrol and realized that the world of ledgers and balance sheets was not for him. By late 1942 he had 1,050 operational hours and was rested before being retrained to attack U-boats at night with Leigh Lights and a posting to his present squadron. He flew on until the contact was astern and then he lost it. It was in 'the quiet loneliness just before dawn.' He turned directly towards where he thought the target was but still there was no contact. Suddenly, after passing astern of the supposed U-boat, the contact was picked up again, at short range. The Leigh Light was switched on to reveal what he called 'a fat, juicy U-boat,' dead ahead. The crew drill of the months of training went like clockwork and he did not have to give an order. The bombs were dropped and Potier flew over the spot many times, but neither bodies nor wreckage appeared. Four hours after, they again flew over the scene of the attack and there was a big patch of oil on the sea. The ambiguous judgment of the attack is, 'Insufficient evidence of damage,' but this does not mean that the U-boat got away unharmed.

On the morning of 21 June Mike Ensor on 224 Squadron arrived back in a bad temper. He was on patrol about midnight, near Ushant and so bored that he tried to remember and sing old songs of his childhood. He was half-way through *Onward Christian Soldiers* when a shower of flak burst about the Liberator. All Ensor said was 'A chap can't even sing without being interrupted these days.'

At five o'clock in the morning on 23 June a 224 Squadron Liberator piloted by Flight Lieutenant W. A. S. Blackden carried out an attack on a U-boat. Sergeant McConaghy was second pilot and Flight Sergeant Berry, who saw the attack from the bomb bay, was wireless operator. They were patrolling between Falmouth and Roscoff Point off the north coast of Brittany and they were about half-way across the Channel when Sergeant McConaghy said, 'There's a sub ahead.' He hadn't much to do as second pilot so he got up and yelled 'Come on:' As he said, his chief contribution was 'moral support.'

Blackden was doubtful when McConaghy said there was something 'like a field-kitchen chimney' making a faint ripple on the sea. Blackden had about 1,100 operational flying hours and he might have become pessimistic about U-boats as he had never seen one. 'I could hardly believe it,' he said: 'It was rather unusual, to say the least of it.' The U-boat was making straight up the Channel. Blackden flew in and dropped his depth charges. Flight Sergeant Berry had the best view of what followed. A hardened Coastal Command type, Blackden had already made three attacks on U-boats and one on a destroyer. He returned from this last attack, on Christmas Eve, with thirteen feet of one wing missing.

Berry was in the bomb bay when this latest attack was made. He said, 'I got down under the flight deck ready to hold the bomb bay doors open and to work 'the camera when the depth charges had been released. I looked down, expecting to see a U-boat move into the scene. I could see a few whitecaps but the sea was mostly smooth. I leaned out when I saw the depth charges fall and I saw an object moving towards the place where the depth charges would enter the water. But-it was not the shape of a U-boat. It was my first 'schnörkel'. There were two splashes on either side of it and I did not see it again.'

Blackden said that they turned in again to photograph the result but there was nothing on the surface of the water except the scum from the depth charges. Blackden flew around to wait for the bodies he hoped to see, but none came. The crew were feeling rather depressed until a blot of rainbow-coloured oil began to form on the surface of the greyish green water. The area of the oil grew until it was 100 yards wide and the Liberator then resumed its patrol, satisfied that at least one more U-boat had been held back from its task.[84]

Off Trondheim on 24 June a Canso on 162 Squadron RCAF piloted by 34-year old Flying Officer David E. Hornell found U-1225 commanded by 30-year old Oberleutnant zur see Ernst Sauerberg, who was outbound for a weather-reporting patrol. As Hornell began his attack Sauerberg stayed on the surface and threw up heavy flak that blew off the starboard engine of the Canso and set the wing on fire. Undaunted, Hornell attacked and sank the U-boat with depth charges and then he ditched. He and his co-pilot Bernard C. Denomy and six other airmen piled into a single life raft. Two of the crew died before a 333 Norwegian Squadron Catalina and a Warwick on 281 Squadron found six survivors and directed an air sea rescue launch to the scene. The Warwick dropped an airborne lifeboat which fell 500 yards down wind. The men in the dinghy struggled to reach it but they were too weak. Hornell wanted to strip and swim to it but the others persuaded him not to. A little time after this he lost his sight. The Catalina then left them, after a heroic vigil of twelve and a half hours. It homed surface craft before flying back to base and the six survivors were picked up but Hornell was still blind and so exhausted that he died on board the launch before it could reach Ireland. Hornell was awarded a posthumous Victoria Cross. Denomy received the DSO and four other men were decorated. U-1225 sank with all 56 hands.

Hector Bolitho had a long talk on the afternoon of the 25th with Philip Hill who made an attack about half-past one the previous morning. 'He was flying over a hazy calm sea when he got a definite radar contact. He was not certain whether it was a U-boat so he maintained course and watched it, so that he could estimate its speed and decide whether it was only another aircraft. He then flew in to attack. He has done nine hundred hours of operational flying. I asked him if he felt excited. He said, 'Yes, I began to wonder what the Leigh light would illuminate. I called to the navigator to turn on the light. I looked out and saw a stack-like object. It was a 'schnörkel'. Then I heard our depth charges thumping off and the explosions. I had no time to think very much. All my attention was taken up in getting the aircraft round for a second attack. Yet one is able to do some sort of thinking with one's second mind and while I was calculating each moment what I should do, I was also wondering in the back of my mind, working out the possible position of the U-boat under water. We had dropped a flame float and after I had flown away for about four miles I came in again and realized that we had missed it. For the next four hours I circled that flame float, wondering what course the U-boat had taken and how far it would be before the surface vessels got to it. We had sent a message to base and all we could do in the end was resume patrol.'

'Philip Hill has seen only one other U-boat in his long story of patrols and this sighting also ended in disappointment. He was ordered to do a patrol over an area in which bombing was forbidden. He had no idea why he was sent and imagined it might be to track the German fleet. He saw a submarine and circled it, thinking it might be British as it was in the area forbidden for bombing. It was not until he landed back at base that he realized it was a damaged U-boat and that he had missed the first big chance of his career.

'I asked him if he felt anything personal about the Germans in a U-boat when he attacked. He said, 'No. The crew is not made up of individuals for me. I might feel different if I saw any of them struggling in the water after an attack.' He told me that he has only once seen a pilot depressed about his attack on the enemy. The man, who was inclined to be a pacifist, returned one Christmas Eve after sinking a U-boat. He sat in the mess, his head in his hands; silent. Somebody asked him why he was so quiet and he answered, 'A fine Christmas present I have given some German wives and mothers.' 'But such incidents are rare. Phil Hill said that he does not have time to analyse what the U-boat means during an attack. It is no more than a target.'[85]

On Saturday 1 July New Zealand Flight Lieutenant John W. Barling a seasoned U-boat fighter on 224 Squadron who had ditched twice, once in the Atlantic and once during bad weather in Gibraltar harbour, arrived back in the afternoon but he and his crew were too excited to sleep and they sat about, bleary-eyed abut alert, waiting for the news everyone hoped for. On Friday night the Liberator crew and four frigates had attacked U-988 commanded by 24-year old Oberleutnant zur see Eric Dobberstein. The aircraft was on the second circuit of its patrol when Barling got a contact just after midnight. The radar operator, Warrant Officer Faulkner was certain there was 'something there' so Barling decided to investigate. He flew a level course over the position, saw nothing, flew on and then picked up the contact again. They saw a dark object and Barling let out a yell. The second pilot, Benny Benson, who looked so young that Hector Bolitho had imagined him swinging a bundle of school books rather than flying a heavy Liberator over the conning tower of a U-boat, was taking part in his first attack on a U-boat and he said that 'it was like an Indian seeing a white man for the first time.'

'It's a U-boat,' he cried.

Barling turned a complete circle and came in towards it. Three members of the crew saw it at the same time. It was a schnörkel. Benny Benson was very pleased. 'I had done ten trips and hadn't seen a sausage. I was very browned off and had taken off that evening, expecting another binding trip. We were patrolling off the English coast and I had no idea there would be a U-boat there. We came straight up the moon-path and saw the schnörkel making a V-shaped ripple as it moved slowly through the water.

'It was so light that the skipper was able to run in and track right over it.' Hubert Jessell, the second navigator, was in the nose of the aircraft; he said that the attack was like something out of a training manual. At one mile from the target Peter Hurn, the first navigator, turned on the Leigh light which made the target a little clearer. Jessell could see the schnörkel 'like an iron flue.' Hurn dropped six depth charges; the radar operator saw them go down and the rear gunner saw them explode. The engineer, Sergeant E. Hannawin, was so keen to see the results of the explosions that he leaned too far out of the bomb bay. His earphones were pulled off and they went hurtling down with the depth charges. When the attack was over- the aircraft came in again and swept the area with the Leigh light, revealing a patch, 100 feet wide, where the depth charges had beaten the seas into foam. In the centre of this appeared a faint patch of oil. The aircraft circled round and round and the patch of oil grew until it covered an area a mile wide, with one slim streak two miles long in the direction of the course of the crippled U-boat.

Johnny Barling sent signals back to base and about 5.30 in the morning, six frigates came on the scene from the south-west. The Liberator guided them to the oil patch and one of them steamed right into it. After handing over the fate of the U-boat to the Navy, the Liberator resumed its patrol.

News came in the evening of 1 July. The frigates had got the U-boat and were bringing some of the crew back to the coast. 'It's been a long time,' 'Benny' Benson said, 'but it was worth it.'

The Admiralty credited the kill originally to the corvettes *Lotus* and *Poppy* but a post-war reassessment saw the sinking awarded to Barling. It was the New Zealander's second submarine kill. On 14 November Pilot Officer Barling was flying a Hudson on 233 Squadron when he sank U-605 commanded by 25-year old Kapitänleutnant Viktor Schütz, which went down with all 46 hands.

On 4 July 224 Squadron crews returned from their patrols, bored at having seen nothing; except Tug Wilson and Bill Tye who had created their own excitement. A few gashes on Bill's face were the result. They were near Ushant about half-past seven this morning when Tug thought he saw a ship among the islands, near Ile Vierge. They flew in at 800 feet to investigate but there was nothing. They were just doing a circuit to resume patrol when they saw the flak towers on the north-east corner of Ushant. Tug said, 'We were so fed up after hours of seeing nothing that we just felt we had to fire at something, so we flew in and Bill opened fire with the nose gun. It jumped out of its mounting and hit him in the face. We were then level with the flak tower so the side and mid upper gunners opened up. The tracer performed a perfect arc as it fell. It was lovely to watch. The three flak towers fired back at us, with tracer flak and red star shells. Their aim was good but we were too high and the bursts were underneath us. Then we flew on over the mainland. It was peaceful, just like England, with green fields and hedgerows. We saw a motor-car on the road and people going to work. There was a level strip of open country undefended and quiet and I was sorely tempted to land and capture it.'

'Their audacity in flying so low over the coast' wrote Hector Bolitho 'makes one think of the change that has come in the attitude of aircrews towards enemy aircraft and flak since D-Day. The coast of France used to be a menace to them. They had learned from continuous experience that as they flew in towards any of the U-boat bases or ports down the French coast, enemy aircraft would fly out to intercept them. The Junkers sometimes came out in packs and Liberators and other heavy aircraft were often attacked by six or seven agile German fighters. One crew returned after eight German aircraft had formated on them. It was a miracle of escape. Coastal pilots began to love clouds for the chance of escape they offered. But sometimes the clouds were not there and these heavy aircraft would have to fight off the Junkers for perhaps an hour and come home riddled with bullets. Or not come home at all. The Bay of Biscay became a horror to them and one day an intelligence officer briefing a crew about to fly down the Bay heard one of them whisper, 'I'm not bloody well going there.' Of course he went, 'but the whisper revealed the fear that harassed most of them. - When D-Day came there was no reason to suppose that the danger would not increase. But the German fighters have not come out to attack and it is now known that they were sent north to join the forces over the invasion area. A month has passed since D-Day and only five enemy aircraft have been seen and of these three were shot down. The effect on the crews is encouraging. Now they fly in over the coast, even when they are not ordered to do so. Instead of bringing home stories of enemy fighters, as in the old days, they talk of French peasants crossing bridges, of the smoke of the seaweed fires at Brest and of fishermen waving to them from the shallows off the coast.

On 17 July the nine man crew of Catalina JV928 on 210 Squadron captained by Flying Officer John Alexander Cruickshank sighted a U-boat on the surface 190 miles west of the Lofotons. This was Cruickshank's twenty-fifth patrol and the first on which he had sighted a U-boat. 'Blip up, skipper - 'bout sixteen miles away!' Cruickshank was roused from a reverie by the shout from Dickson his navigator who was operating the radar. Cruickshank was taking his Catalina on U-boat patrol inside the Arctic Circle. The navigator's shout seemed to mean business. OK. Home us on to her,' he called back. The aircraft made its way towards the spot and then, slightly to starboard, the crew saw the tell-tale plume of foam. The sub surfaced. Without a doubt it was a U-boat and one of the latest type. It had a tonnage five times as great as the standard model. From his pilot's seat Cruickshank could see 37 and 20 mm anti-aircraft cannon behind the conning tower. 'Pilot to crew,' he called, 'it's a U-boat. We're going in.'

It was U-347 commanded by 31-year old Korvettenkapitän Johann de Buhr. Cruickshank, an ex-bank clerk, born in Aberdeen, Scotland, originally enlisted in the Royal Artillery but in early 1941 he had volunteered for transfer to the RAF for pilot training.

Cruickshank flew into the wind so that his engine noise would be carried away from U-347. There was no sign that the 'Cat' had been seen. Nearer and nearer it dived on to the German boat. Then 'Click,' the bomb-aimer's thumb stabbed the release button. But nothing happened. The depth charge had jammed. Levelling up at fifty feet Cruickshank cursed his luck and began a turn for another run. By this time the 'Cat' had been seen and the U-boat crew were scrambling to their positions on the guns. It seemed no time before the shells were flashing past the Catalina. Cruickshank banked his air¬craft. 'Hold on, we're going back,' he shouted into the mouthpiece. This really was business. He began his second run over the U-boat. Suddenly there were bangs inside the aircraft. Dickson was killed outright and two other members of the crew were also wounded. The nose-gunner had a leg riddled with red-hot shrapnel and Cruickshank himself was badly wounded, gasping for breath. Fire broke out on board the Catalina and, while Cruickshank struggled to hold the aircraft to a steady course, another gunner fought the flames with an extinguisher.

Cruickshank himself pressed home the bomb release and this time there was no mishap. The depth charge was well aimed and the U-boat sank in a frothy white sea. With 72 wounds, of which the most serious were two in the lungs and ten in the legs, Cruickshank then passed out and Flight Sergeant Jack Garnett, the second pilot and also wounded, took over the controls. Cruickshank recovered shortly afterwards and, aware of his responsibilities as captain, insisted on taking over the controls from Garnett until he was satisfied that the damaged aircraft was under control and that they were on course. Even after this he refused morphia in case it should prevent him from carrying on if Garnett collapsed. Several times during the five and a half hour flight back to Sullom Voe, in the Shetlands, Cruickshank passed out, but, when the base was reached, he insisted on being propped up in the second pilot's seat in order to be in charge once again. It was dark when they reached Sullom Voe and Cruickshank would not let the damaged aircraft land until the dawn. For a full hour he sat up and gave orders until finally, with his assistance, the Catalina was brought safely down on the water and taxied on to the beach where it was easily salvaged. Cruickshank was given an immediate blood transfusion and lived to receive the Victoria Cross he had so richly earned. U-347 was lost with all 49 hands. Cruickshank received his VC from King George VI at Holyrood House, Edinburgh and was the first to be decorated there during the war. At the same ceremony Flight Sergeant Garnett was awarded the DSM.

On 19 July Terry Bulloch was flying a Liberator III, 'a rather ancient machine by that time. It had the old-fashioned radar, which we were not allowed to use while we were operating right off the North Cape, because the Germans were triggering it off all the time. We were flying from Tain, in north-east Scotland, near Inverness at about 200 feet, in and out of cloud. Suddenly we came out of cloud and this U-boat, which had obviously been tracking us, was dead ahead of me. He opened up at a range of about three-quarters of a mile and hit my two starboard engines. No. 4 was on fire and the other one disabled, with an oil leak. He also shot away the starboard fin and rudder. We were rather taken by surprise.'

Bulloch and his co-pilot, Pilot Officer Lord flew back the 900 miles to Tain on two port engines. They became sore and stiff through holding out against the unequal control forces and threw everything out of the aeroplane, guns, ammo, to lighten it.

'We went straight over Scapa Flow at about 2,000 feet. It is a wonder the Navy didn't shoot at us, because they were always very trigger-happy, but we got it in all right, though it was full of holes. It was rather an abortive sortie: fifteen hours and fifty minutes, quite exciting.'

Bulloch took over to make a safe landing with the crippled aircraft.[86]

On 25 July Hector Bolitho noted that 'The limelight has moved from our part of the U-boat war, to the Halifaxes based in Wales. There is such a pall of silence on anti U-boat operations that few people seem to know that Halifaxes play their part over the sea, as well as in raiding Berlin, Hamburg and the other targets within the Reich. During this month Halifaxes have been looking for any U-boats that might sneak along the French coast under cover of their own escorts and shore based guns. The success in holding back the ships from reinforcing the enemy in Brittany and Normandy has been remarkable during the past few days.

'On the night of 22/23 July the Halifaxes were given eleven jobs and they attacked at least three U-boats and four escort vessels. Two plums fell to the Halifax captained by Lieutenant Caspar Kramis, of Montana, who sighted two fully-surfaced U-boats near Lorient. They had been contacted about a quarter to four in the morning and when the Halifax sighted them they tried to evade, one turning to port and one to starboard. Kramis attacked the one on the port side, from 1,500 feet. As he ran in the U-boat turned again, but the aircraft followed in level flight. Kramis flew in through a slight burst of flak which ceased when he had dropped his bombs. There was haze and no moon to help him judge his results, but after the attack one of the contacts disappeared. Another Halifax of the same squadron flew over the position thirty minutes later and saw only one of the U-boats, with five enemy vessels nearby. As Kramis was circling after the attack, four blips were picked up, possibly from the enemy vessels and another, indicating a fifth vessel. Flight Sergeant Stetsko, mid upper gunner in the Halifax, has had a lucky tour for this was the second time he was the first member of the crew to sight a U-boat.

'A Scotsman, Flight Lieutenant I. J. M. Christie, on 58 Squadron, followed Kramis on this patrol and illuminated four patrol vessels travelling in line astern at twenty knots.[87] He met intense and accurate flak and had to evade the targets. A little later he met three more ships, on the same course. At four in the morning he got a contact and as he approached the contact broke up into six separate blips. His flares illuminated a fully surfaced U-boat escorted by a destroyer and four minesweepers in two lines of three. Christie climbed, ran in and attacked through flak.

'A third Halifax on the same patrol also had a busy night. The captain, Flying Officer Shiack, sighted two 'M' class minesweepers which fired on him and half an hour later he contacted lour enemy vessels heading for St. Nazaire. The flashes of his bombs were reflected in, the clouds through which he made his attack. A few minutes later he saw more minesweepers, in line astern, but he had no bombs left.

'On the night of the 24th, the Halifaxes again came into their own. All four detailed for the patrol sighted ships or U-boats. This time it was a Fijian, Flight-Lieutenant G. D. Aidney on 502 Squadron, who saw a U-boat escorted by three minesweepers, all of which fired on him during his bombing run. There was every indication that his bombs fell near enough to damage, or at least hold the U-boat up on its patrol.

'Enemy shipping attacks were made by aircraft of 58 and 502 Squadrons. Flight Lieutenant Bentley of 58 sighted five enemy vessels in line astern, covering a distance of about three miles. As he circled to get the target in his flare path he saw flak being fired at the 502 Halifax, captained by Flight Lieutenant James. He then saw other Halifaxes, from 502, attacking the biggest of the enemy vessels. There were some encouraging explosions before he flew in to add to the attack. He must have shaken them considerably. He was still in fighting mood and he made a second attack later, when the vessels seemed to be bunched together. A second aircraft on 502 saw the first attack and reported bomb explosions on the starboard side of the target.

'The patrol was continued and again the Halifaxes brought home good stories. Flight Lieutenant Unwin-Smith on 502 Squadron saw two merchant vessels off Ile d'Oleron and attacked what was afterwards believed to be an ammunition ship. The explosions which followed were vivid blue and they came from water level. Unwin-Smith flew about for some time afterwards and the explosions continued for over half an hour. He could still see them when he was thirty miles away.'

The month of August began with two empty days. One hundred and seventy sorties were flown over the South-Western Approaches and in the Bay in the 48 hours ending on the morning of 3 August and not one U-boat was seen. Enemy shipping seemed equally shy and there were only three units reported. A Halifax on 58 Squadron attacked a convoy of six vessels on the afternoon of the 1st and explosions were seen alongside one of them. But there was haze and the results could not be judged. On 4 August one U-boat was seen on the surface by a Halifax on 502 Squadron at about half past three in the morning but the aircraft had already dropped its depth charges on three enemy vessels, one of which was left smoking, so it had no 'gifts' left for the U-boat. On the 5th the lull ended. There were two U-boat attacks during the past 24 hours, by a Halifax on 502 Squadron and by a Wellington on 179. Umpherson on 502 was flying off the Brest Peninsular half an hour after midnight when he saw a U-boat in the moonlight. He dropped his depth charges and saw an explosion very close to the wake of the U-boat. When he flew in again the enemy had disappeared. Becker on 179 Squadron was flying between Brest and the English Coast about nine o'clock in the morning when his rear gunner saw: a 'suspicious looking object' six miles astern. The captain then saw it and described it as 'an oval-shaped object on the edge of the sun-path.' The 'object' began to submerge. Six depth charges were dropped on it, fifteen seconds after it went under, leaving a thin trace of oil. Twenty minutes after the attack there was a bubbling oil streak big enough to be seen half a mile away.

On 7 August U-608 commanded by 25-year old Kapitänleutnant Wolfgang Reisener left Lorient bound for La Pallice. By the early afternoon of 9 August the U-boat was shallow-submerged at a spot 40 miles south of Belle Ile, off Ile de Noirmoutier when the submarine was spotted by a patrolling Liberator, EV877 'C-Charlie' on 53 Squadron at St Eval. At the bomber's controls was Wing Commander Richard T. F. 'Dick' Gates DFC AFC, 53's commander, flying his last operational sortie with the unit prior to promotion to a desk job at Command headquarters. His mid-upper gunner, Pilot Officer A. S. Dantzic told Hector Bolitho the story:

'They were tootling along to have a look at an oil slick which covered an area of about a mile, shimmering on the sea. They looked out hopefully and the beam-gunner called up on the intercom, 'Skipper, there's a sub down there.' They were practically over it and most of them were able to look down and see the wonder of a submerged U-boat. 'It was like a nice long greenish cigar, with a darker green circle which was the conning tower. It was a lighter green than the sea because the sun was shining on it. The pointed nose was quite clear, but the stern was low.' Pilot Officer Dantzic said 'you know how the painted line around the edge of a swimming bath trembles in the water, well the U-boat seemed to shiver like that.' Wing Commander Gates was in the pilot's seat at the time and he gave the order to attack. The first time the aircraft went over, the bomb doors failed to open and the pilot had to make a circuit to port and come in a second time, dropping the depth charges nicely between the end of the immense oil slick and the stern of the U-boat. Dantzic said that they were flying at about 100 feet and the explosion was so terrific that he seemed to be looking up at the column of water. They climbed to starboard and saw the residue of the depth charges and, flying in again, they saw oil. Somebody said, 'It might be a decoy,' so they stayed around and watched. The oil still surged to the surface, so the captain flew off and homed naval vessels [HMS *Wren* and HMS *Killin*] to the spot. The Navy picked up some U-boat planking and samples of the oil after the Liberator resumed patrol. When it flew over the spot again sometime later, the oil covered a terrific area, with streaks spreading out beyond the main mass. The U-boat had apparently gone down and was no doubt struggling with its injuries.

'About half-past two the next morning a 224 Squadron Liberator piloted by Flight Lieutenant John Barling got a contact. As they closed in the blip split up into two and then into three spots of light on the screen. One, which turned out to be U-608, was on the starboard side and the others, which were our own frigates, were to port. Barling saw a U-boat in the moonpath, stationary and in the centre of a big patch of oil. He was about to attack when one of the frigates signalled that it was a 'sinking U-boat' and that the survivors were getting into their dinghies. Barling continued his patrol and when he flew over the spot later in the morning he saw the frigate picking up the Germans from the water. There were about thirty of them, in two groups of one-man dinghies, five hundred yards apart. When the German prisoners were interrogated they said that they had been attacked by an aircraft about 2.30 the previous afternoon, so the story fitted together nicely and brought Coastal another kill. The U-boat left Lorient only two days before, with supplies for fourteen weeks. Their enterprise was therefore nipped in the bud.'[88]

On 15 August Flight Lieutenant Gilbert Potier came home with another victory claim for the Liberator crews on 53 Squadron. He caught one more of the U-boats - U-618 commanded by 23-year old Erich Faust - which had escaped from the pens in Brest and was trying to make its way to the Gironde River to La Pallice. About half-past ten on the 14th Potier flew off to patrol off St. Nazaire. 'It was a lovely sunset,' he told Hector Bolitho 'and the stars were peeping out. As we passed Brest I could see a thunderstorm ahead. I summoned all the courage I have because I don't like thunderstorms. In peace-time I used to put my head under the bed clothes. I knew that every fork of lightning would send a shiver of terror through me. As we approached, the stars went out and the night became black. The lightning was terrine, each jagged fork seeming to run from the sky to the sea, turning night into day. It seemed hours before we were in the middle of it. Every time one of the blinding flashes came I thought it would hurl our thirty-ton aircraft into the sea below. Then we were through and beyond it all. I relaxed and soon the stars' peeped out again. The calm after the storm was very sweet. It was just before midnight that the radar operator said, 'Hullo skipper, radar here, contact just appeared.' 'The contact persisted so I ordered, 'Action stations, everybody! Action stations!'

'The gale was too strong for us to approach across the wind, so I turned away from the target until we were finally on a course into wind. Everything depended on the Radar operator. If he failed we might easily be shot into the sea. We were flying at 200 feet but we could not see the water. A little needle, green with phosphorescence, kept winking up and down on my radio altimeter to tell me that the sea was still there. I felt a little tense, wondering if there was a U-boat slinking along in the blackness, aware that we were there. I hoped not. The radar operator was guiding me splendidly, in his strong New Zealand voice. The others had nothing much to do for the moment except listen and peer into the blackness. Then, 'Steady, skipper, steady and 'Oh, she's a wonderful blip, steady as a rock, skipper. Oh, she's a beaut.' Then excitement came into his voice as he said, 'Slightly right!' Then the Leigh light went on. For a fraction of a second I could see nothing at all, then hell broke loose.

'Our front guns were blazing away for all they were worth and, I saw little balls of red fire coming up towards us and racing away beneath our starboard wing. I put my head into the cockpit to concentrate on the instruments and then came Pop's quiet, 'Bombs gone.' The Leigh Light went out and the blackness was intense. I could feel our rear turret guns firing, then nothing but the steady drone of the engines. I relaxed and called up to see that nobody was injured. All answered except the rear turret. I called again, anxiously and there came back, 'OK Skipper.' It was Butterfield and this was his first ops trip. The astonishing luck of attacking a U-boat within the first two hours of his first trip robbed him of his voice for a moment.

'The Leigh light had been on only fifteen seconds, but a lot had happened - Pop, the navigator, called me up to say we had straddled the U-boat just abaft the conning tower. Bill, in the nose turret, had done a wizard job. He is a nineteen year old Scotsman. He had scored hits all around the conning tower and had started a sizeable fire which was seen by everybody. His accurate fire no doubt saved us from being hit. The rear gunner had also given them a few rounds. The U-boat must have just surfaced and the crew must have been shaken, being attacked within ten minutes. At one in the morning we began homing the Navy and at two-thirty a Wellington arrived and illuminated the scene. We saw two significant oil streaks. At 7.30 the Navy found the U-boat, limping along under the surface, so badly damaged that it was moving at only a mile an hour. They finished what we began and one more of the bastards went to the bottom.'[89]

A few hours after Hector Bolitho arrived at Portreath on 20 August there was 'a curious sensation of suspense in the mess during these hours until it was known that 'Tug' Wilson of 224 had been diverted from patrol to search for the dinghy.'

'He saw it just before dusk and dropped five flame floats so that it would be encircled with light when darkness fell. He then flew off, found a naval vessel thirty miles away and directed it to the dinghy. About eleven o'clock at night, the Navy picked up the crew and brought them to the coast. The suspense in the mess was something one does not know with a Liberator squadron because, if a Liberator meets disaster in the dark, there is little chance of the crew being picked up. I felt this difference all the more because only a few days ago, Ted Lindsay's Liberator was lost, with its crew of ten. Ted, who was one of the flight commanders of 224, was on an anti U-boat patrol when his aircraft was shot down. It was seen crashing into the sea.

'Ted and his crew just didn't come back and there was neither suspense nor hope. The awful gloom, which I have known before, descended on the mess. It was all the more horrible because everybody tried to cover it up with chatter. There was but a momentary flash of realization, 'This might have happened to me.' But this passed because even death and grief become a habit which men learn to conquer.

'Ted Lindsay was different from most of the people in the squadron. They are mixed from the great bowl of humanity; some devoted to noisy poker, some to solitary walks. Some are mashers with well-pressed uniforms and exaggerated tales of conquests over blondes in Newquay and some play good music or read good books in hollows on the hills. Some tinker with cars and are always covered with oil and some are pickled in shop talk so that nothing else but flying interests them. Ted was an old Etonian through and through. From Eton he went to Cambridge and the system had taught him repose and to be frugal with pleasures. He drank, but never too much; he was capable of stern statements without swearing and he was tidy and correct. He covered the ground without fussing and he had authority without need of raising his voice.

'My heart jumped when I saw his luggage already packed outside his bedroom door, within a few hours of the time when he failed to come back. I had liked all he represented and so did everybody else in the mess. The Canadians and Australians did not know that what they loved in him was the essence of a class which can cope with responsibility because responsibility is part of their inheritance. When you define this quality to the men from the new countries they often say 'old school tie' and leave it at that. But when they come upon the quality, they respect it and even love its influence. Ted learned to fly with the Cambridge University Air Squadron and although he had no decorations and had not been in any terrific battles, he had gone through the Services to the rank of squadron leader and the responsibility of being a flight commander by sheer force of character. He could exact obedience without being angry and inspire only by example. This example caused life to be a fragment less noisy and less superficial, whenever he entered a room.'

By this stage of the war anti-U-boat operations were an almost perfect science, as U-1060 discovered to its cost on 27 October. Herbert Brammer had left Bodø the day before bound for the Far East with a minesweeper escort. The submarine had 144 men on board, having picked up 28 survivors from U-957, which had been badly damaged in a collision with a German steamer a week earlier. North-west of Namsos the submarine was attacked by a swarm of Fairey Fireflies on 1771 Squadron FAA from HMS *Implacable*. One bomb sank the minesweeper. Another fell precisely through the conning-tower hatch on U-1060 killing Brammer and eleven other crew. U-1060 was beached later that day on the island of Fliena. Seventy-one crewmen were rescued. On 4 November two Liberators on 311 (Czech) Squadron flown by Flying Officer F. Pavelka and Squadron Leader A. Sedivý and two Halifaxes flown by Flight Lieutenant W. G. Powell and Squadron Leader H. H. Holderness DFC AFC on 502 Squadron demolished the submarine.[90] On the night of 30 October a Leigh-Light equipped Wellington on 407 Squadron RCAF piloted by J. E. Neelin and a Liberator on 224 Squadron flown by Flight Lieutenant W. A. S. Blackden converged on U-1061 which had left Bergen on 28 October and caused heavy damage to their quarry with depth-charges. The submarine limped into Malöy.[91]

On Tuesday, 19th December 1944 the Dutch cruise liner *Nieu Amsterdam* left Greenock bound for Halifax, Nova Scotia with many servicemen aboard. None were more happy to be going home than Clayton Moore, a Canadian rear gunner from Saskatchewan who had completed two tours before getting a well-deserved posting back to Canada where his father worked an isolated ten-acre plot of land near Prince Albert. 'The crossing' Clayton Moore recalled 'took considerably longer than it would have taken on one of 'the Queens' but the food and the accommodation was excellent, so there was a total absence of complaint from the many time expired fellow Canadians on board. For us, the war was ended - at least we were given to believe that it was. But, on Christmas Day, we got an unpleasant reminder that we were still within a war zone. We were nearing the port of Halifax and I had just entered one of the dining halls, intent on enjoying my third Christmas dinner away from home, when an announcement on came over the ship's Tannoy ordering all passengers below decks. No reason was given, but the urgent tone of the message and the sound of bells ringing all over the ship made it plain that we must be under attack. The order was followed by numerous others, but these, being directed at the crew, were in Dutch, a language foreign to most, if not all of us.

'During the voyage I had become friendly with a fellow RCAF officer and he, being with me when the balloon went up, suggested that we should make our way to see what was going on. This we did and were thus afforded an unrestricted view of the action from our carefully selected vantage point behind one of the lifeboats, our ship was engaged in some quite violent evasive action and we could see a Sunderland flying boat approaching from a westerly direction. As we watched, we saw a salvo of depth charges leaving the Sunderland and these splashed into the water about half a mile off our starboard beam, but we were unable to observe anything other than the waterspouts that they produced. The Sunderland, apparently having exhausted the supply of depth charges, then turned and left the action, but was soon replaced by a Catalina. This dropped two more 'ash cans' in the same area, after which it began to circle where they had fallen. At last my companion and I were able to see something of what had caused all the confusion, as a German U-boat rose slowly to the surface. As we watched, a number of dark figures were seen to leave the conning tower and move out onto the narrow deck. One was waving something white at the 'Cat', which then turned in a westerly direction and disappeared over a gathering grey fog bank. The Nieu Amsterdam ceased its weaving and sailed steadily past the unfortunate German submariners and their stricken craft, not daring to stop for survivors because of the danger of coming under attack from another member of the pack.

'The action as over, so my friend and I returned below and joined the line-up for our Christmas fare.

'Later that evening our troopship docked at Halifax to find the city blanketed in thick fog and with the temperature well below freezing. As we lined up on the dockside waiting to be processed, I found myself wondering how the German U-boat crew had fared out there in the icy waters of the Atlantic. Had they been picked up, or had they just been left there to die? During the past two years I had watched many of my friends and colleagues perish at the hands of the same enemy, such were the horrors of war. But I couldn't help hoping that the U-boat crew had been picked up and taken prisoner.'[92]

Edward Bailey recalls the last few months of the war on 86 Squadron:

'On this squadron the crew, of which I was a member, did no convoy escort duties but just flew anti U-boat patrols between the Shetland Islands and Norway. We had no sightings and I flew my last operational flight on 1 May 1945. I found the Liberator an excellent aircraft to fly in and only once in the 750 hours flying time did we have engine trouble.'

With the Atlantic, Bay of Biscay and the English Channel purged of the U-boat all that remained was to accept the surrender of these small craft, crewed by brave and daring men, who at one time had almost brought Britain to her knees. After VE Day U-boats were ordered to surface and fly a black flag in surrender. Laurie Lloyd, a second pilot on 59 Squadron recalls:

'We were on patrol on VE Day and arrived back at Ballykelly to find that everything, including the searchlight crews, was lit up. At the end of a thirteen hour 'stooge' we needed all our collective sense of humour to appreciate their high spirits. A day or so later we were sent out to pick up any surrendering U-boats. I don't know who was more surprised when we actually found one. We picked up U-1109 but were very uneasy during our first run over it. They were not sure whether we were going to be bloody-minded and drop cans on them and we couldn't be sure they were not going to let fly at us. But we passed over without incident and spent the next seven hours flying round U-1109 in tight circles until a destroyer appeared to take over escort. When the U-boat docked in Londonderry we went over to take a look. The souvenir hunters had been at work but the whole atmosphere inside was untidy and depressing. I finished the European part of the war feeling acutely sorry for the crews we had been trying to destroy!'

In June 1945 the bomb bays were removed from most Coastal Command Liberators and their doors sealed. Canvas seats were installed and the aircraft were transferred to Transport Command for trooping flights to India.

Had more Liberators been available in sufficient quantities during the early part of the war, the U-boat menace might have been better contained. As it was, the Liberators, together with other stalwart anti-submarine aircraft like the Sunderland, Hudson and Catalina, did a magnificent job. Success might also have been greater had the Allies shown greater co-operation. For the most part, America's zone of responsibility lay in the Moroccan Sea Frontier between the two British areas - Gibraltar and West Africa. Britain's ally preferred to adopt local protection rather than send anti-submarine aircraft into the Bay of Biscay where Britain considered the U-boats most vulnerable and it was not until 1944 that effective co-operation, originally proposed by the American Secretary of War but initially rejected by both the British Cabinet and Air Vice Marshal Slessor was satisfactorily resolved.

Footnotes

75 The Savoia-Marchetti SM-79 Sparviero (Hawk) was the most successful land-based torpedo bomber of thje war and was produced in greater numbers than all other Italian multi-engined bombers combined.

76 On 26 May Kapitänleutnant Kurt Petersen commanding U-541 stopped the Serpa Pinto, which was carrying 200 Jewish refugees, and seized two American passengers and took them aboard but they were released on Dönitz's orders. It had been a disappointing war cruise for Petersen. On 14 May he had found a convoy off Florida and fired seven torpedoes but none hit. U-541 surrendered to the Allies on 10 May 1945.

77 Flying Officer Ethan Allen DFC was a direct descendant of the celebrated Ethan Allen who fought in the American War of Independence. Hector Bolitho, *Task For Coastal Command*.

78 U-989 was attacked and damaged by Wellington HQ149/C flown by Squadron Leader Farrell and Flying Officer W. P. Johnston on 407 Squadron RCAF and Liberator BZ942/M piloted by Flying Officer E. Allen DFC on 224 Squadron, both of which were shot down by the U-boat's gunners. The other aircraft that was lost were a Liberator on 53 Squadron piloted by Squadron Leader Crawford which crashed at Poullan-sur-Mer. *Over the Beaches; The Air War Over Normandy and Europe 1st-30th June 1944* by John Foreman (Red Kite 1994).

79 It will be remembered that Coastal Command gave credit for the damage to U-989 commanded by 26-year old Kapitänleutnant Hardo Rodler von Roithberg to W. J. Hill and his crew of the Leigh Light-equipped Wellington on 179 Squadron.

80 *Search, Find and Kill* by Norman Franks and Axel Niestlé (*German U-boat Losses During WWII*, Greenhill Books 1998).

81 *Submarine: An anthology of first-hand accounts of the war under the sea, 1939-1945* edited by Jean Hood (Conway Maritime 2007).

82 *Hitler's U-boat War: The Hunted, 1942-1945* by Clay Blair (Random House 1998)/*Task For Coastal Command* by Hector Bolitho.

83 The submarine was bombed and nearly sunk by two Whitleys on 502 and 51 Squadrons on 31 August 1942 and was almost scrapped on its return. On 11 March 1944 U-256 shot down Wellington H flown by Flying Officer H. C. Sorely on 407 Squadron RCAF and was damaged on 7 June by Halifax L on 53 Squadron. *U-boat Fact File* by Peter Sharpe (Midland Publishing Ltd 1998).

84 *Task For Coastal Command.*

85 *Task For Coastal Command.*

86 In all, Terry Bulloch was credited with sinking four U-boats and severely damaging two more. The next highest score is that of Wing Commander Oulton who was credited with two submarines sunk. When the war ended Bulloch had attacked no fewer than 19 U-Boats in 4,568 hours of operational flying. He finished the war flying C-87s and later RY-3 aircraft, in RAF Transport Command. In the 1950s Bulloch was still flying the Atlantic, as Captain of a BOAC DC-7C airliner and he still had the knack of breaking records. A short while before Christmas 1957 he flew from Montreal to London in 8 hours, 10 minutes; 15 minutes faster than the previous record. In 1958 Bulloch was rapidly approaching his 500th Atlantic crossing. And by some strange chance, his flight engineer on many of these trips was a Scotsman called Jock McColl. Bulloch retired in 1974.

87 On 2 January 1944 U-415 was returning to Brest after a successful patrol having intercepted the escort vessels of Convoy OS62 in the early hours of Christmas Eve and sinking HMS *Hurricane* north-east of the Azores. Early in 1 January Flight Lieutenant Christie located the U-boat south-west of Lorient and carried out a night attack, damaging the U-boat but it reached Brest on 6 January. *Handley Page Halifax: From Hell to Victory and Beyond* by K. A. Merrick (Chevron Publishing 2009).

88 The 51 survivors from the U-608 were rescued by HMS *Wren*, which had also depth charged the submarine and HMS *Killin*.

89 The frigates *Duckworth* and *Essington* depth-charged the U-boat. Potier was awarded the DFC.

90 *U-boat Fact File* by Peter Sharpe (Midland Publishing Ltd 1998)/ *Hitler's U-boat War: The Hunted, 1942-1945* by Clay Blair (Random House 1998).

91 On 7 February 1945 U-1061 ran aground at Alvo and had to be towed to Bergen due to considerable damage to her hull. The submarine was not operational again. Ibid.

92 *Lancaster Valour; The Valour and The Truth* by Clayton Moore (Compaid Graphics 1995). The only U-boat in the area that failed to report in was U-869 commanded by Kapitänleutnant Helmut Neuerburg, which was discovered by amateur shipwreck divers in September 1991. 'The fatal blow could have been delivered as a result of an Allied ASW ship or aircraft attack that has not yet come to light.' Off Halifax after Christmas, Kurt Dobratz commanding U-1232, the last U-boat to reach the Nova Scotia area in 1944, fired three torpedoes at the *Nieuw Amsterdam* but they all exploded harmlessly in her wake. *Hitler's U-Boat War: The Hunted, 1942-1945* by Clay Blair. (Random House 1998).

Chapter 5

The Strike Wings

*'The sky around us seemed to fill with filthy black puffs of smoke - everywhere
I looked they appeared, burst and whipped past our Mossie and my stomach
began to feel distinctly uneasy. My pilot, a calm Devonshire chap who
wouldn't say boo to a goose in the Mess but was hell-on-wheels when behind
a control column, took all this without a word and continued to plunge
through it all, keeping station with the chap slightly to port and ahead of us.
Looking over his shoulder further to port, towards the next Mossie I was
horrified to see that its starboard engine was streaming thin grey smoke; then
saw it wing over sharply and dive. We were too low down for that sort of
manoeuvre - he must have gone straight into the sea at full power. It
happened so quickly I thought I'd dreamed it; then knew I hadn't...
'Then the Mosquito ahead of us bought it - one second he was there, the next
he'd disappeared in a blast of orange-yellow flames and smoke and I felt the
thumps of bits of him hitting our wings and fuselage as my pilot fought to
keep us steady. He only said, 'Kee-ristmas!', then went quiet again. Once on
track and steady again we checked as best we could for any serious damage to
our own kite. The dials stopped spinning and seemed OK everywhere, though
on my side I could see a chunk of wing scored from front to trailing edge out
near the wingtip. Both engines continued at full steam, so we carried on.
Ahead of us I saw a large vessel broadside on to us and my pilot eased the
nose down and gave him three short bursts as we passed over him - probably
just to relieve his feelings at seeing his drinking buddy buy it earlier.'*
**20-year old Terry 'Chalky' White, Mosquito Strike wing navigator,
mid-1944.**

In March 1941 the Bristol Beaufighter IC began to replace the Blenheim
IVF as the standard long-range fighter of Coastal Command, some of the
first aircraft going to 143 Squadron at Aldergrove in Northern Ireland.
In December a decision was made to separate the Fighter and Coastal
Command versions of the Beaufighter I on the production line. The first
production Ic was the 217th aircraft, delivered in February 1941. The first
aircraft were modified only after they had come off the production line
so as not to disrupt night fighter production. The first coastal Beaufighter
was R2152, which was modified by removing the wing guns and fitting
fifty gallon fuel tanks in their place. A navigation table was fitted in the
fuselage and the camera-gun replaced with a DF loop. 252 Squadron was
the first Coastal Command squadron to receive Beaufighters to use in the

strike-fighter/long-range escort role. The aircraft arrived in March 1941, but the extra tanks had yet to be made and as an interim measure, Wellington fifty gallon tanks were fitted on the floor between the cannon bays. The Beaufighter X with torpedo gear began to replace the Beaufort in Coastal Command service from 1942. All production aircraft were fitted with a 0.303 Browning machine gun in the observer's position for rearward defence. AI (Airborne Intercept) Mark VIII radar was installed in a nose radome for ASV work, the torpedo gear with gyro-angling, radio and navigation equipment moved the centre of gravity and increased instability problems. To cure this, the elevator area and fin area were increased on later aircraft.

The Beaufighter eventually became operational in Coastal Command in early 1942 and it soon showed what the Command had lacked on anti-shipping operations since the outbreak of war. It was fast, rugged and strong and like the Mosquito it had a wide choice of armament including cannon, machine guns, rockets and bombs and a modified version - the 'Torbeau' could carry a torpedo. As early as March 1942 a Beaufighter had been successfully tested as a torpedo-carrier at the Torpedo Development Unit at Gosport and in September 1942 a Mark IVC became the first Beaufighter to be armed with rocket-projectiles. The rocket-firing version of the Beaufighter VIC, which would enter squadron service in May 1943, was first used on 22 June that year and the type became known as the 'Flakbeau'. A form of attack was evolved in which the 'Torbeaus' were escorted by 'Flakbeaus' to blanket the enemy ships' defences with fire while the torpedo aircraft launched their torpedoes during the diversion. Nos. 235 Squadron and 236 and 248 Squadrons were the first three Coastal Command squadrons to receive Beaufighter ICs. Originally they were used as long-range fighters over the North Sea hunting for Luftwaffe aircraft, several of which they destroyed and also flew escort to several Hampden bomber raids. Because of the increased enemy opposition and the operational limitations of the Hampden aircraft, it was decided in 1943 that Coastal Command's anti shipping squadrons should convert to Beaufighters.

It was in June 1942 that 27-year old Flight Lieutenant Ken Gatward on 236 Squadron first came into the glare of press publicity when volunteers were called for to drop a French tricolour over the Arc d'Triomphe in Paris. Gatward had joined the RAFVR in 1937 and had flown Blenheims on reconnaissance and bombing operations on 53 Squadron in 1940. The origins of the audacious undertaking dated back to September, 1941 when Major Ben Cowburn of the SOE (Special Operations Executive) was dropped into occupied France. He made his way into Paris where, when strolling along the Champs Elysees one day, he heard in the distance the sound of a military band and as it came nearer he saw a German detachment, led by an officer on horseback, marching towards the Arc de Triomphe. Cowburn noted what a wonderful target the parade would make and what a wonderful boost to French morale an attack would be. Back in London Cowburn put his proposal to the SOE who approached the AOC-in-C Fighter Command. The original proposal was to send three Spitfires equipped with long-range tanks to lay red, white and blue smoke - the colours of the tricolour - over the French capital. The plan was abandoned and instead it was decided to send a single Beaufighter. Gatward and Sergeant George Fern on 236 Squadron were selected from among the volunteer crews in Coastal Command. Major Cowburn back in France once again, provided a timetable for the Germans' daily parade along the Champs Elysees and on 5 May 1942 Gatward and Fern began training. Every day they made practice gunnery attacks on a ship wreck in the Channel, pored over detailed maps of Paris and studied photographs of all the buildings in the parade area. They also visited Portsmouth Dockyard to collect a new and grand-looking Tricolore, for which they signed several forms. Back at Thorney Island nearby they cut the flag into two and the parachute section sewed iron bars on each piece. Secretly they practised dropping the wrapped flags from the top of a hangar to see how they unfurled when descending.

On 13 May the weather augured well for the raid, but as they crossed the French coast the cloud cover cleared and, obeying orders, they returned disappointed. Three more attempts were made, but the weather conditions imposed by did not materialise and back to base they came. By the fifth try on 12 June, Gatward's patience was almost exhausted. He took off from Thorney Island in T4800/ND-C and was determined to get through at all costs. Ken Gatward later recalled:

'Cloud was forecast, but it had broken up when we reached the French coast. This time we carried on. We flew close to the deck all the way, rarely more than 100 feet up and often as low as 30 feet, hedge-hopping trees and buildings. We cruised in at about 220 mph, navigating with a map. Fern did a difficult job magnificently and guided me straight into Paris on course. The parade was timed for midday. Just before noon we picked up the shape of the Eiffel Tower and at 12.02 we were over the Champs Elysees, I climbed to 300 feet and banked for the attack - but there was no parade. The boulevards were almost deserted. Somehow, it seemed, the Germans had learned of our mission. Filled with rage and frustration, we dived on to the Champs Elysees, roared along at below-rooftop height and climbed over the Arc de Triomphe. As we flashed past it Sergeant Fern flung the flags out through the flare-chute. They went out rather like harpoons and that was the last we saw of them. By now we were approaching the Place de la Concorde and the Kriegsmarine Headquarters. This was my secondary target and as we passed we sprayed the place with cannon shells. We got a glimpse of terrified sentries running for their lives and then we were on the way home. We flew back to the coast as low as we had come, but met no ack-ack or enemy fighters. We got away with the whole operation scot-free. The only incident was a minor collision with a big crow that crashed into our starboard radiator. Apart from that our only opposition came from swarms of small flies, which, low flying, we had collected in a solid mass on our wind-shield. By the time we got back to Northolt it was difficult to see through them.'[93]

In July 1942 the offensive in the Bay, which had promised so well with the advent of the Leigh Light in June, was now petering out in failure. In June German aircraft had managed to intercept only three aircraft over the Bay, but with the arrival of the twenty-four Ju 88s which Dönitz had wrung from Göring, opposition warmed up. In July RAF patrols had to fight twenty-five combats, in August thirty-three and in September forty-four. But though losses increased from eight aircraft in July to sixteen in October, those of the enemy rose far more abruptly. In July Coastal Command destroyed in the Bay one German aircraft; in August, four; in September, twelve; and in November (when RAF losses were only seven), twelve again. All this was not accomplished without sacrifices in other directions, for the whole effort of two Beaufighter squadrons (235 and 248) had to be directed against the enemy. But it was worth diverting squadrons to new tasks when they could record episodes like the following:

No. 235 Squadron. St. Eval. 18.9.42. Beaufighters N, C, A, H. E, P, J and O. At 1755 hours, aircraft sighted FW 200 Kurier on easterly course, height 200 feet, over armed trawler of 300 tons. E, P and N attacked FW 200 from port while 'O' dived from 2,000 feet head on and remainder attacked from starboard. FW 200 burst into flames, disintegrated and dived into sea. Three crew were seen in water and one attempting to climb in dinghy. Aircraft H saw C dive into sea from 200 feet, apparently damaged by flak from trawler. 1820, three Ju 88s were sighted flying at 1,000 feet over fishing vessel flying French flag. Aircraft P climbed and attacked while other Beaufighters converged from various directions. Hits were seen on port engine of one Ju 88 which was further attacked by 0 and E; flames appeared in cockpit and enemy dived into sea enveloped in flames. When Beaufighters left, tail planes of two Ju 88s were protruding from sea. Aircraft A followed third Ju.88 and delivered two successive attacks, but Ju. disappeared into cloud.

The AOC-in-C, Coastal Command Philip Joubert, pressed Air Ministry to approve the formation of Beaufighter 'strike wings' and these became reality in September 1942 when a decision was taken to equip Coastal Command with 15 squadrons of Beaufighters by April 1943. The first Strike Wing was formed in November 1942 at North Coates Fitties in 16 Group. It consisted of three Beaufighter squadrons; 143 (fighter), 236 (fighter-bomber) and 254 (Torbeaus). By November 1942 the work of the Beaufighter patrols was virtually complete. For the time being German interference from the air almost ceased and anti-U-boat aircraft were again able to carry out their patrols unmolested. The Beaufighter Strike Wing's first operation came on 20 November when Spitfires of 12 Group, Fighter Command, reported a convoy of twelve to sixteen ships steering south-west towards Rotterdam. 236 and 254 Squadrons were at once dispatched to attack the convoy but the weather was bad, the formations lost touch and the convoy was protected by FW 190s. The largest merchant ship and two escort-vessels were hit, but three Beaufighters were lost and four were so seriously damaged that they crashed or made forced landings on return. The Wing was immediately withdrawn for intensive training and it did not become fully operational again until the following spring.

In April 1943 the Beaufighter wing at North Coates was ready for action. It had been Slessor's intention to put three such wings into operation by that month but a shortage of Beaufighters, combined with the need for fighter protection for the anti-submarine squadrons operating in the Bay of Biscay, together with the demands of the air force in the Mediterranean, delayed the outcome until the end of the year.[94] On 18 April the Beaufighter wing at North Coates took off on its first 'strike' since the unfortunate episode of November. The target, located earlier in the day by one of the wing aircraft, was a heavily escorted convoy off the Dutch coast; and the attacking force consisted of nine Torbeaus on 254 Squadron, six Beaufighter bombers on 236 Squadron and six Beaufighters on 143 Squadron, all covered at high level by Spitfires and Mustangs of Fighter Command. 'The role of the escorting Beaufighters', records 236 Squadron, 'was to attack the escort vessels with bombs, cannon and machine guns and silence their fire whilst the torpedo carrying 'Beaus' attacked the large merchant vessel. Rendezvous with single-engine fighter escort was to be made over Coltishall. The operation went entirely according to plan except that the convoy was encountered some ten miles further north than had been expected (off Texel). Two 'M' class mine-sweepers were hit with bombs, cannon and machine-gun fire and left on fire and an armed trawler was also hit. Two certain torpedo hits were made by 254 Squadron on the largest merchant vessel (the target vessel of the strike), which was left on fire listing heavily and thought to be sinking. Many excellent close-up photographs of the attack were secured. The whole operation was outstanding not only in the success of the attack but also in that between 1535 and 1550 hours everyone of the 21 Beaufighters engaged landed safely back at North Coates. Only very slight damage due to enemy fire was sustained by two or three aircraft and no casualties whatsoever to crew'.

Before the end of April a similar operation resulted in the destruction of two merchant vessels and a trawler, besides damage to several escorts, all at a cost of one Beaufighter. The key to success thus seemed within our grasp. A notable indication of this was soon to come. In May 1943 a tally was made of the active shipping in Rotterdam, the most convenient port for the great industrial area of Rhenish Westphalia. It amounted to only 37,000 tons, as against 106,000 tons a year earlier. The work of the strike-wing, coupled with raids on the port and ceaseless mining, had forced the Germans to halt most of their traffic at Emden, where handling and transport facilities were greatly inferior. By the spring of 1943 the anti-shipping offensive thus promised great things but the demands of the Mediterranean theatre ensured that the planned compliment of five strike-wings in Britain was delayed though by the summer of 1943 the

Beaufighter Squadrons began to justify the faith initially placed upon them, performing well in the roles of air escort for anti-U-boat aircraft in the Bay of Biscay and proving more than a match for enemy Ju 88s and Focke Wulf 190s. In May 1943 the North Coates Wing received its first rocket-armed Beaus and used the new weapon in action for the first time on 22 June 1943. Up to a dozen 'Torbeaus' were used against any target first, covered and followed by up to 20 rocket or cannon-armed Beaufighters to apply the coup de grace.

Throughout the year 'Rover' patrols continued to be flown by the obsolescent Hampdens on 144 Squadron and 455 Squadron RAAF at Leuchars and 489 Squadron RNZAF on Wick. They harried enemy shipping off Norway. The Strike Wing at North Coates, the first to come into action, aided these efforts, which became stronger and more effective as Beaufighters began gradually to take the place of the outmoded Hampdens. While the 'Rovers' of Air Vice-Marshal A. B. Ellwood's 18 Group - single aircraft, or small formations not exceeding five - quartering the seas, ranged far and wide up and down the long Norwegian coast, the Strike Wing at North Coates struck further south against enemy convoys, strongly escorted by flak vessels. In May the Wing received a number of Beaufighters equipped with the new rocket projectile, a singularly effective weapon against shipping. It was first used in force on 22 June 1943. The manner in which the Wing was henceforth to operate was this. Up to twelve aircraft carrying torpedoes attacked the enemy convoy, being covered by as many as sixteen rocket and eight cannon firing Beaufighters whose duty it was to engage the escorting vessels. Such, for example were the tactics followed in the assaults on convoys - delivered on 18 July and 2 August. If the enemy was found within range of Spitfires and Mustangs of Fighter Command, these also joined in the battle. Of three ships sunk in that month by aircraft of Coastal Command two fell victims to the reorganized Strike Wing. Soon the Wing was scoring considerable successes and the enemy had to divert manpower, fighter aircraft and escort vessels needed for other duties in order to protect merchantmen. The enemy also was almost unable to make use of Rotterdam thanks the joint efforts of the Strike Wing, the minelaying aircraft of Bomber Command and the light surface craft of the Nore Flotilla of the Royal Navy. In 1943 the Strike Wing sunk thirteen ships of a total tonnage of 34,076 gross tons. The losses inflicted upon him by other anti-shipping aircraft of Coastal Command were nineteen ships of a total tonnage of 50,683.

Among the first Beaufighter pilots to use the 3-inch rocket on Coastal operations was Wing Commander R. H. 'Hugh' McConnell DFC (later DSO) on 235 Squadron. McConnell recalled:

'Our first attack followed a report by a Norwegian Mosquito pilot of a medium-sized merchant vessel which had become stranded in a Norwegian fjord just east of North Christiansund, not far from Trondheim. We stood by all day hoping to be led to the target by a Mosquito, but the weather closed in and we had to wait patiently for it to clear. Owing to the difficulty of keeping formation in bad weather and trying to keep up with a much faster Mosquito, it was decided that the Mosquito pilot should stand behind me in my leading Beaufighter and direct us to the enemy ship. On the Sunday six of our Beaufighters took off at six o'clock in the evening. Three from my squadron were to shoot up the ship with RP, while the other three were to act as fighter escort. The crews were warned that they had to be careful when approaching the target owing to the steep hills surrounding the fjords. We had to approach over the hills, coming in low, firing quickly and passing out over the heavily defended harbour entrance.

'The weather was bad at the start, but after 15 minutes' flying we came out into a cloudless sky and unlimited visibility. I led the formation very low up the Norwegian coast. Three small escort ships signalled us with an Aldis lamp and we flashed back a reply. They took us for Hun aircraft. Then we flew low over the inhabited islands and could see the islanders in their Sunday clothes taking an evening stroll. We came to a field where some Germans were playing football and they ran for their lives.

'It was 1930 when we climbed over the hills to make our attack. The enemy had been firing at us for some time but had not come near us. There was also a hail of fire from the shore ack-ack. batteries. When we had flown over the hill we had to be quick on the trigger or we would have passed over the enemy ship. In fact, I didn't have sufficient time to fire at first, nor did my No 2 Beaufighter, but No 3 spotted the ship a

---

Beaufighter/Mosquito Strike Wings

North Coates
236 Squadron (November 1942 - May 1945)
254 Squadron (November 1942 - May 1945)
143 Squadron (December 1942 - October 1945)

Wick
144 Squadron (October 1943 - May 1944)
404 ('Buffalo') Squadron RCAF (October 1943 - May 1944)

Leuchars
455 Squadron RAAF (March 1944 - April 1944)
489 Squadron RNZAF (March 1944 - April 1944)

Langham
455 Squadron RAAF (April 1944 - October 1944)
489 Squadron RNZAF (August 1944 - October 1944)

Davidstow Moor
144 Squadron (May 1944 - July 1944)

Strubby
144 Squadron (July 1944 - September 1944)
404 ('Buffalo') Squadron RCAF (July 1944 - September 1944)

Banff
144 Squadron (September 1944 - October 1944)
404 ('Buffalo') Squadron RCAF (September 1944 - October 1944)
143, 235 and 248 Squadrons made up the Banff Wing with Mosquitoes.

Dallachy
144 Squadron (October 1944 - May 1945)
404 ('Buffalo') Squadron RCAF (October 1944 - March 1945)
455 Squadron RAAF (October 1944 - May 1945)
489 Squadron RNZAF (October 1944 - May 1945)
404 ('Buffalo') Squadron RCAF (May 1944 - July 1944)

little sooner and opened fire with his RP. I turned round up the fjord and made a second attack, this time scoring hits on the ship; No 2 following me scored several more. Meanwhile the Beaufighters of the other squadron were circling as protection against enemy fighters. I saw the ship catch fire at the stern and she was burning brightly when two Messerschmitt Bf 109s appeared and attacked No.3 Beaufighter. At the time the Beau's observer was busy holding camera over the side, taking photographs and he first he knew that enemy fighters were about was when a bullet hit his camera.

'We flew out to sea and managed to shake off the fighters, but No.3 Beau was badly shot up, with the undercarriage out of action and a hole in one of its petrol tanks. One of our escorting Beaus, which was also attacked, turned away from the coast and was subsequently missing. We regained base and No.3 Beau made a successful belly-landing on a small runway; its observer was slightly wounded.

'Trips to Norway averaged 300 miles each way from our base at Wick. The journey out was always done at low level, a mere fifty feet to stay below enemy radar detection. This produced a great sensation of speed as we sped over the wave tops, until sighting our target when we had to climb to 1,500 feet. Immediately one had a contrasting sensation of being about to stall and that the Beaufighter was hardly moving at all. Although this happened scores of times as we prepared for attack, I always had the same fear of stalling which I was never able to suppress... Especially when operating off the Norwegian coast, a long way from home and in range of enemy single-engined fighters, we much preferred bad weather and good cloud cover. At Wick the saying was 'we prefer to fly when even the seagulls are walking' - and Wick seagulls were a very large and hardy breed! During 1942 and early 1943 we usually carried a pigeon with us in the Beaufighter on our shipping strikes off the Norwegian coast. The bird was housed in a sawdust and shavings filled tin box which, being loose in the aircraft, sometimes got chucked around, particularly when we were taking violent evasive action. The bird was, of course, intended to be used should we ditch to carry our position home. On return to dispersal after an 'op' we were sometimes told to release the pigeon, whereupon it invariably perched on top of the aircraft's rudder and showed no inclination to fly anywhere, not even back to its loft. We decided that 'rough rides' must have upset its gyro-compass navigational system and eventually didn't think there was any real point in continuing to carry the bird. This very much upset one of our better navigators, Peter Bassett, who always said that his accuracy was due to the fact that he never gave a course to the pilot to fly until he had shown it to the pigeon who somehow indicated whether the gen was 'pukka' or 'duff'.'

In 1943, to help Coastal Command in their onerous task, Mosquito fighters were detached to Scotland and to Predannack at the southern tip of Cornwall, for sorties far out to sea. From 1943 to early 1944, a few NF.II squadrons in Fighter Command assisted Coastal Command with Instep anti-air and anti-shipping patrols in the Bay of Biscay and the Western Approaches. One of them, 307 (City of Lwow) Squadron, flew its first such patrol on detachment from Predannack on 13 June. Bad weather however, caused the Poles to abort the operation. Next day four more Polish-crewed NF.IIs led by Squadron Leader S. Szablowski took off and headed for the Bay, accompanied by a 410 Squadron RCAF NF.II. Szablowski and his navigator, Sergeant M. Gajewski, spotted five U-boats on the surface and went in to attack from line astern. Szablowski fired and hit the second U-boat before hitting the third submarine. The U-boats returned heavy fire and Szablowski's port engine was hit and put out of action. Flying Officer J. Pelka, the No.2, attacked but found that his cannon would not fire, while the third and fourth Mosquitoes did not attack because by now the flak was intense. Szablowski nursed his ailing Mosquito back 500 miles to Predannack, while the others completed their patrol and he belly-landed successfully. Szablowski had in fact inflicted so many casualties among the men on the bridge and at the guns of both U-68 and U-155, from Lorient, that both had to abort their cruise and return to base.[95] Five days later, on 19 June, Szablowski's three Mosquitoes and a 410 Squadron NF.II destroyed a Blohm und Voss Bv 138 three-engined reconnaissance flying boat in the Bay.

Another of Coastal Command's tasks was to attack German capital ships which lurked in the Norwegian fjords ready to break out for raids on the rich shipping lanes of the North Atlantic. One of the capital ships that posed the greatest threat to Allied shipping in 1943 was the *Tirpitz*, but sinking it with conventional weapons was out of the question. 618 Squadron therefore was formed at Skitten, a satellite airfield for Wick in Coastal Command, under strict secrecy, on 1 April 1943 and just one month before 617 Squadron's attack on the German dams on 16/17 May, for the sole purpose of using Dr. Barnes Wallis' 'Highball' weapons against the *Tirpitz* and other capital ships at sea. 'Highball' weighed 950lbs with a charge weight of about 600lbs and a diameter of 35 inches. Based on the 'Upkeep' 'bouncing bomb' which 617's Lancasters had dropped on the German dams in May 1943, Highball was significantly smaller and lighter (about 10 per cent of the weight of the larger weapon). Each modified Mosquito B.IV could carry two 'Highballs', launching them at low level with a back spin of approximately 500 rpm from about three quarters of a mile. 618 spent much of 1943 perfecting the weapon and flying assimilation sorties but by 14 May, the day before Operation 'Servant', the intended strike on the *Tirpitz*, only six suitably modified B.IVs were available at Skitten and the strike was called off. 'Highball' trials continued but by September the Squadron had been reduced to a cadre at Benson.[96]

During October 143 Squadron, Coastal Command, which was equipped with Beaufighters at North Coates, shed its virtual OTU status and moved to Banff to convert to the Mosquito as part of the Banff Strike Wing, commanded by Group Captain Max Aitken DSO DFC. On 7 November 143 Squadron entered the fray for the first time since relinquishing its Beaufighters when two Mosquitoes flew a patrol off the coast of Norway. In November the Mosquitoes of the Banff Wing operated in increasingly larger formations of up to two-dozen aircraft.

In December 1943, 455 Squadron RAAF began replacing its Hampden bombers with Beaufighters. Wing Commander J. R. N. Davenport DFC, who had been a flight commander, became 455 Squadron's CO, with Squadron Leaders A. L. Wiggins DSO and C. G. Milson DFC as his flight commanders. This trio of Australian ship busters each won other awards in the remaining months of the war, Davenport adding a George Medal, DSO and a Bar to his DFC. Milson a DSO and Bar and a Bar to his DFC and Wiggins a DFC. The Australian squadron were given the role of 'Flakbeaus' and the torpedoes were launched by 'Torbeaus' on 489 Squadron RNZAF. Because of the Australia-New Zealand combination the wing soon became known as the 'Anzac Wing.' On 6 March 1944 455 Squadron RAAF flew their first operation on Beaufighters when their eight 'Flakbeaus' escorted four 'Torbeaus' in an attack on a convoy of six ships located off Norway. The convoy was protected by no fewer than ten escort vessels, four Me 109 fighters and a Bv 138 float plane. Despite the odds, the Anzac Wing attacked and as the 'Flakbeaus' raked the escort ships with cannon fire the 'Torbeaus' successfully launched their torpedoes in spite of the attacks of the enemy fighters. One merchant vessel was left sinking and others, both merchantmen and escorts, were damaged, without loss.

In October 1943 248 Squadron at Predannack which was equipped mainly with Beaufighter Xs on anti-shipping operations in the Atlantic began receiving a detachment of five crews and 34 ground crew on 618 Squadron. They flew Mk.XVIII 'Tsetse' Mosquitoes, so named because of their fearsome 6lb Class M (Molins) 57mm gun for use against U-boats on the surface, which was installed in the nose in place of the four 20mm cannon. An arc-shaped magazine, holding twenty-four rounds of 57mm armour-piercing HE shells capped with tracer, was positioned vertically about midships, feeding into the breech-block behind the crew. The barrel extended below the floor of the cockpit, the muzzle protruding below the fairing of the nose. Two, sometimes four .303 inch machine guns were retained, however, for strafing and air combat. All these guns were sighted through one reflector sight, the firing buttons being on the control column. The Molins gun had a muzzle velocity of 2,950 feet/second and the ideal range to open fire was 1,800-1,500 yards. The gun and its feed system were sensitive to side-ways movement and attacking in a XVIII required a dive from about 5,000 feet at a 30° angle with the turn-and-bank indicator dead central. The slightest drift would cause the gun to jam. Operations on XVIIIs commenced on 24 October 1943 when Squadron Leader Charlie Rose DFC DFM and Sergeant Cowley and Flying Officer Al Bonnett RCAF and Pilot Officer McD 'Pickles' McNicol attempted to track a U-boat in the Bay of Biscay but they returned empty-handed. On 4 November Charlie Rose and Flight Sergeant Cowley and Flying Officers Douglas 'Royce' Turner (who owned a Rolls-Royce) and Des Curtis headed south to the Bay of Biscay. Rose and Cowley failed to return when they crashed into the sea during a diving attack on an enemy trawler. Rose got off two shells and was either hit by return fire or knocked out of the sky by a ricochet from one of his shells in the second of two attacks on the vessel.

Three days later, much to their astonishment, at 0945 Bonnett and McNichol, flying at 300 feet in the Bay of Biscay found a surfaced U-boat. It was U-123, commanded by Oberleutnant zur see Horst von Schröter, which was returning to St. Nazaire at the end of a fruitless 84 day patrol - her twelfth - to the Trinidad area. von Schröter had been ordered home on 11 October due to the lack of refuellers. (The mine-swept channels off the French Atlantic coast leading to the U-boat bases at Brest, Lorient, St. Nazaire, La Rochelle and Bordeaux, were ideal killing grounds because the water depth was too shallow to permit the U-boats to crash-dive if attacked). On the first run in Bonnet opened fire with eight 57mm rounds at 1,600 yards and at 200 feet. The gun crew returned fire and one shot hit the oil tank but strikes were observed on the foredeck, which struck between the conning tower and the deck gun, then aft of the conning tower and U-123 spurted clouds of yellow and black smoke. von Schröter was unable to dive because of a hole in the conning tower. However Bonnett too had problems. After the first dive his cannon jammed and he was forced to strafe the U-boat with machine gun fire, which killed one crewman and wounded two others. As a result of Bonnet's attack on U-123 the Kriegsmarine was forced to provide escort vessels for its U-boats from now on. After repairs U-123 made one more war cruise, to West Africa, in April 1944 and was blown up at Lorient on 19 August as it was unseaworthy.[97] Exactly one year after the war ended, J. B. Lawson, who had commanded the SS *Holmbury* when von Schröter sank her on 5 May 1943, received photographs taken of the sinking of his ship through the post. One showed the sinking of the SS *Holmbury*, the other the Commander of German submarine U-123. Von Schröter had kept his word.

By 1 January 1944 248 Squadron Mosquito Conversion Flight mustered sixteen 'Tsetses' and four FB.VIs available for fighter reconnaissance and support for anti-shipping operations in 19 Group, Coastal Command. On 11 January Flight Lieutenant Noel Russell DFC and another Mosquito pilot shot down a Bf 109 during an anti-shipping strike in Flekkefjord by 14 Mosquitoes and 18 Beaufighters. The Mosquitoes returned to Leirvik harbour on 15 January 1945. This time they destroyed two merchantmen and an armed trawler before fighting their way back across the North Sea pursued by nine FW 190 fighters. Six Mosquitoes failed to return to Scotland. On 16 February 248 and 618 Squadrons were moved to Portreath and the former would now provide fighter cover for the Tsetses for 618. On 20 February 248 Squadron flew their first interception and anti-shipping patrols in the Bay of Biscay. On 10 March four FB.VIs which escorted two XVIIIs to an area about 30 miles north of Gijon on the Spanish coast, got into a vicious dog-fight with eight to ten

Ju 88s flying top cover for a German convoy of four destroyers and a U-boat. One of the Ju 88s immediately fell to a head-on attack by the four VIs and a second was shot down into the sea in flames shortly afterwards. The XVIIIs, meanwhile, went after the convoy. Squadron Leader Tony Phillips carried out four attacks on the U-boat and Flying Officer Doug Turner, two. They damaged a destroyer and Phillips blasted a Ju 88 out of the sky with four shots from his Molins gun. One of the shells literally tore an engine from the Ju 88 and it spiralled down into the sea. Coastal Command Liberators waded in and continued the attack on the convoy.

On 25 March two 'Tsetses' crewed by Flying Officers Doug Turner and Des Curtis and Flying Officer A. H. 'Hilly' Hilliard and Warrant Officer Jimmy Hoyle, escorted by four FB.VIs on 248 Squadron came upon a formation of two armed minesweepers and a destroyer. In the middle of these escorts was U-976, a Type VIIe of 769 tons, commanded by Oberleutnant zur see Raimund Tiesler, which was returning to St. Nazaire after being recalled from her second war cruise. The two pairs of escorting FB.VIs dived on the escorting ships down sun and opened fire with cannon and machine guns. A heavy fusillade of fire from the ships came up to meet them. Doug Turner opened the attack on U-976 and got off five rounds with the Molins. Every burst was accompanied by recoil which whipped the needle of the airspeed indicator back to zero. Turner made four attacks in all and fired off all his twenty-four rounds. One of the shells in the first diving attack destroyed one of the guns on the U-boat. Hilliard attacked U-976 on the waterline below the conning tower before breaking off. About ten hits were seen on the conning tower and on the forward deck near and below the waterline. After the attacks U-976 sank and Jimmy Hoyle saw an oil patch which he estimated to be 100 yards long and 30 yards wide. Survivors from the U-boat were picked up by the minesweepers.

On 27 March the same 'Tsetse' crews, but with six FB.VI escorts on 248 Squadron (which had begun conversion from Beaufighters in December), set out for the same area again. Intelligence had monitored the course taken by U-769 and U-960, which were due to arrive at La Pallice escorted by four 'M' Class minesweepers and two Sperrbrechers (merchantmen converted to heavily armed flak ships). RAF anti-shipping aircrews regarded these vessels, used primarily as a defence for the enemy's coastal shipping, as their most dangerous enemy. U-960 was commanded by Oberleutnant zur see Günther 'Heini' Heinrich, who had enlisted in the Kriegsmarine in October 1938 and had taken command of U-960 on 26 January 1943. Hilliard's intercom and VHF set in HX903 went u/s, but he decided to continue. Rounding the northwest peninsular of France the formation was spotted just over two hours after take-off. When they reached 2,000 feet heavy flak began bursting all around them. Hilliard banked to port and his Mosquito escort did the same, so the pair broke from the formation for an attack, while the rest climbed. The escort went for a Sperrbrecher while Turner and Hilliard dived on U-960, firing off seven shells during their run-in, 'five of which I claimed as hits,' recalls Hilliard, (One of the shells hit the armoured conning tower.) He goes on.

'We screamed over the U-boat at zero feet and I noticed the gunners stripped to the waist pulling their 37mm gun into a vertical position. Then I heard and felt a thud, seconds later followed by the machine gun inspection panels in front of my windscreen splitting open. I thought that the nose section had split from the shell I had collected, but looking around there was no apparent damage. [The 37mm shell had hit the Mosquito right on the nose cone but fortunately, the armour plating under the instrument panel cushioned the impact of the flying shrapnel]. Flak by this time had opened up from coastal batteries.'

Altogether, the four mine-sweepers fired forty-five 88mm shells and 1,550 20mm shells and claimed one Mosquito 'definitely' shot down. Hilliard and Hoyle however reached Portreath safely despite the ruptured nose cone protruding into the slipstream and they landed almost out of fuel. Turner had started his dive as Hilliard cleared the target and in all, four shells were seen to hit the metalwork. Five other Mosquitoes were hit in the attack. Flight Sergeant C. R. Tomalin managed to put his FB.VI down at Portreath despite a large hole in the starboard main plane. Flight Sergeant L. A. Campton and Sergeant Peters crash-landed also, with the hydraulics shot out. Aboard U-960 the conning tower, periscope and control room were badly damaged by Hilliard's 57mm shells. Ten men, including Heinrich, who was hit above the left knee, were wounded, some of them badly. U-960 managed to put into La Pallice for repairs. A year later she put to sea again and was sunk in the Mediterranean on the night of 18 / 19 May by the combined efforts of two Wellingtons, a Ventura and two US destroyers.[98]

The first ten days of April produced no results and then on the 11th two Tsetses escorted by five FB.VIs on 248 Squadron and six on 151 Squadron at Predannack took off on another coastal patrol from Portreath. One Mosquito crashed into a hill on take-off and one of the 'Tsetses' returned early with mechanical problems. The others pressed on to St-Nazaire where they came upon a U-boat with an escort of a Sperrbrecher, a flak ship, two trawlers and an air umbrella of about a dozen Ju 88s. The FB.VIs attacked the escort ships and then turned their attention to the Ju 88s while Flight Lieutenant B. C. Roberts in one of the Tsetses went after the U-boat. He saw spouts of water near the hull of the U-boat as he fired his Molins but could claim no definite hits. Flak was extremely heavy and Wing Commander O. J. M. Barron DFC, CO of 248 Squadron and another Mosquito, were shot down. Two of the Ju 88s were claimed destroyed. Flight Lieutenant Stanley G. 'Baby' Nunn and Flying Officer J. M. Carlin flying Mosquito LR362/T fired at shipping and at its escorting Ju 88s, one of which put shots through the starboard propeller which severed the hydraulic oil pipe supply and the aileron-trimming controls and blew off the port flaps. Nunn dived to sea level and, escorted by another Mosquito, cruised back to Portreath 350 miles away on one engine. He could not lower his flaps or undercarriage and made a belly landing.

In April it was seen that the increasing German mosquito fleet of fast torpedo and gun carrying motor boats, known as E-boats, might constitute a serious menace to the east coast convoys off Britain and to the future invasion fleet. It was imperative to restrict their reconnaissance activities and deny the enemy information about Allied shipping movements. The Anzac Wing's Beaufighter squadrons transferred to Langham, Norfolk and an intensive bombing training programme was carried out, interspersed with shipping reconnaissance off the Dutch coast and the Heligoland Bight. Shipping sighted in these areas was being attacked by Beaufighters of a RAF anti-shipping wing at North Coates, just south of the Humber. When the Anzacs' bombing practice period ended, it joined in these operations. Sorties were carried out at a moment's notice and the ground crews worked hard and long hours under difficult conditions to maintain the squadron at a state of maximum serviceability. From the middle of May 1944 anti-E-boat patrols were carried out in the Channel and along the French, Belgian and Dutch coasts by Beaufighters armed with cannon and carrying 1,500 pounds of HE bombs. Soon the enemy found it necessary to provide lanes of heavily armed escort ships and 'Sperrebrecheren' (flak ships) along the lines of the Allied patrols. In places four to seven of them were placed close inshore to tempt the Beaufighters within near range of shore batteries. The battle with these craft was still going on as the invasion of Western Europe approached.

At the end of April 248 Squadron began attacks on land targets and in May the 'Tsetses' made attacks on surface vessels as well as U-boats. Their technique was to fire the armour-piercing shells through the wooden deck planking of the ships while rocket-firing Beaufighters went in at 500 feet in a shallow dive. On 26 May off Trondheim, 'N' and 'E', two Mosquitoes on 333 Norwegian Squadron, one of which was flown by Jacob M. Jacobsen and Hans Engebrigsten, hit the U-958 commanded by 27-year old Kapitänleutnant Gerhard Groth, who had left Bergen on 22 May. The 'Tsetse's' 57mm cannon fire killed one German crewman and wounded two others. After repairs in Bergen and Kiel, the boat was transferred to the eastern Baltic.99

On D-Day, 6 June 1944 248 Squadron flew five operations from 0445 until 2215 hours, being employed on preventing U-boats and ships from attacking allied craft, affording cover to air strike forces and flying blockading sorties in support of the seaborne attack forces off the Normandy, Brittany and Biscay coasts. On the third operation at mid-day two 'Tsetses'[100] found two freighters in the Gironde Estuary but held their fire hoping for more offensive targets. Late in the afternoon three Seetier-class heavy destroyers from the 8th Zerstorer Flotilla were spotted by Coastal Command reconnaissance off Brest, heading north into the Western Approaches at high speed. Immediately, an air strike was mounted. Ten Mosquitoes took off at 1845 to escort seventeen anti-flak Beaufighters on 144 Squadron and fourteen rocket-armed Beaufighters on 404 'Buffalo' Squadron RCAF in the Biscay area, arriving in the area of Belle Isle at around 2030 hours. A U-boat was seen to crash-dive and a few moments later the formation came across three destroyers steaming north line abreast at fifteen knots. 248 Squadron climbed to cover the Beaufighters and then dived out of the sun en masse, attacking the flak gunners aboard the vessels with cannon fire. Flight Lieutenant S. S. Shulemson DSO led the 'Buffalo' pilots on 404 in behind them, four releasing rocket salvoes at the leading warship. Nine more Beaufighters assailed the second in line, leaving both destroyers in a badly damaged condition. The last Beaufighter strafed the third ship. The middle ship was left on fire and the rear one holed below the waterline was left sinking and seriously damaged. Such was the speed and violence of the attack that not a single rocket-Beau was hit. A shadowing He 111 was spotted near St. Nazaire and Mosquito (HR120/G) fired shots at it and the enemy aircraft was destroyed by LR339/F flown by Flight Sergeant Stoddart. A second strike took place shortly after midnight, when five more 404 'Buffalo' Squadron crews attacked the vessels, causing even more damage. The three ships managed to reach Brest, where hasty repairs were effected. Two nights later they set off again, only to be caught by the Royal Navy. The 10th Destroyer Flotilla sank ZH1 and Z42 and forced the third, the *Tartar*, ashore near the Ile de Batz. Here it was 'finished off' by twelve rocket-Beaufighters of 404 'Buffalo' Squadron the following night. The door from the west was firmly closed.[101]

On D-Day+1 two 'Tsetses' flown by Doug Turner and Des Curtis and Al Bonnett and 'Pickles' McNicol, each made a run on a surfacing U-boat. A dozen 57mm shells were fired at the veteran U-212 which was commanded by 27-year old Kapitänleutnant Helmut Vogler. He had put to sea on her 11th war cruise on D-Day but on his second run, Bonnett's cannon jammed and he only made a series of dummy runs on the U-boat which crash-dived, leaving a pool of oil and a crewman on the surface.[102] Turner's 'Tsetse' was hit by flak in the port wing and engine nacelle but he and Bonnett made it back to Cornwall safely. Bonnett and McNicol were killed two days later, following a search for survivors of a German destroyer aground near Ile de Bas, north of the lighthouse. Seeing little point in attacking, Bonnett's Mosquito and another flown by Wing Commander Tony Phillips DSO DFC, now CO of 248 Squadron, headed homewards. As Bonnet broke to port for landing Phillips' Mosquito collided with it slicing off its tail. Bonnett's Mosquito fell into the sea, while Phillips, with six feet chopped off the starboard wing and almost out of control, raced in to land with 15 degree flap and travelling at 160 knots landed safely.

Attacks on U-boats were the order of the day throughout the summer of 1944 but in early June there was a lull in the Western Approaches. Although 143 sorties were flown in the 24 hours to midnight on the 9th, only three U-boats were seen and attacked. Four 248 Squadron Mosquitoes at Portreath flown by Flying Officer G. N. 'Gerry' Yeates

(MM399/T), Flight Lieutenant Stanley G. 'Baby' Nunn DFC (LR347/T), Flight Sergeant W. W. Scott (HP907/V) and Flying Officer K. Norrie (HR158/W) attacked U-821 three miles or so north-west of Ushant with such ferocity that the commander, 23-year old Ulrich Knackfuss ordered the crew to abandon ship. The U-boat, which was bound for the English Channel, shot down Flight Lieutenant E. H. Jeffreys DFC and Flying Officer D. A. Burden on 248 Squadron before it was sunk by a Liberator.

The sky was cloudy, but visibility was good. The Mosquitoes broke away to starboard and made a succession of attacks over a period of eight minutes. During the twenty-four attacks five thousand rounds of ammunition were poured-into the U-boat. 'Baby' Nunn told Hector Bolitho that he could see the Germans rushing to man the guns.

'The first aircraft to fly in received a smattering of flak from them and a small hit in the starboard radiator. But this was all and after the second attack the enemy guns were apparently silenced. The Germans continued to come up from below but as they appeared on deck they were shot down by our guns and they could be seen tumbling into the sea. After the sixth attack one of the navigators counted about twenty Germans struggling in the oil track behind the U-boat, most of them in life-jackets. One shower of our bullets hit the ammunition locker on the deck of the U-boat and there was an explosion. The Mosquitoes left the U-boat with her stern awash, oil trailing from her riddled tanks and her bow turned towards the coast.

Towards the end of the Mosquito attack a Liberator on 206 Squadron [EV943/K piloted by Flight Lieutenant Alexander D. S. Dundas DFC] arrived on the scene. I saw Flight Lieutenant Dundas afterwards and he told me that he flew in just as the Mosquitoes had finished their ammunition. It was the first U-boat he had seen after five hundred hours' operational flying. Dundas had the satisfaction of knowing that his depth charges fell three on either side of the U-boat. There was a fierce disturbance in the water, the bows heaved out of the sea and then the whole U-boat slid back and sank. There were big green bubbles and a chaos of wreckage, with three survivors in yellow Mae Wests.'

It was the first U-boat that Dundas had seen after five hundred hours' operational flying. Dundas had the satisfaction of knowing that his depth charges fell three on either side of the U-boat. There was a fierce disturbance in the water, the bows heaved out of the sea and then the whole U-boat slid back and sank. There were big green bubbles and a chaos of wreckage, with three survivors in yellow Mae Wests. They were rescued by a German motor launch which was promptly sunk by a flight of Mosquitoes on 248 Squadron led by Squadron Leader 'Jean Maurice' the nom de guerre adopted by Max Geudj, a Frenchman of the Jewish faith, to safeguard his family. He had received reports on 26 March 1942 that his father had been imprisoned in Morocco because of his pro-British sympathies. Max Geudj's operational flying had commenced on 248 Squadron in February 1942 with his navigator Flight Sergeant Charles Corder. Geudj had flown 75 operational sorties on Coastal Command Beaufighters and he was the first French airman to receive the DSO, in March 1943.

Hector Bolitho found that 'getting a story out of this French pilot is like opening oysters with your bare hands. His dark eyes, like polished damsons brook no interference with his authority and he had the rare blessing of believing that he was always right. He was what is described in wartime as 'a born leader.'[103]

Beaufighters on 144 and 404 Squadrons found a destroyer aground off Ile de Batz where it had beached after naval action a few days' earlier. The Beaufighters made a low level bombing attack through flak from the shore but they were not harmed and their left the destroyer in flames. The smoke from the fire could be seen six miles away and it was not likely that the ship would ever be used again. Another Beaufighter on 235 Squadron piloted by Flight Lieutenant R. R. Wright shot down one of the few Ju 88s seen since D-Day. The Junkers exploded as it hit the sea.

On 13 June Flight Lieutenant Lewis Bacon DFC on 248 Squadron was flying his Mosquito in formation two miles north of Ushant, he saw a German aircraft flying north and he followed. The leader of the formation, Flight Lieutenant Cobbledick, said that he would fly ahead and cut the Junkers off. He did this and Bacon followed. The Junkers climbed and turned into Cobbledick, thus placing Bacon on his tail. The action was quick and simple. Bacon fired three bursts and the Junkers dived towards the sea. Bacon fired another burst on its way down. The Junkers lost one wing hit the water and exploded. The aircrews arrived home astonished at their freedom from air attack. Before D-Day they preferred to fly at night when close to the enemy coast, because there was less danger of being attacked by German fighters. Now they preferred flying by day because there was less danger of homing on to flak ships, minesweepers and other well-armed surface vessels before there is time to identify them.[104]

On 14 June U-290, which had left Egersund on the first of the month, was damaged in an attack by Mosquito 'H' on 333 Norwegian Squadron which wounded eight men aboard the submarine. Next day Beaufighters sank a merchantman of 8,000 tons, a naval auxiliary of 4,000 tons and a minesweeper. Four escort vessels were also damaged. The Norwegians were active again on the evening of 16 June. Mosquito HP864/H flown by Lieutenant Erling Ulleberg Johansen attacked U-998 75 miles north-west of Bergen. The boat, which had left Kiel on its first war cruise on 12 June, was so badly damaged that the commander, Hans Fiedler, was forced to put into Bergen where the submarine was withdrawn from service as beyond repair. Lieutenant Jacob M. Jacobsen was flying Mosquito 'R' with Per C. Hansen as his navigator when they hit U-804, commanded by 33-year old Oberleutant zur see Herbert Meyer. This boat was on its first war cruise; having left Kiel four days' earlier. Eight crewmen were wounded, three seriously. The Mosquito crew were shot down by return fire from the submarine gunners and they were rescued by U-1000 two days' later. Meyer was forced to abort to Bergen and on 19 June he re-sailed to the Atlantic but the Mosquitoes would get their revenge on U-804 on 9 April 1945.[105]

On 16 June meanwhile, Squadron Leader Barnes on 235 Squadron, also at Portreath, made the unit's first operational flight. By the end of the month thirty-two sorties by the squadron's Mosquitoes had been completed. On 22 June, in addition to more conventional bombs, cannon and machine gun fire, wing-mounted 25 lb Mk.XI depth charges and A.VIII mines were used operationally by Mosquitoes for the first time while 235 Squadron at Portreath, which had been equipped with Beaufighters, flew their first Mk.VI sortie. The final Beaufighter sortie was flown on 27 June when six Mosquitoes on 235 joined with nine on 248 to provide escort for Beaufighters on 144 and 404 'Buffalo' Squadron RCAF. They were unable to attack the ships that they found because they were too inaccessible.

The Mosquitoes now flew escort for the Beaufighters and they were also used to intercept Dornier 217s which carried Henschel Hs 293 glider bombs for attacks on Allied shipping. The first successful strike by 144 and 404 'Buffalo' Squadron RCAF came on 29 June. Two dozen Mosquito FB.VIs and two 'Tsetses' attacked a convoy comprising a tanker, two escorts, two ASTs and two trawlers. Ten Mosquitoes swept in with cannon and machine guns blazing, followed by two with 500 lb Medium Capacity bombs and then Mk. XVIIIs. The tanker was left blazing. On 30 June Pilot Officer Wally Tonge and Flight Sergeant Ron Rigby were shot down by flak whilst on an anti-shipping strike by 21 Mosquitoes and nine rocket-firing Beaufighters on four naval vessels off Concarneau in Brittany. Tonge successfully ditched a mile or two from the shore and the two men were seen in their dinghy shortly afterwards but they did not survive and were buried in the grounds of a small church in the village of Combrit.

On 4 July Wing Commander Tony Phillips with Flying Officer R. W. 'Tommy' Thomson DFC and Squadron Leader 'Jean Maurice', the Free French pilot, with Squadron Leader Hal Randall, flew a costly 248 Squadron operation to the Brest Peninsula. The two Mosquitoes found a group of mine-sweepers anchored in Penfoul Cove and the Kercreven docks. For greater accuracy they closed right in on their targets, skimmed over the masts of the enemy ships and dropped their bombs. AA guns were firing from Creach-Conarch heights and the ships. It is unclear if the Mosquito crewed by Phillips and Thomson was hit by flak. A witness claims that they hit the top of the mast of one of the ships. The Mosquito crashed near the Keranguyon Farm and the crew were ejected in the explosion. Phillips was found near the aircraft, Thompson falling a hundred yards away, in front of the doorstep of Madame Berrou's farm, which caught fire after being hit by flying debris. Two farm workers, Yves Glernarec and Yvonne Laurent, a young girl, had their clothes set alight. Glernarec badly burned, survived, but Yvonne died twelve hours' later. For two days the airmen were left where they lay before a German officer gave the order to bury them.

Flight Lieutenant Charles Corder was the long-serving navigator of the Mosquito flown by 'Jean Maurice', which managed to return against all the odds after it had been severely damaged by a Luftwaffe fighter. It was their 71st operation together. When they encountered a Ju 88 long-range fighter, Guedj attacked and sent it crashing into the sea. Return fire from the German fighter's gunner severely damaged the aircraft. Guedj was wounded during the attack and the intercommunication in the aircraft was put out of action. With the situation appearing hopeless, Corder crawled forward to assist the pilot before returning to his seat, where he obtained radio bearings and gave Guedj a course to steer for their base in Cornwall, 180 miles away. One of the two engines failed and Guedj had difficulty keeping control, forcing him to fly a few feet above the sea. Corder once more crawled forward to assist him, having managed to repair the intercommunication system. Just before they reached the English coast the second engine caught fire, which spread to the cockpit. Corder transmitted an SOS and fired distress cartridges to attract the attention of those ashore. As they approached Cornwall, it was clear that the aircraft had either to ditch in the heavy seas or clear the cliffs. As Corder guided Guedj to the cliffs' lowest point, observers on the ground were convinced that the aircraft would crash; but Guedj managed to clear the cliffs by a few feet before making an emergency landing as the second engine finally failed. Corder's navigation had been so accurate that they managed to crash-land on their own airfield at Predannack.

On 5 July no U-boats were seen but three Mosquitoes on 248 Squadron attacked two minesweepers and a coaster in 'the River Odet the afternoon before and certainly damaged one of the minesweepers. The price was one Mosquito. The enemy fighters had been as scarce as the U-boats and during five days only one 'possible' had been seen, by a Sunderland on 228 Squadron. The Ju 88 fired on the Sunderland which came home unharmed. One-hundred and forty aircraft flew over the patrol area for 1,151 hours during the twenty-four hours up to midnight on the 4th and results were more encouraging. About half-past five the next morning a Liberator on 53 Squadron saw a schnörkel. The aircraft flew in twice to attack but the depth charges hung up. It flew in again and dropped one depth charge near the target and, on the fourth run in, six more were released. They fell about 30 feet ahead of the schnörkel. Results could not be assessed but an hour later a Wellington, flown by a Polish crew on 304 Squadron, saw a swirl and the submerging conning tower of a U-boat one and a half miles away. Two depth charges were dropped about fifty seconds after the conning tower submerged and they were seen to explode close to the swirl.

On 11 July fifteen Mosquitoes of 235 and 248 Squadrons went out to attack a convoy north of Croisia Point, off St. Nazaire, with cannon and bombs and one vessel was left on fire. Two 'Tsetses' flown by Doug Turner and Des Curtis and Flying Officers' Bill Cosman and Freedman and escorted by sixteen FB.VIs, made an evening raid on the approach to Brest harbour where a surfaced U-boat was proceeding slowly with no wake along the Goulet de Brest, escorted by three minesweepers and a Sperrbrecher. The shore batteries combined with the ships to put up an intense flak barrage yet Cosman made a diving attack on the U-boat, breaking off at 50 yards and claiming two possible hits out of four shots fired. Doug Turner scored five hits on the Sperrbrecher and Cosman's parting shot was a salvo of two 57mm shells at the leading minesweeper, as the Mosquitoes weaved their way through the flak to the mouth of the harbour.

Next day Mosquitoes on 248 and six Mosquitoes on 235 Squadron attacked three 'M' class minesweepers and two Sperrbrechers which were stationary off Toulinguet Point outside Brest. Some of the crews thought they saw a U-boat also, lurking between the rear minesweepers. The leading minesweeper was left in flames; there was a small fire on the rear minesweeper and an explosion on one of the Sperrbrechers. One of the Mosquitoes attacked the supposed U-boat and claimed to have hit it. There was flak from the ships as well as from the shore, but the seventeen aircraft all returned to base, three of them damaged and one navigator wounded. Next day the weather became sour again but before the weather closed in, a U-boat was seen by shipping reconnaissance aircraft, between Ile de Croix and the mainland. Two Mosquitoes on 248 Squadron were sent to investigate. They found three small trawlers and two coasters near the island and, ten miles away, a fully surfaced U-boat with a Sperrbrecher protecting it. The leading Mosquito prepared to attack but the U-boat moved nearer to the Sperrbrecher and two minesweepers and an armed trawler appeared. In view of the overwhelming force against them the Mosquitoes wisely came home.

On 16 July Flight Lieutenant Stanley 'Baby' Nunn on 248 Squadron was leading a section of three Mosquitoes on an anti-shipping strike off St. Nazaire when his cannon had a stoppage so he dived to 200 yards to fire at a patrol vessel with machine-guns. There was a bang and a bump as flak from the ship hit his port engine. As he broke away he could see oil and coolant streaming from the engine, in which there was a red glow. He climbed as he flew over land fearing his fuel tank would catch fire and warned his navigator to prepare to bail out, but the emergency exit door was jammed. Nunn headed out to sea and dived to sea level only to find himself between two ships which opened fire on him. On one engine he weaved his way out to sea. He now called up the formation, which he was able to join and, flying on one engine, again belly-landed at Portreath where he found that the starboard mainplane and the rudder, elevator and trimmer were badly shot up.[106]

The tempo of operations ran higher in the second half of 1944 as the Allies consolidated their hold in Normandy and the enemy made strenuous efforts to run supply convoys to his troops in Holland and Belgium. These convoys were attacked by Coastal Command from the Norwegian coast right down to the south Dutch coast and E-boats were harried at night along the French coast around the Cherbourg Peninsula. The enemy convoys grew larger and more heavily escorted and on 21

On 8 August 1944 Wing Commander A. K. 'Ken' Gatward DSO DFC commanding 404 'Buffalo' Squadron RCAF led a formation of 15 Beaufighters and nine more on 236 Squadron of the North Coates Strike Wing against a reported gaggle of enemy ships between Belle Ile and the French mainland. Four minesweepers were sunk off Bourgeneuf but three Beaufighters and three of the escorting 8th Air Force P-51 Mustangs were lost.

Beaufighters on 236 Squadron making an attack on the armed enemy motor vessel *Magdeburg* off Royan, France on 13 August 1944.

On 24 August 1944 20 Beaufighters on 236 and 404 RCAF Squadrons of the Davidstowe Moor Strike Wing attacked the German destroyer Z.24 and the Torpedo boat T.24 near Le Verdon in the Gironde Estuary. The torpedo boat was sunk immediately and the destroyer capsized early the next morning.

Wing Commander (later Air Commodore) A. K. 'Ken' Gatward DSO DFC who took command of 404 'Buffalo' Squadron RCAF on 1 April 1944, was famous for his daring exploit in a Beaufighter on 12 June 1942 when he and his navigator, Sergeant Fern, dropped a French flag over the Champs Elysées.

Beaufighters on 455 Squadron RAAF attacking an 'M' class minesweeper on 25 August 1944. The minesweeper was leading a convoy of about eight ships when sighted and attacked north-west of Borkum. Taken from a 455 Squadron Beaufighter (with the camera directed backward), the picture shows no fewer than thirteen 'strike' aircraft, all of which, except for two in the top right corner, are coming out of the attack. On either side of the vessel under attack are the tracks made by salvos of rockets entering the water. The smoke trails in the middle of the picture are also from the rockets, and the white specks are tracer bullets from the ships. The minesweeper was left smoking heavily.

Fully armed Beaufighters on 236 Squadron on stand-by in October 1944. Each aircraft carries a battery of eight 3 inch rocket projectiles under the wings with 25lb Semi-Armour Piercing (SAP) rocket heads for the anti-shipping role. As a safety measure the electrical leads ('Pigtails' remain unplugged until the aircraft start engines.

Beaufighter NE831 PL-O on 144 Squadron at Dallachy, which was hit both by flak and fire from a FW 190 during a strike on Z-33, a German 'Narvik' Class destroyer, two 'M' Class minesweepers and several flak ships in Førde Fiord on 9 February 1945. Despite having its hydraulics put out of action and an elevator shot away, Flight Sergeant Stan Butler managed to belly land on the grass at Dallachy safely.

ockets from Australian Beaufighter 'Q for Queenie' speed down the cliff, on 8 March 1945, in
n attack on one of six enemy ships sighted in Midgulen Fjord, Norway. Seven other
eaufighters on 455 Squadron RAAF took part and thirteen RAF Beaufighters, an escort of
ourteen Mustangs and two Air Sea Rescue Warwicks completed the force, which was led by
quadron Leader J. M. Pilcher, DFC* RAAF. The attack was made with both rockets and cannon.
wo of the three motor vessels in the convoy were set on fire. The third motor vessel and one of
ne three auxiliary ships were left smoking. One 455 Squadron Beaufighter failed to return. Its
rew were Warrant Officer W. D. Mitchell and Flight Sergeant I. H. Jury.

They flew so low to attack an enemy ship that the ship's masthead became embedded in their Beaufighter's nose; Flying Officers S. Sykes (left) and his navigator, Lee Turner on 455 Squadron RAAF beside their damaged aircraft. Sykes received the DFC for this operation and in May 1945 was awarded the DSO for his courage in an attack on a merchantman in Ardals Fjord, Norway. Although his arm and leg were severely injured when his Beaufighter was hit by flak 400 yards from the ship and he was wounded in many other places, he attacked and then flew 350 miles back to a perfect landing at base.

On 21 April 1945 a formation of Mosquitoes returning from a strike in the Kattegat intercepted 18 German torpedo-bombers and destroyed nine of them within minutes.

Cannon and machine gun ammunition for a Coastal Command Beaufighter.

Air VCs

Top Left: Flight Lieutenant John Alexander Cruickshank, a Catalina pilot on 210 Squadron, wh[o] received the Victoria Cross on 21 September 1944. Bottom Left: Flying Officer Kenneth Campbell, a Beaufort pilot on 22 Squadron who was posthumously awarded the Victoria Cross on 13 March 1942. Top right: 29-year old Flying Officer Lloyd Allan Trigg RNZAF on 200 Squadron who was posthumously awarded the Victoria Cross, on 2 November 1943. Bottom right: 34-year old Flying Officer David E. Hornell, a Canso pilot on 162 Squadron RCAF, who was posthumously awarded the Victoria Cross on 13 March 1942.

Underside view of Beaufighter TF.X NT850 on 236 Squadron showing D-Day invasion stripes and rocket rails.

On 9 April 1945 35 Mosquitoes on 143, 235 and 248 Squadrons of the Banff Strike Wing attacked U-boats in the Kattegat sailing from Kiel, Germany to Horton in Norway. They were accompanied by two Mosquito outriders on 333 Norwegian Squadron and one from the RAF Film Unit and escorted by Mustangs from Peterhead. Two U-boats – U-804 and U-1065 - were sunk by rocket and cannon fire but an explosion destroyed the FU Mosquito, killing the two crew.

Opposite page: A Fordson tractor eases a twin-trolley load of depth charges under the wing of Liberator GR. VI KG904/E-Z on 220 Squadron in the Azores mud and rain in April 1945. Note the Leigh Light in the upper foreground. (IWM)

Top Left: Wing Commander Gage Darwent 'Bill' Sise DSO* DFC* was born on January 22 1917 at Dunedin, New Zealand. After being educated at Otago Boys' High School and Otago University, he trained as an accountant, and joined the RNZAF as an aircraft hand on the outbreak of war. He was regarded as Coastal Command's leading 'ship-buster', serving on 254 and 248 Squadrons (which he commanded) While serving at Portreath in 1944 he met Section Officer Mary Hollingworth Crear and they married in January 1945. (IWM)

Top Right: Wing Commander Richard Ashley Atkinson DSO DFC* RAAF (born 1913) CO, 235 Squadron and his 20-year old navigator, Flying Officer Valentine 'Val' Upton, were killed on 13 December 1944 during an attack on merchantmen at Ejdstjord. Atkinson, originally from Emmavilla, NSW, had a brief spell as a mining engineer, then bought a passage to England and joined the RAF and was a flying officer before the outbreak of war. He had seen operational service on 205 Squadron and had flown Catalinas and Sunderlands in the Indian Ocean.

Bottom Left: Wing Commander Max Guedj DSO DFC, a Frenchman of the Jewish faith, born on 8 June 1913 in Sousse, Tunisia, who adopted the nom de guerre, 'Jean Maurice' to safeguard his family in France. He was killed while leading a Mosquito strike against shipping in Narvik Fjord on 15 January 1945. (IWM)

Bottom Right: Group Captain (later Sir) Max Aitken DSO DFC who commanded the Banff Strike Wing

Left: Flight Lieutenant William 'Bill' Roxburgh, a Glaswegian on 206 Squadron, who piloted Fortress II FK195/L on 25 March 1943, 380 miles SSE of Iceland and sank U-489 with depth charges. (IWM)

Below:
Fortress IIA (B-17C) FL459/J one of sixteen (FL449/464) on 220 Squadron 15 Group Coastal Command at Terceira, Azores late in 1943. (Note underwing and nose ASV radar antennae.) Pilot Officer G. Roberson and crew on FL459 sank U 624, a Type VIIC submarine, on 7 February 1943 and on 7 March 1943 Flying Officer Bill Knowles and crew, again in FL459, sank U-633. Moving to 247 Group in the Azores, Flight Lieutenant R. P. Drummond and the crew on FL459/J sank U-707 300 miles east of the Azores on 9 November 1943. On 13 March 1944 Flying Officer W. R. Travell shared in the sinking of U-575 with Fortress FA700/R of 206 Squadron and a Wellington of 172 Squadron. FL459 equipped 519 and 251 Squadrons and was finally scrapped in 1945. (IWM)

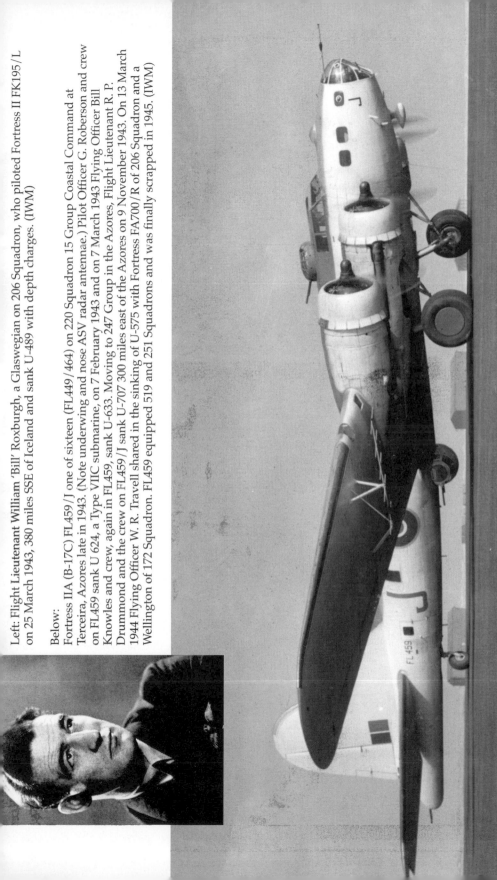

Beaufighters attacking an enemy vessel close to the shore-line of a Norwegian fjord on 5 May 1945.

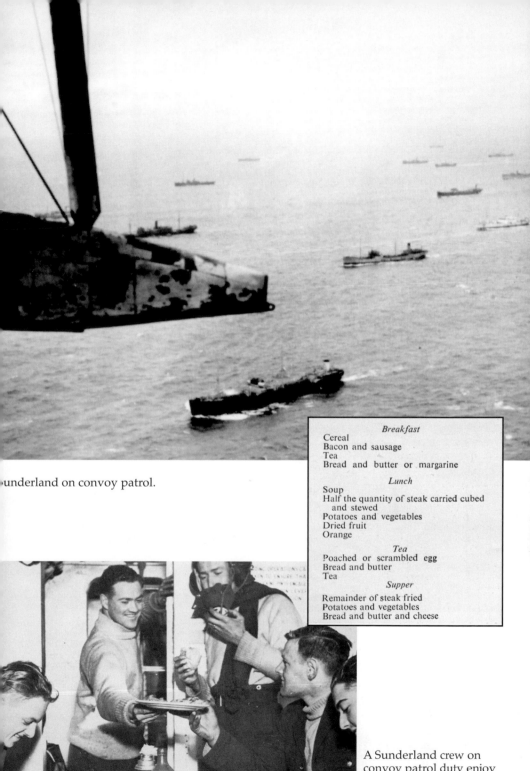

...underland on convoy patrol.

A Sunderland crew on convoy patrol duty enjoy a meal in the galley. *Inset:* A typical crew menu on a long North Atlantic convoy patrol.

A Sunderland taking-off.

The 6,000 ton cruiser *Nürnberg* making its last voyage, en route from Copenhagen to Wilhelmshaven on 20 May 1945, escorted by GR.VI Liberators on 547 Squadron.

July a convoy of nine merchantmen, escorted by more than thirty escort vessels was attacked in the Heligoland Bight. 455 Squadron RAAF sent eleven Beaufighters to the attack, led by Squadron Leader Milson. Despite the intense barrage from ships and shore batteries and rockets trailing steel wires which were sent up by the ships, the Beaufighter combination tactic again enabled the 'Torbeaus' to launch their torpedoes successfully. Two of the largest merchant vessels were sunk, two other merchant vessels and five escorts were left burning furiously and most of the remaining ships were damaged by cannon fire. No Beaufighters were lost, although two aircraft had to fly 300 miles over the sea each on one engine and others were damaged.

On 21 July Mosquitoes HR127 and LR346 on 235 Squadron were ordered to fly an air umbrella patrol above a naval destroyer escort group off Ushant. Weather conditions were foul, but the two Mosquito crews set out, having received a report that the destroyers were being harassed by several Dorniers, carrying Henschel Hs 293 glider bombs. Boring their way through dense clouds and mist down to sea level, through continuous driving rain, the two aircraft deliberately separated to avoid any possible air collision, but as they did so one Mosquito dipped a wing into the sea and crashed at high speed. The second Mosquito eventually returned to base, to report that weather conditions were nigh impossible to penetrate. Thirty-eight year old Wing Commander John V. Yonge, was highly conscious of the need to provide air cover for the destroyer group and decided to fly the sortie himself, in company with one volunteer crew (Flying Officers M. J. 'Jack' Frost DFC and Fuller). Yonge, who was first commissioned in the RAF in December 1925 and had commanded 235 since April, recalled:

'When Frost and I took off the weather had cleared a little over base, but we had to fly blind, in close formation, to get through the rain and low cloud. We finally broke cloud at 1,400 feet while approaching the patrol area. Then we came into a patch of weather the like of which I had never seen before. We were in a col, with a thunderstorm to the south, sea fog over Brest and Ushant and continuous rain to the north; it was the most extraordinary combination of weather. Then we reached the patrol area and it was comparatively clear, but we had to vary our height and fly blind from time to time to keep at our task. At 20 minutes past one I had still not found either the destroyers or the reported Dorniers. Then, half an hour later, we sighted two Dornier Do 217s, with a Mosquito from another Wing opening fire on them at long range. I learned later that the Mosquito was an ADGB[107] aircraft and that it was still trying to attack after being hit in its port engine. The pilot had to give it up and fly home as best he could.

We jettisoned our wing tanks, opened up to full boost and revs and attacked the second Dornier at 300 knots. I was just about to open fire when I saw that Frost had already set its port engine on fire. I therefore swung my gun-sight on to the leading Dornier and attacked with several bursts of cannon and .303in, opening at 800 yards. I closed right behind its tail, although he was doing his best to dodge me. Out of the corner of my eye I saw the first German, which Frost had hit, diving in flames and three parachutes floating down to the water.

'My burst was effective. The Dornier blew up, 100 yards in front of me, so close that streams of his oil blacked me out completely. I had to jerk back the stick to avoid hitting him and then to fly on instruments until the windscreen wiper had cleaned some of the oil away. Then I could just about peer through the relatively clear spots between the thick German oil and saw the two Dorniers blazing on the sea and several of the crews in dinghies.

'It was only then that we saw the destroyers we were defending from the Dorniers for the first time. I spoke to the Navy and told them that both Germans had been shot down in flames and that the survivors were waiting in the water to be picked up. Frost and I became separated in the thick cloud on the way back, but we landed at base within five minutes of each other. Then I handed the Mosquito over to the ground crew, always there to make us feel that they were part of the effort. They wiped the thick oil from the fuselage and painted a swastika on it, for our victory.'

The operations in 1943 of the Strike Wings were a prelude to stronger action in 1944, when disciplined co-ordination in the execution of attacks had been perfected. By the beginning of that year, 455 Squadron RAAF and 489 Squadron RNZAF had at last received their torpedo-carrying Beaufighters or 'Torbeaus' as they were known. They at once began to operate from Leuchars as a second Strike Wing, having spent the previous autumn and summer in 'Rover' work off the Norwegian coast. Here, too 'A' Flight on 333 (Norwegian) Squadron, operating Catalinas from Woodhaven were indefatigable in reconnoitring the rugged coastline of their country, which they knew so well and in maintaining the traffic in secret passengers. The 'Rover' patrols and the assaults carried out by Strike Wings were the responsibility of 18 Group covering Norway and of 16 Group (with headquarters at Chatham covering the German and Dutch coasts.[108]

On 1 April 1944 Wing Commander (later Air Commodore) A. K. 'Ken' Gatward DSO DFC took command of 404 'Buffalo' Squadron RCAF, the first Canadian unit under the aegis of RAF Coastal Command. On 8 August he led a formation of 15 Beaufighters and nine more on 236 Squadron in a strike against a reported gaggle of enemy ships between Belle Ile and the French mainland. Taking off at 1620, Gatward led his men straight out to sea towards the indicated area, but on arrival found nothing to attack. In Gatward's words:

'We saw a few old fishermen who waved to us and there were children in some of the fishing boats, who waved too. We flew south and just as we approached the extreme end of Bourgeneuf Bay, I spotted four German minesweepers, all stationary and bunched together, on a calm sea. We wheeled to port and I gave the old cry of *Attack, Attack*; ordering the port section to take the port ship and the starboard section to take the starboard ships, leaving the middle one to me. Flak came up from the shore, 1,000 yards away and the minesweepers opened fire at two miles' range. They kept it up until we opened with our cannon at 1,000 yards after which the fire from the ships died down. However, it continued to come fairly thick from the shore, near Fromentine. One of our Beaufighters bought it; R. S. Forestall was the pilot and I. C. Robbie his navigator, both Canadians. I had seen their tracer coming in with mine, so they must have been shot down during the attack, just before their aircraft crashed close to the ships.

'As we closed range to about 400 yards we fired off our rockets. Soon three of the ships were on fire and the fourth was smoking. There were great clouds of smoke - very satisfactory. It is always miserable to look back after any attack and see ships unharmed on the water. We went over the tops of the ships and broke out to sea. Then the pilot of one Beau called up to say that he had 'lost' an engine and if I'd escort him home. At that moment a second Beau pilot called up to say 'It's all right, I'm with him' and a third signalled 'I'm with you chap, carry on'.

'As I had the rest of the formation with me and saw that the crippled aircraft was escorted on either side, I went on. Then one of our naval vessels called us up, saying that they understood from our chatter that we had some luck. I signalled back, 'We think it's too small for you to bother about', but they answered, 'Nothing is too small for us!' So I answered, 'Right, go ahead and good luck'. So we left the three minesweepers in flames and toddled home along the coast, seeing nothing on the way but a few fishing boats.'

Wing Commander Gatward made one of the important contributions to the story of D-Day by attacking the destroyer which had to put back into dry dock at Brest. His next successful attack was on a destroyer aground off the Ile de Batz. Then came an attack on two 'M' Class minesweepers, a trawler and a small tanker near St. Laurent. Again he flew off with the satisfaction of seeing most of them in flames. These attacks in the Bay were wedged in between sorties in the north. One of Gatward's attacks was off Heligoland when his squadron beat up a convoy of about thirty ships. Two big ships and one escort vessel were confirmed sunk, another was 'seriously daamged' and the rest 'damaged'. The technique of attack with RPs was perfected by this time and since D-Day Gatward's squadron was able to do a great deal of damage to shipping moving out of the Bay. On 14 August Gatward made the last attack of his second tour of operations when he led a formation of Beaufighters into Arcachon Bay where a floating dock and eight vessels were attacked. All the targets were hit but Gatward's aircraft was badly damaged when he flew into the heart of the flak and he came home covered in oil. Two other aircraft were also damaged but no one was injured and the formation came home complete. Gatward, who flew up the Champs-Elysées two years earlier, to drop a tricolour over the Arc de Triomphe, walked up it on his two feet in the second week of August. He had been sent there as the first Coastal Command liaison officer since the delivery of Paris from the Germans.

During the first week of August more and more Sperrbrechers were sighted. At half past nine in the morning of 6 August two of them were seen with two merchant vessels off St Nazaire and in the early afternoon an Avenger of the Fleet Air Arm saw a convoy of four merchant ships off Belle Ile. Two more merchant vessels were seen near Ile de Groix at four in the afternoon, escorted by an Elbing destroyer and a Sperrbrecher. Two more of the heavily armed ships, together with ten smaller minesweepers, were seen, also near Belle Ile. No U-boats were sighted on the 7th but there were twenty-two sightings of enemy shipping and seven attacks, the most satisfying being on a Sans-Souci escort vessel which was sunk in the harbour of Les Sables d'Olonne. The attack was made about half past nine on the night of the 6th and the flak from the Sans-Souci and other escorting vessels was 'pretty terrific', supported by flak from the shore. The formation of Beaufighters flew in, attacked and saw two 'splendid' explosions, followed by fierce blaze and black smoke. The aircraft passed through the merciless flak and only one was damaged. Otherwise the formation arrived back unharmed.

Do 217s with glider bombs were again discovered on 9 August when twelve Mosquitoes on 235 Squadron and two Mk. XVIIIs on 248 Squadron, on a Biscay patrol, found four bombers and shot down two and damaged the others. Hector Bolitho was at Portreath and gathered the details of the attack:

'The formation was flying between Belle Ile and the mainland in search of enemy shipping which was believed to be evacuating Service men from St. Nazaire, but they found Dorniers instead. They were flying over the sand dunes and lighthouse at the entrance to the Gironde River when they saw two Dorniers flying from the coast, no doubt heading out to attack one of our naval forces in the Bay. One of the Dorniers was under the leader's left wing before he recognised it as a German. He called up the other aircraft, 'Two bandits ahead. Attack! Attack!' He then turned to port and chased the leading Dornier. The rest of the formation turned to pursue the second one. They were strung out in a circle so that each of the Mosquitoes saw the Dornier from a different position. The leading Dornier opened his throttles and flew straight out to sea, jettisoning the glider bomb which was no doubt intended for our Navy. He took evasive action and being so much lighter without his bomb he was more manoeuvrable. The leader began shooting close, at about 200 yards and the Dornier returned the compliment with tracer which passed below. Then he did a very tight turn, causing the Mosquito to overshoot. The leader then turned also and found that the Dornier was heading back to the land, with both engines smoking. He climbed and took more evasive action and the leader fired several more bursts at him. As he came near the coast the Mosquito pilot closed in again but found that he was out of ammunition.

The Dornier disappeared inland but it was too dark then for our pilot to see the smoking engines of the enemy. The leader of the Mosquito formation then looked down the coast and saw that a third Dornier had joined in the fun. It was dusky then. He saw two Dorniers crash into the water; pools of burning petrol on a hazy grey sea. The leader said to me, 'There were Mosquitoes all over the place it seemed and I did not find out until later that two of our aircraft had attacked a fourth Dornier. One of them chased it inland and saw one of its engines on fire. Just as he was closing in he found that his cannons would not work - a bullet had penetrated the pneumatic pipe line. When we landed at base we found that five of our Mosquitoes had been hit by the Dorniers, but no one was hurt and the damage was not serious.

'A formation of Mosquitoes of 248 Squadron also made an audacious attack on the 9th. It is a classic example of the way the aircraft are daring everything to penetrate enemy harbours to kill the shipping before it can make the open sea. One of the observers who took part in this strike told me the story. The aircraft had been standing by for some days, waiting to attack enemy ships if they attempted to evacuate or reinforce the Brittany Peninsula and on the 9th thirteen of them were detailed to sweep the Biscay Coast as far south as the Gironde River. The observer said, 'We searched every nook and cranny except where the water was too shallow for shipping and while we were off Benodet on the coast of Brittany, we sighted a force of minesweepers. We noted them for future reference; we kept them in the back of our minds in case we saw nothing better. We flew south, between Belle Ile and the mainland and on to the Gironde. The flak came up thick for their fingers were pretty light on the triggers. Three of our aircraft had to withdraw from the task, one with engine trouble and later one of our anti-flak aircraft was hit from the shore. The pilot was wounded and the aircraft was escorted back by one of the bombers.

'We found one of our naval groups and escorted them for eighteen minutes, but we found no enemy shipping to speak of, only a small coaster and a merchant vessel in Bourgneuf Bay. So we flew up the coast again, back to Benodet to confirm that the minesweepers were still there. It was about half-past eight in the evening when the leader arrived south of the river mouth. While eight of the aircraft were perfecting their formation, the leader and the deputy leader flew into the river to make sure the minesweepers were still there and to see how they were disposed. There was no flak then, but the Germans had plenty of time to have a cup of tea and load up for us when we flew in for the actual attack. The leader and deputy leader rejoined the formation and gave us our orders.

'The formation flew north up the river which is about half a mile wide at the mouth, past the town of Benodet. All secrecy was lost by then and the Germans must have guessed our intention. We found the minesweepers lying just beyond the town and there was another alongside a floating dock and sheltered by the trees. We all made head-on attacks and when we were 2,000 yards away the minesweepers opened up with heavy and light flak. And there was a carpet of flak from the shore for us to dive through. We could see the rows of black puffs below. We were at 800 feet and the puffs at 400, but we were hit twice, just as we had the misfortune of a stoppage in three cannons. The flak passed through the starboard side of the nose and hit a parachute and there was a hit in the starboard wing. We had to break away because of the cannon breakdown so we flew over the tree-tops, towards the sea. We passed over a lovely chateau we know well now. We always say we will go to rest there when the war is over. It is a lovely place, with a park.

'Observers have little to do while the actual attack is on,' he said. 'So we rival each other in taking the photographs. The ones taken on that strike show that all the minesweepers were hit; all were smoking and two were in flames. The results were satisfying; damage to four minesweepers and only slight damage to one of our aircraft.' I asked the observer if he experienced any excitement during the attack and he said, 'No, one would be surprised if nothing happened. The satisfaction comes afterwards, when we break away from the attack, realize that we are all right and look around for the other blokes.'

'Mosquitoes from Portreath' wrote Hector Bolitho 'sighted a big bag at about 10 o'clock in the morning off Royan, including an 'M' Class minesweeper which was blown up with a direct hit and left in flames which leapt 200 feet in the air. The Mosquitoes then strafed two small escort vessels, armed with flak. They also attacked a 3,000-ton Sperrbrecher off Le Verdon and there was a concentration of cannon hits on the hull. The superstructure of one of the escorting vessels was left on fire and at least two more were damaged.'

The Mosquito flown by Warrant Officers Frank Chew and 'Jock' Couttie was so badly hit by flak that it lost both its engines and was forced to ditch in the Gironde at about ten o'clock in the morning. The aircraft broke in halves as it hit the water and when the pilot and observer were free of the wreckage they saw that the rescue dinghy had drifted fifty yards away. They swam to the dinghy, climbed in and considered their misfortunes and their chances of escape. Frank Chew had lost his shoes in the water and there were no paddles in the dinghy. There was flak from both banks of the river and Chew could hear the other aircraft of his formation pounding a ship in the estuary. They tore two pieces of wood from the wreckage to use as paddles and then had to decide whether they would make their way to the south bank where the wooded country offered shelter and possible escape, or paddle to the open sea where one of our escort vessels might find them.

They chose the open sea and after paddling for half an hour they heard the chug chug of a boat, louder and then dying away, then louder again. They could do nothing but sit and wait until a sixty-foot fishing vessel came alongside, with twenty Germans on board and an ominous cannon. Frank Chew quickly sank his French money over the side of the dinghy. As he said, he didn't see any reason why they should have it. The Germans threw a rope and when Chew had made it fast the Germans started their, engine so quickly that the dinghy overturned and threw

Chew and Couttie into the water. 'That was a bit of a bind,' said Chew, 'because Jock had baled out the dinghy with a shoe and both his shoes and socks were drying on the side when we went over. He lost them. Neither of us had any shoes. The Germans weren't rough with us. They hauled us on board the trawler, made us hold our hands up, took our Mae Wests and then our identity cards. When the aircraft crashed I had bruised two of my finger nails. One of the German sailors bandaged my fingers for me, quite gently and then we were ordered to stand at the stern of the trawler, while we were steaming towards Royan, but nobody spoke. I did not quite know what to think.

'As we came near Royan two of the Germans led us to the shelter of the fo'c'sle, so that as we came alongside we would not see any damage from our attacks. Just as the trawler touched the wharf a funny little German officer with blazing blue eyes and three stars on his epaulettes, jumped on board, called us 'Swine, bastard, gangster,' and began to thump me in the kidneys. Behind him stood four or five men with rifles. He was funny and he did not hurt and when he had pounded me about a dozen times he packed up and had a couple of bangs at Jock. Jock looked across at me and I looked across at him. I said, 'Never mind, Jock, take no notice of him.' The German officer was glaring mad and it wasn't very pleasant to have to stand there and let him do what he liked. If ever I saw him again I would remember him. He said, 'Swine, bastard, gangster,' again and left us.

'Then another officer motioned us on to the pier. He flourished a big automatic; so big I thought it ought to be on wheels. As we walked along I could see the minesweeper my pals had hit during the attack. One bomb had landed between the funnel and the bridge and I could see that the ship would never be used again. The officer saw me looking at it so he muttered something in German, waved his big gun towards the minesweeper and then at me. I thought I'd better not laugh, but I must say that I wanted to. They took Jock and me to separate rooms and after an hour a French civilian came and asked us in English where we were from. I gave him my name, rank and number, but no more. Two more hours passed and the guards put us into a small van, closed all round. There were two guards with us and they would not let us talk, but there was a blanket in front which swayed a bit so we could see through. They were running us round and round the streets to confuse us and we saw the same buildings two or three times.

After about an hour of this we left the town and were taken to a Luftwaffe base in the country. There an Oberleutnant took everything from us; fountain pens and cigarette cases, all except the gold ring which was on one of my wounded fingers. The Oberleutnant was kind about that. Of course, they made a list, like one of our stores' chaps would have done. I suppose those store types like lists, whatever country they come from. Then they let us sit in the sun, with nice open farming country about us, to dry our clothes. In the afternoon the same van came again and we set off for another place. I hadn't the slightest idea where we were until there was a puncture. They let us out while they were mending it and we saw a signpost which said, Cognac, 8 kilometres.'We climbed back when the tyre was fixed and drove on to what was left of Cognac aerodrome. It was really knocked about by our bombing, with all the hangars down, no aircraft and a skeleton staff. We were taken into the Commandant's office, but he didn't seem to know what to do and we just stood there for an hour, while the officers stared at us. Still nobody spoke, except the Commandant when he asked us whether we belonged to the British or Canadian Air Force. I didn't think much of his English. They were well dressed but they didn't seem to be a very bright bunch of fellows. Nobody seemed to know what to do with us until the late evening, when they put us in separate cells in the local gaol. Jock and I had no chance of speaking before that. We had just looked at each other and grinned. Even if we opened our mouths they would shout, 'Verboten.' They turned the keys on us and left us there all night, next day and next night, with nothing to eat or drink: I just walked up and down. I was supposed to be going on leave next day and I just said to myself, 'And here I am in Cognac local gaol instead.'

'It was Saturday night, 12th August, when they locked us up. On Monday afternoon, 14th August, one of the German guards came in with bread, coffee, greasy soup and a meat ball swimming in gravy. I was pretty fed up by then and the smell of the meat ball was all over the cell, so I picked it up with the spoon and threw it out of the window. The guard was about my own age and he was so mad at me that he gathered everything up and went out. I just prowled up and down, looking at the bars of the window. There were seven of them, with two cress pieces and the cement that held them was new. The angry guard had left the combined spoon and fork behind so when night began to fall I used the spoon to dig the cement away from one of the bars. I was soon able to wrench one of them free. My window was in the outside wall of the prison and there was another lower wall at right angles, on to which I could have jumped and perhaps got away. While I was working on the second bar I heard a noise outside the cell, so I quickly shoved the concrete back on the loose bar, put the spoon on the table and waited. It was another bind because the guard came in and led me out of the cell before I could finish my work on the window. If I had been able to remove the two bars I could have forced the other back.

I joined Jock in the passage and they let us talk for the first time. I asked him what he had been doing by himself. He said, 'Nothing' but he grumbled because the mosquitoes had bitten him. He had been bitten all night. I'd put my battle dress top over my head to keep them away, but he had used his for a pillow. We were taken to three trucks and a car in which two officers and two girls were sitting. There was a good deal of chattering and I realized that they were talking about the Maquis and that they were frightened. We were pushed into one of the trucks and the procession set off for Bordeaux. We had one adventure on the way when we stopped for a puncture. A French chap on a push bicycle overtook us and as he passed the convoy he bowed politely and said, 'Bonjour, Bonjour'; but directly he had passed he jumped off his bicycle, whipped out a revolver and fired at the Germans in the front truck. Then he jumped on his bicycle again and made off, with the officers in the car following him. I do not know what happened, but one of the guards came to us afterwards, pointed in the direction of the cyclist, then to his stomach and said, Kaput.

'There was an alert when we were outside Bordeaux, but we drove on to the Luftwaffe headquarters, We were still walking without shoes and the officer there made signs to us, apparently asking us what size we took. I said eight and he said acht and then we were marched to the Bordeaux goal, where we were put into a cell with three other prisoners. One was a German seaman who spoke English. I don't know what he was in gaol for. He told us that we would soon be in a prisoner of war camp, but thank goodness he was wrong. The cell was seven foot square and when I climbed on Jock's shoulders I could see that we were four storeys up and that there were six feet of solid concrete above us, without any foothold. There was no chance of escape, but every now and then a guard came in and tapped the bars with a piece of metal. Perhaps they had found out about the bar I had moved in the last cell and they were taking no chances.

They let us out for half an hour to wash and we met some of the other prisoners. There were ten Americans, a Canadian and an Englishman, who had been in France since last December. They had no idea how the war was going, so we gave them all the gen. Then we got into the good old argument with the Americans, which were the best aircraft, theirs or ours. The guards seemed very restless and anxious. I suppose they were worrying whether they would be able to escape. We had hardly settled down when Jock and I were moved into a small cell on the top floor, with just enough room for both of us to lie down. We were there all one day, with bread and coffee in the morning, soup for dinner and more bread at night. We didn't talk much. Weld known each other so long there was nothing new to say. We were allowed out for an hour then for some exercise and to talk with the other prisoners. Everybody was very cheerful and we laughed when one of the Americans told us how they had pinched a fire engine in the north of France and travelled many miles in trying to escape. They had been shot down on a bombing raid. Others had pinched bicycles but the Germans had got them before they travelled very far. Some had dared to get on trams, although they could not speak a word of French or German.

'On Wednesday the 16th a Lancaster crew joined us, after being shot down during an evening raid on Bordeaux.[109] There were so many of us then that the Germans had to put us into the prison chapel where we were quite gay, talking our heads off. Next day when Jock was looking through the bars of one of the Chapel windows he saw two chaps from our station. Warrant Officer Genno and Flight Sergeant Goodman. They were old friends. We had to laugh, they looked so dejected, but they were brought into the chapel with us and we had a good natter.

'The officer had not forgotten about our size acht shoes and on the Wednesday morning they were brought in to us. It was just like home; forms to sign in triplicate, vouchers, bags of paper, exactly the same as home.

'The chapel was used as a gaol for Germans also; Luftwaffe officers and naval officers, who had refused to go to sea. One of them spoke English. He was a Christian Scientist and a conscientious objector and we had quiet little talks with him, but he was an unhappy little man: The others talked of flying bombs and said, 'London kaput, Plymouth kaput,' but I said, 'Flying bombs kaput' and told them that our Spitfires were shooting them down before they could reach London. They would not believe me.'

Next day there was absolute panic. I could hear them saying, 'Maquis' every now and then as they packed, boxes and suitcases. They were obviously frightened and that afternoon the German prisoners were taken away and we were left alone. Then the Luftwaffe and the army fought about us. We had been the prisoners of the army up to then and the Luftwaffe claimed that we belonged to them. There were twenty-two of us left. Two of the Americans had already escaped two miles into Spain, but the Spaniards caught them and sent them back. Six other Americans had got to Bordeaux where they met a Frenchman, who hid them and promised to get them over the border. He let them hide for five days and then handed them over to the Gestapo. The Americans won't forget that Frenchman's face if they ever see him again.

'The Luftwaffe won us and took us away to Merignac aerodrome, which was the headquarters of the French Air Force. It was from here that the Germans controlled all the Ju 88s, Dornier 217s and Heinkel 177s, with which we had been dealing in the Bay, but that was over. The headquarters had been well and truly plastered by the US bombers and we were put in the only serviceable building. The Luftwaffe seemed quite friendly and they treated us well. We couldn't understand it. I suppose they knew their number was up with our armies moving over the land and the Maquis advancing, so they thought it just as well to be kind. They took us to the hospital to sleep and there we waited for three days, while they demolished the runways and cookhouses, setting fire to everything before we moved on. We had one little trick that annoyed them. On the wall of the room there was a photograph of Hitler and one of Goering. When the guard came in he always found us standing in front of the photographs staring at them without saying a word. They did not like that so one of them came in and took the photographs away.

'Then we moved again, at night and twenty-two of us were packed into an open truck. A convoy of 3,000 men moved out of that aerodrome in the most terrible trucks I have ever seen. Some had no tyres and travelled on the wheel rims; all of them used charcoal because they had no petrol. The rain fell on us in that open truck, all night and next morning and when daylight came we supposed we were being taken to

Germany, but they were still quite kind and they gave us the same rations as their own men. All the time we knew the Maquis were coming nearer and nearer and we passed truck after truck blown off the road. Sometimes there were explosions. Then we arrived outside Chateau Neuf, but there was something wrong. Nobody told us what it was, but we stayed alongside the road for four days, beside a farm. The trucks were all cleverly camouflaged, with sods of earth piled against the wheels to make a grass bank. You couldn't see those trucks at twenty yards. Nine Spitfires flew over us on the second day, but they did not see us and nobody fired at them, but we were proud to see them. The Germans were a poor lot. They went into the woods and hid and they put us in a barn when the Spitfires flew over. I wasn't impressed by what I saw of those Germans at all. There was one, a tall chap of about twenty-four. His name was Joseph Ludwig and he came from Munich. When darkness was falling he would come to us, put his finger to his lips and whisper, 'No Hitler,' and there was one of the guards who spoke a little English, a miserable little chap from Freiburg. I felt a bit sorry for him although I shouldn't. He looked the hen-pecked sort. He hated the war, he said he wanted to see England and learn to speak more English so we told him, 'You'll learn plenty of English in one of our prisoner of war camps. We have special classes for chaps like you!' We laughed at that but he didn't.

'Whenever the truck stopped on the way and we got out, the little man would hand one of us his rifle while he jumped out after us. When he was off duty he would come to us and drowse off to sleep with his rifle and bayonet at his side. We could have slit his throat but it would have been foolish. And there was one, very young, learning English from a story book for children; a story about Peter and Elizabeth having a day at the farm and he asked us to explain the words to him. The guard who gave us his rifle to hold was named Otto and he was the only one not from bombed cities. They used the ones from the bombed places to guard us, hoping they would not be too kind I suppose. The ones who weren't on guard got very drunk and they sang Lilli Marlene all the time.

'Then came the day when five of them took out a map and began jabbering very quickly. They told us of the landing of our troops in the south of France and what parts of the country we had taken, but they weren't bitter. At least those who came near us weren't. Those who were bitter had to stay away at a distance glowering at us and howling at us in German. I don't know what they said, but I don't suppose it was very nice. Some of them would come to us at dusk and talk and they admitted that they had very little chance of getting back to Germany.

'Just about this time the rain and hardships got the better of some of the boys and they had stomach trouble, dysentery and rashes. There was no medical officer with all the 3,000 Germans, so our four officers demanded medical attention for the prisoners. Having those officers with us pulled some weight with the CO and fourteen of the boys were sent to the civilian hospital in Angouleme.

'Then the Maquis attacked the camp. It was dusk and there was great shouting and yelling going on. There were bursts of gunfire all along the woods. We were put back in the barn and the door was locked. There was machine-gun fire near the barn for a few minutes and we ducked down. We saw poor Otto through a chink, raising his rifle, then thinking better of it he just lowered it again and disappeared. We could hear the gun fire and the grenades, but none came our way. The attack went on for about an hour and next day we heard a rumour that the Germans were fighting their way out and that they intended leaving the sick ones behind. Of course the rest of us went sick immediately. So they sent us off to the civilian hospital so that we were all together again.

'We hadn't been in that French hospital five minutes when the whole town knew. Oh you should have seen them! They came with flowers, wine and champagne and they even smuggled a radio into our room so that we heard an American dance band, then the English news. That was good to hear. We heard that our soldiers had taken Rheims and that they were almost at Lyons. So we brought out a map and saw what a hole the Germans were in. There were 20,000 of them in that part of the country and the gap through which they could escape was getting smaller all the time. Their chances were pretty hopeless. We were in that hospital for two days and everybody in the town seemed to come to visit us. Some of the girls came and we got the marine lieutenant, who could speak French, to write a few French phrases on pieces of paper for us. When the French girls said, Bonjour we said, Bonjour, enchante so quickly they thought we could speak French. So they rattled on but we didn't understand a word.

'On the evening of 31st August, we heard firing in the streets. The Maquis had arrived at Angouleme and at three o'clock in the morning a Maquis officer came to our beds and said, 'You are free.' They made Jock and I and the others get up and dress. 'This is no time to stay in bed,' they said, so we had to get up at three in the morning and join the parade through the streets. They had produced hundreds of flags, Union Jacks and Stars and Stripes, which they had been hiding. They were big flags and the streets suddenly went wild. There were bonfires and everybody went mad. I'll never forget that march. They cheered us because of our RAF uniforms and they just showered kindness on us. They gave us breakfast in a big hotel and when we walked around the streets we were mobbed everywhere.

'On the evening of 2nd September we met an American captain and a Canadian officer, who had been dropped by parachute to help the Maquis. They told us to be at the hospital at seven o'clock that evening and said, 'You're leaving by air for England.' That night Jock and I went to a small landing strip outside the town and there were two Dakotas from England, full of supplies for the Maquis. We took off in the dark and landed in England on 3rd September, at five o'clock in the morning. It was the fifth anniversary of the war.

'There was only one sad bit after that. Jock had got a bottle of brandy in France and he had nursed it all the way, like a baby in his arms. After we arrived in London we went to the RAF Stores and as we walked in, Jock dropped the bottle of brandy on the road and broke it. I shall never forget the expression on his face as long as I live.'[110]

Footnotes

93 The reason for the changed time of the parade that day has never been explained, but the flight was still considered a tremendous success and it convinced many doubting Thomases in France of the efficiency and reliability of the RAF and the SOE organisation. News of it spread through France like wildfire. Frenchmen gleefully told each other of how the Germans had been taken by surprise in broad daylight and how the Beaufighter had cocked a snook at all the hundreds of Luftwaffe fighters based in Northern France. Gatward was awarded the DFC and Fern the DFM. Later Gatward was awarded the DSO and a bar to his DFC, becoming one of the most outstanding Beaufighter strike-leaders. As Wing Commander he became CO of 404 Squadron. Fern rose to rank of Squadron Leader. *Beaufighter Squadrons In Focus* by Simon Parry (Red Kite, 2002).

94 On 20 January 1944 Air Chief Marshal Sir Sholto Douglas took over Coastal Command from Slessor, who was appointed Deputy Allied Air Commander in the Mediterranean theatre and C-in-C of the RAF in the Mediterranean and Middle East. In April 1944 Sholto Douglas issued a directive setting out clearly the role of his Command. No.19 Group, at Plymouth, was to provide the patrols in the south-west approaches of the Channel and to escort convoys. No.16 Group, at Chatham, was to perform a similar office in the event of an attempt by U-boats to attack from the north and enter the northerly approaches of the Channel. No.15 Group at Liverpool was to continue to cover convoys in the Atlantic and to attend to the northern transit area; in this they were to be assisted by No.18 Group at Rosyth.

95 *Conflict Over The Bay* by Norman L. R. Franks (William Kimber 1986 and Grub St. 1999).

96 618 Squadron was re-tasked for re-assignment to the Pacific to attack, with 'Highball', the Japanese fleet at Truk, which, because of the distance involved, meant that the Mosquitoes would have to operate from a carrier! The attacks however, never took place.

97 *U-Boat Fact File* by Peter Sharpe (Midland Publishing Ltd 1998).

98 U-960 was bombed by Wellingtons M and U on 36 Squadron and Ventura V on 500 Squadron and depth-charged by the USS *Ludlow* and USS *Niblack* 52 miles NNE of Tennes, Algeria and lost with 31 hands. Twenty survivors were rescued. *U-Boat Fact File* by Peter Sharpe (Midland Publishing Ltd 1998).

99 *U-boat Fact File* by Peter Sharpe (Midland Publishing Ltd 1998)/ *Hitler's U-boat War: The Hunted, 1942-1945* by Clay Blair (Random House 1998).

100 MM424/H and NT225/O.

101 *Beaufighter Strike 1944: The Air War Over Europe June 1st-30th; Over The Beaches* by John Foreman (ARP 1994).

102 U-212 limped into La Pallice for repairs on 9 June. When U-212 put to sea again, on 12 June, a damaged hydroplane forced her return. On 21 July U-212 was depth-charged by the frigates HMS *Curzon* and HMS *Ekins* 24 miles SW of Beachy Head and lost with all 49 hands. *U-Boat Fact File* by Peter Sharpe (Midland Publishing Ltd 1998).

103 *Task For Coastal Command* by Hector Bolitho (Hutchinson & Co Ltd 1944).

104 Flight Lieutenant Lewis Bacon DFC and his navigator Flying Officer William Miller DFC were killed on 24 February 1945 during a tactical demonstration on the R/P range near Tarlair when after firing his rockets, the port wing of Bacon's Mosquito came off and the aircraft broke up.

105 *U-Boat Fact File* by Peter Sharpe (Midland Publishing Ltd 1998).

106 Following repairs LR347/T served on 248 Squadron until July 1945.

107 Air Defence of Great Britain.

108 Group Captain Max Aitken wanted youth at the helm and in October 1944 he told Younge that he was wanted for operational duties at Northwood, London. He was replaced by Squadron Leader Richard Atkinson. *A Separate Little War* by Andrew D. Bird (Grub St 2008).

109 Lancaster PD237 VN-D on 50 Squadron at Skellingthorpe was shot down on the daylight raid on an oil depot at Bordeaux on 13 August. The pilot, Flight Lieutenant P. D. A. Lorimer RAAF and one other member of his crew evaded. The other five were captured. Chorley.

110 As quoted in *Task For Coastal Command* by Hector Bolitho.

Chapter 6

Mosquito Merry Making

*There was joy among the Mosquito crews who respond to victory like children.
It is extraordinary to go into a room where they make their report to the
Intelligence Officer after a strike and see how the results affect their manner
and even their appearance. If the strike has been abortive they look tired and the
very young ones have unusual lines on their faces and are pale. If they come
home with success, they are all cock-a-hoop, young and fresh, without a trace of
tiredness. I slowly realise the difference between the crews who fly in the big
aircraft and these shipping strike individualists. The anti U-boat crews are
more solemn in their celebrations, as if the long monotony of the ocean was still
with them. Only on great occasions do they fling themselves whole-heartedly
into ridiculous pleasure. But the pilots and observers of the Mosquitoes and
Beaufighters become reckless over the slightest event. And they need little to
amuse them. They have improved on the tie chewing vice. They will not test
until every tie in the room has been set on fire so that one has to resign oneself
to seeing one's tie sizzling until the room stinks of the burning stuff. Their
favourite celebration is a sort of heathen ceremony for which the metal seats in
the bar are turned upside down and beaten, like tom-toms. In the midst of this
mad rhythm a fire is lighted and over this the victors will dance in a frenzy
until the flame dies down. A crazy affair when described, but harmless, idiotic
fun to watch.*

Hector Bolitho

The day after Chew and Couttie were shot down, on 13 August, eleven
Beaufighters on 236 Squadron and twelve on 404 attacked two
Sperrbrechers off Royan and sank them at about 0930 that morning. One
of the aircraft crashed into the sea. The first Sperrbrecher, the 6,128 ton
Magdeburg, was badly hit by cannon and RP and there were hits on the
superstructure. The aircrews saw clouds of smoke pouring from the centre
of the ship. The second Sperrbrecher was the *Schwanheim*, which was also
left smoking with hits on the deck and bridge and twelve hits below the
water mark. An aircraft flew over the spot again on the 14th and brought
back satisfying photographs. The *Magdeburg* was already at the bottom of
the sea and the *Schwanheim* was burning fiercely with her decks awash.

Flak was intense on the evening of 14 August when 26 Mosquitoes on
235 and 248 Squadrons at Portreath led by Wing Commander Bill Sise DSO*
DFC, CO of 248 Squadron, carried out a shipping strike on a Seetier-class

destroyer, a Sperrbrecher of 4,000 tons and two trawler type auxiliaries all stationary at Le Verdon in the Gironde Estuary with rockets, cannon and the six pounder 'Tsetse' gun. The Sperrbrecher was set on fire and the trawlers were hit by cannon. Warrant Officer Harold Arthur Corbin and his navigator Flight Sergeant Maurice Webb in Mosquito HP866 attacked the Seetier Class destroyer and a there was an explosion on board but they drew heavy AA fire from both ships and land batteries. Corbin was born in 1923 and joined the RAF in November 1940, four days after his 17th birthday. He joined 235 Squadron flying Beaufighters on anti-shipping sorties from Portreath, but after a few operations he was posted to 248 Squadron at Predannack. The Mosquito was hit in both outer fuel tanks by heavy flak. The port inner tank was also pierced and all the fuel lost. One shell smashed into the Mosquito through the floor of the fuselage and wrecked the IFF and 'Gee' apparatus. Corbin set course for Vannes airfield in Brittany, now occupied by the Allies, with fuel streaming from his punctured tanks, the port engine U/S and the starboard engine damaged. When he arrived over Vannes, Corbin climbed to 4,000 feet and ordered Webb to bail out and then he went out himself. Both made successful landings and spent the night under a hedge before making contact with American troops the next day. [111]

On 17 August seven Mosquitoes on 248 and six on 235 sighted six coasters and ten lesser vessels at the mouth of the Loire at ten o'clock in the morning but they did not attack. The leader decided to search for bigger fry and at 1128 some of the aircraft attacked a vessel ear Penmarch Point. It turned out to be the wreck of a ship attacked by the Navy some time before. Three days' later twenty-one Beaufighters on 236 and 404 Squadrons attacked two armed trawlers in the harbour of Les Sables D'Olonne. They were hit so violently, that parts of them were thrown 200 feet in the air and both of them were burning when the Beaufighters turned for home, unharmed. At six that evening a Mosquito piloted by Flight Lieutenant J. H. B. Rollett developed engine trouble and was ditched. The crews of two other Mosquitoes saw the mishap and reported the position to the Navy, but some hours passed before Rollett and his navigator were found. Next day Mosquitoes on 235 and 248 Squadrons attacked two minesweepers and an armed trawler near Le Verdon. The trawler was left on fire and there were explosions on both the minesweepers. Four of the aircraft were damaged but all crews came home in safety.

About this time an intensive training programme was carried out by 455 Squadron RAAF in the use of rocket projectiles. Four of these weapons were carried under each wing, giving the rocket Beaufighter ('Rockbeau') a striking power comparable to that of a broadside from a cruiser bearing six-inch guns. Opportunities to use the new weapon came quickly and on 13 August 1944, a convoy of five merchant vessels with nine escort vessels was attacked by the Anzac Wing off the East Friesian Islands. The escort vessels included the *Artevelde*, a vessel said to have been built before the war as a private yacht for King Leopold of the Belgians and converted by the Germans to the role of a fast escort vessel. This was hit by a salvo of rockets and intensive cannon fire and heavily damaged. Another of the escorts - it had eight aircraft painted on its bridge, indicating a claim of eight aircraft shot down -received cannon fire and two salvos of rockets and was left in a near-sinking condition. Another important operation of this type took place on 25 August.

The day before the Beaufighters bagged the final prize. They sank the two destroyers; the last ships sufficiently armed to menace Allied surface craft operating in the Western Approaches. About nine o'clock in the morning twenty Beaus on 236 and 404 Squadrons led by Squadron Leader E. W. Tacon, a New Zealander, found the destroyers in the mouth of the Gironde River. Flight Lieutenant C. Gregory was deputy leader and the aircraft on 404 were led by Flight Lieutenant W. R. Christison, a Canadian. They had been told to attack a supposed U-boat near the mouth and they flew in over the flat farm land north of Bordeaux and then down the river. They found the supposed U-boat, but it was only the hull of a Sperrbrecher attacked some days before. The twenty aircraft then approached the mouth of the river and saw the destroyers, opposite Le Verdon. They made all this journey without any opposition but the moment they came in sight of the destroyers, which were stationary, the flak came up at them. The leader got the aircraft into position for a beam attack as the destroyers got under way smartly and tried to move out to sea. They were too late. Their fire continued and the shore batteries joined them in giving the aircraft a terrific pasting as they flew in. Only three of the twenty got through unharmed. Tacon led the formation into the heart of the barrage. Two aircraft were hit so badly that they had to finish the attack on one engine. The cannon fire from the aircraft was accurate and the rockets were fired perfectly, leaving both ships shrouded in flames and smoke. Three of the damaged aircraft had to land in France and one crashed into the sea, but the others did not give up even when the choice targets had been hit. They shot up ground defence posts and blew up an electric power house, on their way out to sea. The end is wholly satisfying. Although the aircraft suffered many hits, the crew that crashed into the sea were rescued by one of 9ur destroyers and the crews of the three aircraft that landed on French soil were shaken but not seriously hurt. They were flown back to England on the 25th.

Next day the Beaufighters were out again but the only targets they found were small vessels already aground in Audierne Bay. They were bombed and left burning. The same force attacked a merchant vessel, probably one of the few surviving Sperrbrechers off Royan, about half-past five in the afternoon. It was left on fire, with smoke rising three hundred feet into the air. One Beaufighter was lost during this task.

As the Allies swept through France and Belgium into Holland and the Allied Air Forces maintained their ceaseless pounding of rail and road communications, the enemy tried to supply his troops through the ports of Emden and Den Helder and maximum effort sorties were the order of the day for the British anti-shipping units. Every available aircraft was put into the air, entailing long and arduous work by the ground crews. The armourers enabled the Anzac Wing to fire 6,500 rounds of cannon ammunition with only three stoppages. Twice two major sorties were carried out within twenty-four hours.

As the nights grew longer and the autumn of 1944 came, the enemy was able to slip ships through under cover of darkness and bad weather. Coastal Command turned to the possibility of striking at the enemy's ships in harbour in spite of the known strength of the harbour defences. On 12 September the Anzac and North Coates Beaufighter wings swept in through the harbour mouth at Den Helder to attack shipping at anchor in the Marsdiep Roads. They were met by a most intense barrage of heavy and light flak both from ships and shore batteries, but the attack was pressed home and a number of ships damaged. After passing over the ships the aircraft shot up gun positions on the shore on their way out.

A Beaufighter on 455 Squadron RAAF piloted by Flying Officer Sykes DSO DFC flew so low over one ship that it struck the mast and brought back three feet of masthead, with electric light fittings, embedded in the nose of the aircraft. The compasses were shot away and the pilot decided to follow another aircraft home. The aircraft Sykes followed, however, was itself severely damaged; the navigator's cupola was blown off, all navigation instruments rendered unserviceable and the navigator, a RAF man, wounded. A fire broke out in the navigator's compartment and he struggled to extinguish it as the Australian pilot, Flying Officer L. W. Farr DFC set course into the setting sun for England. By masterly airmanship both these aircraft were flown back to base where both were forced to crash land because flak had damaged the hydraulics. The crews escaped serious injury, but two aircraft of the North Coates wing failed to return.

It was again decided to raid Den Helder, which the enemy seemed to be trying to use now as an evacuation port for the troops trapped by the Allied advance. On 25 September the largest strike force ever laid on by Coastal Command assembled at Langham. About seventy Beaufighters took part, including twelve Australian aircraft led by Wing Commander Davenport and they were escorted by eight RAF Tempests. The harbour had been carefully photographed on the morning of the strike and the disposition of the shipping there was accurately known. The operation was planned and synchronized with the greatest care. The attack was to be opened by ten aircraft of a Polish Mustang squadron, which were to dive bomb the heavy flak positions on shore with two 500lb bombs each, three minutes before the Beaufighters attacked.

The strike force swept in between the islands to the north-east of the harbour and turned over the Zuider Zee, led by the aircraft detailed to beat up the ship and shore flak positions. The Mustangs bombed at the scheduled time, but although the 'Flakbeaus' made a determined attack the gun positions were so numerous that they could not effectively silence them. Their fire appeared as a veritable wall, with the black puffs of 88mm and 105mm heavy guns and the white puffs of 40mm Bofors guns and the whole area was crossed with bright red 20mm tracer. In the face of this barrage the shipping was attacked with cannon fire and rockets. One M-class minesweeper was seen to blow up and the rest of the ships were left on fire or severely damaged.

As a Beaufighter unit, 455 Squadron RAAF fired 1,833 rockets and 126,963 cannon shells during the war. Its operational hours since its first operation in August, 1941, totalled 11,753. Two months before the Australian Squadron fired the first of those 1,833 rockets, the V-weapon attack on England had begun.

In September enemy activity in the Bay of Biscay had decreased to such an extent and Germany's seaborne traffic travelling daily along the Norwegian coast with large quantities of supplies now assumed a much higher priority. The last operation from Portreath to the Bay of Biscay came on 7 September when six Mosquitoes on 235 and 248 searched in poor visibility for U-boat activity near Gironde. 235 and 248 Squadrons flew to Scotland, joining 333 Norwegian Squadron and 144 and 404 'Buffalo' Squadron RCAF Beaufighter Squadrons to form the Banff Strike Wing under Group Captain Max Aitken DSO DFC. 333 Squadron had formed at Leuchars on 10 May 1943 from 1477 (Norwegian) Flight and commenced its first Mk.VI operations on 27 May. The Banff Wing carried out their first strike on 14 September when 22 FB.VIs and four 'Tsetses' on 235 and 248 Squadrons and nineteen Beaufighters - seven on 144 Squadron and twelve on 404 Squadron which led the formation - attacked shipping between Egero and Stors Toreungen light. A flak ship and a merchantman were sunk. The Mk. XVIIIs left the formation before it struck at four motor vessels sailing north, protected by two escort ships. Hits were claimed on all of them and fires started. On 21 September six Mosquitoes on 248 Squadron escorted twenty-one Beaufighters to Kristiansund in search of U-boats.

On 28 September the Banff Wing Mosquitoes were at last modified to carry eight rocket-projectiles (RP) on Mk.IIIA projector rails beneath their wings just like the Beaufighters. The rails had to be set so that they were parallel with the airflow at correct diving speed, otherwise the RPs would weathercock and either under- or overshoot the target. They would also miss if the pilot dived at the wrong airspeed. At first the RPs were armed with 60lb semi-armour-piercing heads of the type used in the Western Desert for tank-busting. These did not however, penetrate shipping and caused little structural damage, so were soon replaced with 25lb solid armour-piercing warheads. Sometimes rockets would 'hang up' on the rails and fail to fire. If this happened, crews had to bail out because if they tried to land, the RPs were liable to explode.

When making an attack on shipping, the Mosquitoes normally commenced their dive of approximately 45 degrees at about 2,000 feet and then opened up with machine gun fire at 1,500-1,000 feet, before using the cannons and lastly, at about 500 feet, the RPs. The RPs were arranged to form a pattern spread on impact, so that if fired at the correct range and airspeed and angle of dive, four would hit the ship above the water-line and the other four would undershoot slightly to hit below the waterline.

In the Norwegian fjords pilots usually had once chance, so they fired all eight rockets at once. After entering the ship's hull each would punch an 18-inch hole in the far side of the hull for the sea to flood in, while the remains of the cordite motor burned inside the hull to ignite fuel and ammunition in the ship.

On 30 September a 'Rover' involving 17 Mosquitoes and a dozen Beaufighters was flown. Only a few isolated vessels were found and sunk in early October because the enemy operated at night in the knowledge that the strike wing could not fly in tight formation at night. On 9 October the Banff Wing tried out a system that had been tried at North Coates during early August 1944. A Warwick laden with flame floats and markers took off at 0415 and 2 hours later, dropped them to form a circle 19 feet in diameter 100 yards from Stavanger. Half an hour later eight Mosquitoes on 235 Squadron followed by eighteen Beaufighters, traced the same course. At 0620 the first aircraft arrived and began to circle. As dawn appeared, the formation set off heading for Egrsund. Led by Wing Commander Tony Gadd on 144 Squadron, at 0710 they sank a German merchantman and a submarine chaser, while a Norwegian vessel was badly damaged. When they had recovered from the surprise the enemy gunners put up a fierce flak barrage but this was smothered by cannon fire. Three aircraft were damaged but all returned.

On 19 October the flak alarm was raised by lookouts on three vessels at anchor at Askvoy at 1330 as nineteen Mosquitoes streaked towards them. Flashes erupted from the nose of each Mosquito and spouts of water erupted in a line towards the U-boat. Rounds struck the bridge and more triggered a fire which the Tsetses fanned with their 57mm shells. Seven crew were injured. One said later that: '... they had been attacked by an aircraft carrying a big gun, emitting a long flame.' One 235 Squadron Mosquito was lost.

With the departure of the two Beaufighter squadrons on 22 October to Dallachy to form a wing with 455 RAAF and 489 RNZAF Squadrons' 'Flakbeaus' and 'Torbeaus' from Langham, 143 Beaufighter Squadron at North Coates moved north to join the Banff Strike Wing and convert to the Mosquito VI. On 24 October two Mosquitoes on 235 Squadron attacked three enemy aircraft, the first seen by the strike wing. Warrant Officer Cogswell dispatched one Bf 110, while Flight Lieutenant Jacques finished off the second Bf 110 hit by Cogswell, who had set an engine on fire. Jacques then destroyed the third aircraft, a Ju 88C. By the end of the month, five strikes had been made.

On 7 November 143 Squadron flew its first FB.VI operation when two aircraft carried out a search for enemy aircraft between Obrestad and Lindesnes. Frequent snow and hail was a feature of operations on 8 and 9 November when the Mosquitoes looked for shipping off Ytteriene, Marstein and Askvoll. The Banff Wing now began to operate in increasingly larger formations, including for the first time, on 13 November, a combined 'op' with the Dallachy Wing. The largest strike so far occurred on 21 November when New Zealander Wing Commander Bill

Sise DSO DFC, who had taken over 248 Squadron on the death of Wing Commander Phillips led a formation of thirty-three Mosquitoes, accompanied by forty-two Beaufighters and twelve Mustang escorts, in a shipping strike at Ålesund on the Norwegian coast.

On 27 November the Dallachy Wing attacked a convoy of two large merchant ships and four escorts in Sula Fjord. Results of torpedo attacks were not observed but many hits with rocket projectiles seen on 3,500-ton ship and one escort was set on fire and left sinking. Three Beaufighters were damaged but all returned safely. Reports subsequently received showed that the other large ship was the *Fidelitas* of 5,740 tons. She did, in fact, receive a torpedo hit and sank as a result. On 29 November in a diving attack on a U-boat off Lista Flying Officer Woodcock in a 'Tsetse' Mosquito fired eight 57mm shells, scoring two hits, while other XVIIIs attacked with depth charges and cannon. 'Tsetses' were again in action on 5 December when Bill Sise led thirty-four Mosquitoes in an attack on merchantmen in Nord Gullen. On the 7th, Squadron Leader Barnes DFC commanding 235 Squadron led 25 Mosquitoes of the Banff Wing to the Norwegian coast accompanied by forty Beaufighters of the Dallachy Wing, escorted by three 'Finger Fours' of Mustang IIIs on 315 (Polish) Squadron flying to the rear, to attack a convoy in Ålesund harbour. Landfall was made as briefed but Barnes led them further up the coast, towards Gossen airfield, whereupon they were jumped by approximately twenty-five FW 190s and Bf 109Gs. They dived through the middle of the Mosquitoes and attacked singly and in pairs. Flight Lieutenant Konrad Stembrowicz, one of the Mustang pilots, who flew 13 such escorts from Peterhead, recalls.

'As we approached the coast of Norway one of the Mosquitoes had an engine-out and it turned back. I nodded towards my No 2, Flying Officer 'Danek' Nowosielski who turned and followed to escort him home. It wasn't what I intended but it was very noble of him. Very soon afterwards the Germans jammed our radios and all I could hear was one long whistle. Then fifteen FW 190s and Bf 109s appeared at 5,000 feet from behind the small white clouds. They attacked the Mosquitoes and the Beaufighters and we went after them. I saw a 109 attacking and went after him. It was a short combat. I destroyed one '109. He flew through my hail of bullets and a grey stream of smoke appeared. Four rounds hit me in my wings but they all passed between the petrol tanks! We lost Flying Officer Andrzej Czerwinski. [Altogether, the Mustangs downed four fighters and two more collided. Two Mosquitoes were among the four aircraft that failed to return.] When I broke off I found myself alone, so I flew back with a lonely bomber.' The Mustangs shot down four fighters and two more collided but two FB.VIs and a Beaufighter were lost.

In Vilnes Fjord on 9 December Twenty-three Beaufighters of the Dallachy Wing attacked a 2,000-ton cargo ship. Showers of debris were thrown into the air and the vessel was last seen heading for the shore under a heavy pall of smoke. Three days' later December the Mosquitoes returned to Gossen but this time no fighters were seen. On the 13th Wing Commander Richard A. Atkinson DSO DFC* RAAF CO, 235 Squadron and his

20-year old navigator, Flying Officer Valentine 'Val' Upton, were killed when a cable across a fjord cut off the Australian's starboard wing during their attack on merchantmen at Ejdstjord. Atkinson, originally from Emmavilla, New South Wales, had a brief spell as a mining engineer, then bought a passage to England and joined the RAF and was a flying officer before the outbreak of war. He had seen operational service on 205 Squadron and had flown Catalinas and Sunderlands in the Indian Ocean.

On the 16th the Mosquitoes came upon a medium-sized merchant ship and its escort hiding between the steep cliffs of a fjord at Kraakhellesund. Despite intense flak from the escort and surrounding cliff sides, the Mosquitoes dived into the attack in line astern, because there was no space to manoeuvre. Half an hour later a second wave attacked. Two of the FB.VIs were shot down. Three days' later Mustangs escorted the Mosquitoes to Sulen, Norway but no fighters appeared. They destroyed two motor boats in Leirvik harbour but had to contend with attacks by two-dozen Luftwaffe fighters. Each side lost one aircraft. On Boxing Day twelve FB.VIs on 235 Squadron led by Squadron Leader Norman 'Jacko' Jackson-Smith, with two outriders from 333 Squadron, flying at very low-level, attacked two merchant ships at Leirvik harbour, about 70 miles up Sogne Fjord, with machine guns and cannon. They left one sinking, the other blazing. One of the Mosquitoes was crewed by Flying Officer Bill Clayton-Graham DFC and Flying Officer 'Ginger' Webster. Clayton-Graham recalls.

'After attacking the nearest ship I went on to attack the second ship, when I was hit in the port engine. One ship was left sinking, the other on fire. Our strike force totalled twelve aircraft. As I broke off the second attack, smoke was pouring from my port engine, which I feathered and I flew round the headland to go down Bomba Fjord and out to sea, having climbed to 1,000 feet. Heavy flak burst around me in the fjord and then I saw fighters in line astern flying with me about 1,000 feet above and slightly astern to my right - about 24 of them. As they peeled off to attack I turned into them and attacked with machine-guns (my cannon were spent), which forced about twelve of them (Me 109s and FW 190s) to dive past my nose and through my line of fire. I saw one hit well and truly and I must have tickled quite a few others. I was not hit but was a sitting duck with only one engine. I turned back on course out to sea, dived onto the wave-tops with the good engine at full throttle and awaited the second attack, which never came. They had all gone on to attack another aircraft flown by my good friend, Flying Officer Jim Fletcher, whom they shot down. One enemy fighter was reported by the Norwegian underground to have been shot down.

'Our strike leader, Squadron Leader 'Jacko' Jackson-Smith, who had seen my predicament but had lost sight of me, called me up and told me to fire a Very light so he could come and escort me. I replied, 'Not bloody likely, they'll see me, too!' - and pressed on. About 20 miles out to sea, I called up the patrolling Air-Sea Rescue Warwick, which carried a lifeboat. He homed in on me (I was doing about 170 mph) and escorted me back the 300-odd miles over the North Sea to Banff. The Mossie handled beautifully and I made a safe wheels-down landing. A piece of shrapnel was found, which had cut a coolant pipe in my port engine. A change of underpants and several pints of beer were the only repairs needed by me.'

Warrant Officer Harold Corbin and his navigator Flight Sergeant Maurice Webb in Mosquito 'N' had been hit by flak, which had damaged one engine, causing a loss of glycol coolant. Corbin recalls.

'Seeing the German fighters waiting for us as we came out of the fjord I risked full throttle, got down on the deck and hoped the damaged engine would last until we were out of danger and that no German would pick on us. We were lucky and finally out of danger, but the damaged motor, having done what was necessary was finished, so I feathered the prop and once again headed for home on one motor. Having got safely back to Banff I then misjudged the approach and realised that I was going to touch down in a field 100 yards short of the aerodrome boundary and runway. I was not unduly worried until just after touchdown. I saw a stone wall at the aerodrome edge. Just as we hit this I switched off to avoid possible fire and selected 'wheels up' on the undercarriage to allow the wall to knock the wheels back up. I felt we might somersault otherwise and end upside-down. Well, dear old 'N' hit the wall, flat on our belly, both props and wheels torn off but otherwise on an even keel. Maurice and I were trapped in the wreckage but within seconds Max Aitken had raced around the perimeter track in his station wagon and dragged us out. He then took us to the station hospital. We were only slightly injured and soon recovered, but when 248's CO, Bill Sise DSO DFC came to see us he said, 'I'm giving you a rest. No more ops, but I want you to stay with the Squadron to help newcomers.' We then went off to an aircrew officer's course at Hereford. After a month or so we returned to find the Squadron had suffered many losses during our absence. Bill Sise had been posted to 143 Squadron, many friends were gone and the biggest blow of all was that our dear, our beloved, Wing Commander Maurice Geudj had been lost.'

By the winter of 1944/45, shipping moved along the Norwegian coast only at night. During daylight hours, ships hid under the cliffs up fjords, many miles from the coast. This made it impossible for the anti-shipping squadrons to attack in the way that had been developed over the years - a blanket strike by all aircraft virtually simultaneously; anti-flak aircraft first followed immediately by the main armament, rockets and/or torpedoes. In the narrow fjords only two or three aircraft could attack at the same time. One such encounter took place on 9 January when eighteen FB.VIs on 235 Squadron returned to Leirvik with an escort of a dozen Mustangs and attacked eight merchant ships in the harbour. Flying Officer Bill Clayton-Graham DFC recalls: 'We left three ships on fire. The Norwegian underground later reported one ship sunk at its moorings and four others severely damaged: One of the ships on fire had unloaded ammunition, which was stacked alongside the quay. Happily this did not go up during our attack. We had a fighter escort of 12 Mustangs, but they were not needed on this occasion.'

Two days later there was more success when fourteen Mosquitoes accompanying eighteen Beaufighters on an anti-shipping strike in Flekke fjord led by 455 Squadron RAAF were intercepted off Lister. Flight Lieutenant N. Russell DFC and another Mosquito pilot shot down a Bf 109. Only Swedish ships were seen before FW 190s and more Bf 109s tackled the force. Four enemy fighters were then claimed as destroyed for the loss of a Beaufighter, a Mosquito and an ASR Warwick. On 15 January a formation of thirteen strike Mosquitoes, one 'Tsetse' and two 333 Squadron outriders, led by Wing Commander Geudj, now 143 Squadron CO, returned to Leirvik. They completely surprised two merchantmen and an armed trawler and left them burning and sinking before they were jumped by about thirty FW 190s of III./JG5. Tsetse 'Z' fired four shells at a FW 190. Five enemy fighters were shot down but five Mosquitoes, including the one piloted by 'Maury' Geudj, were also lost. The rest fought their way back across the North Sea pursued for a time by nine fighters. This sudden rise in Banff Wing losses caused concern at Northwood and after this attack 248 Squadron's 'Tsetses' were transferred south to North Coates.

On Friday 9 February a formation of Beaufighters in the Dallachy Strike Wing comprising eleven Beaus on 455 Squadron RAAF, eleven on 404 RCAF, nine on 144 and one from 489 RNZAF escorted by ten Mustangs on 65 Squadron, sighted and attacked four naval ships including a Narvik-class destroyer in ice covered Forde Fjord, which is narrow and flanked by steep hills. Consequently it was impossible for all the aircraft to attack together. They also had to fly through an intense barrage put up by both ships and land batteries. The destroyer and two auxiliaries were hit. Because of the extremely difficult position of the ships, the attack lasted about half an hour which gave FW190s from Herdla time to reach the scene. Flak and fighters accounted for nine Beaus and one Mustang. The biggest loss - six - was from 404 Squadron; 455 lost two and 144 lost one. The navigator of the 144 Squadron aircraft piloted by Pilot Officer P. C. Smith DFC recalled:

'We survived the flak but were shot down by a FW190 which got in two bursts and knocked out the port engine and, incidentally, the intercom. I managed to free my loose-mounted Browning and fired until it jammed due to the ammunition belt having been damaged also: To my surprise and relief the FW190 flew off and did not wait to see us ditch in Hoydalsfjord. It seemed almost certain that the single burst of fire from my Browning had caused the FW190 to crash and burn up. The pilot, 28-year old Leutnant Rudi Linz, who had been credited with 69 victories - most of them against the Russians - was killed. By a miracle, we came down close to a settlement of about three farms and were rescued from the freezing water after about ten minutes; the dinghy was in the damaged wing and did not inflate. We were taken to one of the farms were we dried and thawed out. It was clear that I needed medical attention and, as no Norwegian doctor could possibly come to such an isolated spot, where the only communication was by boat, unknown to the occupying Germans, we had to be handed over. A patrol came for us during the evening. After weeks in hospital in Oslo I spent the remainder of the war in Stalag Luft I.' [112]

On 11 February 235 Squadron Mosquitoes fired its rockets in anger for the first time and delayed-action bombs were dropped in a narrow fjord off Midgulen. They rolled, 'Dam Buster'-style down a 3,000-feet cliff and exploded among the ships below. The Mosquitoes began to widen their horizons and operating independently of the Beaufighters now, ranged far and wide over the Norwegian coast seeking specific targets. On 21 February 235 Squadron carried RPs for the first time when a 5,000-ton ship in Askevold Fjord was attacked. Taking part for the first time were spare aircrew on 603 Squadron who had flown Beaufighters in the Middle East, led by Wing Commander Christopher N. Foxley-Norris DSO. Nearly all had joined 235 Squadron.

In March Mosquitoes began seeking out specific targets in Norway. Over the first few days the installation of new, Mk.IB tiered RP projector rails, enabled long range drop tanks to be carried in addition to the RPs. 235 and 248 Squadrons were now able to operate at an increased range, but with a 50 or 100 gallon drop-tank and four RPs under each wing, the Mosquitoes tended to stagger on take-off!

On 7 March a strike led by Wing Commander Roy K. Orrock DFC, CO, 248 Squadron was made against eight self-propelled barges in the Kattegat. Four outriders on 333 Squadron led the formation in and top cover was provided by twelve Mustangs. Two Warwicks on 279 Squadron were in attendance to drop lifeboats to ditched crews if called upon. Two Mosquitoes on 235 Squadron shot up flak ships with machine-guns and cannon and 24 aircraft on 235 and 248 and fourteen on 143 Squadron fired rockets at the targets. Orrock recalled: 'There were eight barges going south and a large merchantman with an escorting flak ship going north. I decided to attack the eight, they seemed more important. They were obviously well laden.' No enemy fighters showed but when 44 Mosquitoes and twelve Mustangs were dispatched on an armed reconnaissance to the Skagerrak and Kattegat on 12 March eight Bf 109s gave battle. Two enemy fighters were shot down for no loss. On 17 March six ships at Ålesund harbour, one of the most heavily defended ports in Norway, were repeatedly strafed by thirty-one FB.VIs on 235 Squadron using cannon and rocket fire after they had been led in by two Norwegian crews in 333 Squadron. Flak was heavy and two aircraft were lost but the Mosquitoes fired their cannon and RPs to deadly effect, leaving three of the ships sinking and the other three crippled. One ship was holed thirty-two times and another 37 times. All except twenty-four of the RPs hit below the waterline. 'Two ships were lying in the inner harbour and four more were just outside as we came over the hills,' reported Flight Lieutenant W. F. Clayton-Graham. 'There was quite a large amount of flak, some heavy.' Squadron Leader 'Robbie' Read reported 'a concentrated attack. There was certainly plenty of flak meeting us, but everyone seemed to be scoring hits with rockets.'

On 21 March 235 and 143 Squadrons rocket-firing Mosquitoes on 128 and 143 Squadrons made short work of an enemy ship at Sandshavn. Two days' later a troopship, the 7,800-ton *Rothenfels*, at anchor in Dals Fjord, was attacked by nine Mosquitoes. The strike leader, Squadron Leader 'Robbie' Read and one other, were shot down. In the afternoon Wing Commander Foxley-Norris led another strike, attacking a motor vessel at Tetgenaes. Next day 404 'Buffalo' Squadron RCAF learned that it would soon be flying Mosquitoes. On the 24th half the squadron moved to Banff to begin conversion while the remainder attacked merchantmen at Egersund with Beaufighters. The rest of the Canadian squadron transferred to Banff on 3 April. On 23 March Mosquitoes on 143 and 235 Squadrons destroyed a ship at Sanshavn with rockets.

On the morning of 24 March Flight Lieutenants Joseph R. Williams and Tom Flower on 235 Squadron set out to fly a search at Utsira and Utvaer but nothing was heard until a report was received from the Royal Navy that a Mosquito had been shot down. The Mosquito crew had sighted the wake of a surfaced U-boat. U-249 commanded by Kapitänleutnant Uwe Kook had set sail from Bergen on 21 March, resurfacing three days later making about nine knots near Skjelanger. At 13.20 hours the single Mosquito was spotted approaching by those on watch and U-249 opened fire as the aircraft made its run in. Williams fired his eight rockets and cannon and machine guns. Steam was coming from the U-boat and one sailor lay wounded but the Mosquito was hit in the starboard engine. Momentarily it seemed to stop under impact and plunged forward, crashing into the water before the entrance to the harbour of Fedje. Flower perished in the crash. Williams escaped through the hatch and bobbed to the surface; he was subsequently rescued by the U-boat crew and pulled onto the deck. Once below Uwe Kook, a large impressive man and a gentleman treated the downed Mosquito pilot well. Slightly damaged, the U-boat returned to Bergen where an ambulance and Red Cross waited for the wounded crew men and Kook docked at 1910. U-249 then resumed his patrol and at 2000 hours, 11 Flotilla Group signalled him that an escort vessel was in position ready to receive the British pilot. Williams boarded the Unitas and the following day the vessel docked in Bergen. Armed guards escorted Williams away from the pier and he was shot in cold blood by Germans. [113]

On 27 March a freight train near Naerbo was attacked by Flight Lieutenant Richard G. 'Taff' Young after patrolling the Utsire-Naze area. The next day two cargo ships and an escort vessel in Egersund Fiord were seriously damaged after an attack by 28 Beaufighters from Dallachy but flak was 'formidable' and four Beaufighters did not return from this strike.

On 30 March Wing Commander Arthur H. Simmonds, 235 Squadron CO, led 44 FB.VIs followed by the RAF Film Unit Mosquito in an attack on Porsgrunn-Skein harbour. No fighters troubled the formation and the Mosquito escorts were able to fire against gun positions in the sides of the fjord. The attackers flew so low against the four merchantmen that they crested the wave tops. One merchantman was hit by 28 rockets, another by 39 rockets and a third by over sixty RPs. 'T-Tommy' crewed by Flight Lieutenant Bill Knowles DFC, originally from Portugal and Flight Sergeant Lawrence Thomas, struck an overhead electric cable and crashed. They were later buried on a joint grave in Skein Cemetery. Three of the four merchantmen were sunk and the fourth was badly damaged while a warehouse on Menstad Quay full of chemicals was also destroyed. Flight Lieutenant Doug Turner said that this was about the best results he had ever seen. 'As we went after the merchantman tied to the quay we could even see the Plimsoll marks on one. We scored hits with all the rockets aimed at one of the vessels and as we came away three separate plumes of smoke were building up to a great height.' Flight Lieutenant Don Clause added: 'A gun position on the side of the hill was firing at our crews as they went in. There were about four guns. I swooped down and sprayed them with cannon and they did not bother later crews going in'.

On 1 April 34 Mosquitoes fired 262 rockets at eight ships anchored in a heavily defended anchorage in Sande Fjord, setting set fire to four of the vessels and scoring over 30 strikes on a tanker in dry dock which then blew up. The Mosquitoes were protected on the raid by four other aircraft on flak suppression duties and 333 Squadron's outriders were used to help maintain the formation and guided it to the correct fjord. Four days' later 37 Mosquitoes escorted by Mustangs flew across Denmark to attack a widely-spread out and heavily-armed convoy in the Kattegat. Every ship in the convoy was left on fire and sinking and an estimated 900 German soldiers were lost. One Sperrbrecher sank with all hands, 200 bodies being recovered by Swedish vessels. An escorting Mustang was shot down over Denmark and a Mosquito crash landed with the crew picked up by the Danish Underground.

On 22 April 404 'Buffalo' Squadron RCAF flew their first Mosquito operation when RF851/H on a shipping reconnaissance using cannon and machine-gun fire, destroyed a Blohm und Voss three-engined Bv 138 flying-boat anchored off Kjevik. It immediately exploded, sending a smoke plume to 500 feet. Meanwhile, 254 Squadron at North Coates equipped with Beaufighter Xs concentrated attacks off the Low Countries on U-boats and midget submarines, which attacked Channel shipping at night. In March the Beaufighter Squadron had been reinforced with five 'Tsetse' Mosquitoes transferred from 248 Squadron to help them and had Spitfire XXIs for cover. The 'Tsetse' Mosquitoes' first went into action from North Coates on 12 April when XVIII 'A' fired its six-pounder at a U-boat, which was also bombed with depth charges dropped by a Wellington on 524 Squadron. Next day 'Tsetse' 'B' fired at a suspected submarine and on the 16th 'D' attacked a schnörkel with no known results. Two 'Tsetses' found five U-boats on the surface on 18 April, but before they had time to attack the submarines had crash-dived and the two rounds fired were near misses.

Mosquito FB.VI crews had yet to get a confirmed U-boat 'kill' all to themselves but all that was about to change on 9 April when 37 rocket-projectile Mosquitoes on 143, 235 and 248 Squadrons were despatched to Norway with five others as fighter cover and DZ592, a 2nd TAF photo-Mosquito on the look-out for enemy shipping. Three U-boats - 804, 843 and 1065 - were spotted in line astern on the surface of the Kattegat coming from Denmark and heading for Norway. Squadron Leader Bert Gunnis DFC, who was leading the strike, ordered the nine FB.VIs on 143 Squadron near the rear of the formation being led by Squadron Leader David Pritchard to attack. The U-boats had not seen the Mosquitoes. Then they did, but it was too late. With the rest of the wing wheeling in behind, 143 Squadron attacked, their cannons blazing as they fired seventy RPs into the U-boats, now frantically trying to escape beneath the waves. Gunnis and Flying Officer Angus A. McIntosh on 248 Squadron, Squadron Leader David Pritchard on 143 and Flight Lieutenant 'Phil' Davenport on 235 sank U-804 commanded by Oberleutnant zur see Herbert Meyer, which was lost with all 55 hands and were primarily responsible for the destruction of U-1065 commanded by Oberleutnant zur see Johannes Panitz, which was lost with all 45 hands. U-843 was sunk by Flying Officer Johnny Rendell on 235 Squadron which went down with 44 hands including the commander, 32-year old Oskar Herwatz.[114] The Mosquitoes were so low, three more suffered damaged engines when they were hit by flying debris and were forced to land in Sweden.

Flight Sergeant John R. Smith, Flight Lieutenant Peter McIntyre's navigator on 248 Squadron, recalls that 9 April was his most memorable day. 'It began with the morning briefing for a wing sweep through the Skagerrak and Kattegat, looking for enemy shipping to attack. We were told that our Mosquito, 'Q-Queen' was unserviceable, but as our new Wing Commander, Jackson-Smith, wasn't flying that day, we were told we could have his 'K-King' - a brand new aircraft. When we readied for take-off it refused to start for some minutes. When we were finally ready, all of the others were airborne and heading for Peterhead to get in formation. We had some difficulty getting off the runway, nearly removing the top deck of a passing bus! We flew flat-out to catch up and take our position in the formation. We went through the Skagerrak without seeing anything and were heading back to Banff when we saw three U-boats line astern on the surface of the Kattegat, coming from Denmark and heading for Norway. We did not hear any order to attack but when the leading aircraft in our formation attacked the leading U-boat, Peter decided to attack the middle one with our rockets and cannon. He scored direct hits and the U-boat blew up. We normally flew at about 50 feet to beat the German radar but we were well below this; probably only about 20-25 feet. As we passed over the U-boat, straight into the explosion, some debris hit us and it knocked out our starboard engine. We had been told that in the event of serious trouble, not to try to get back to base but to make for neutral Sweden. So we announced over the wireless we were making for 'Brighton', code-name for the day for Sweden. We did not hear any reply. It would seem we were transmitting all right, but our receiver was out of order.

'We set off for Sweden on a course I had given and managed to gain several hundred feet. We passed over what I believed to be the Swedish coastline when some anti-aircraft guns opened up. It brought immediate panic from Peter and even though I had been pretty sure I knew where we were, I began to worry a little. He shouted, 'This isn't Sweden; it's Norway! And you know what the Germans are doing to PoWs.' (It was rumoured that they were castrating Alliéd aircrew.) It was Sweden. The Swedish AA gunners must have been practicing, as the shells did not burst near us. We limped on and some minutes later I recognized a viaduct that was marked on my map. It gladdened my heart, for I knew we were spot-on course for an airfield I had headed for. Peter immediately brightened up and told me to get rid of the ARO, which was secret. We came upon the airfield and he made a perfect one-engined landing far superior to the practice ones he had made at home. I pressed the two small buttons on my right, which destroyed the IFF and 'Gee' box. When we got out of the aircraft, Peter got down on his knees and kissed the ground. He got up, put his arm around me and said, 'Good old Smitty. You knew where you were all the time, didn't you?' I didn't say anything. A Swedish Air Force officer with a revolver in his right hand wasn't taking any chances, but he shook hands with us with his left. 'Welcome to Sweden,' he said, in perfect English.' [115]

On 11 April another attack was made on Porsgrunn, by 35 Mosquitoes. Bf 109G-14s shot down two although the remainder left four merchantmen sinking. In the Kattegat on 19 April 22 FB.VIs of the Banff Wing firing rockets and cannon sank U-251 which had just left Kiel two days' earlier bound for Horten in Oslo Fiord. The submarine had been relegated to training duties after a long refit in June 1943 having sunk two Allied vessels on two of its nine war cruises. The U-251 was lost with 39 hands.[116]

One hundred and fifty miles off the Scottish coast on 21 April 42 FB.VIs on 235, 248, 143 and 333 Squadrons, led by Wing Commander Christopher Foxley-Norris, CO, 143 Squadron intercepted a Luftwaffe strike mission inbound from Gardermoen, Denmark to attack the 26 ships in Convoy JW66, the last of the wartime convoys to Murmansk which had left the Clyde on 16 April with a heavy naval escort of two 'jeep' carriers, a cruiser and twenty-two other warships. The Mosquitoes were returning to Banff after a search for enemy shipping which had only produced a few small vessels in conditions of mist and heavy rain which did not justify an attack, when the enemy formation was sighted. The Mosquitoes' escort of 24 Mustangs had gone on ahead after securing permission to return early to Peterhead where a mess party had been planned for the evening. At 2030 hours in bad weather with rain and a cloud base below 600 feet and 150 miles off the Scottish coast, the Mosquito crews suddenly spotted the force of eighteen Ju 88A-17 and Ju 188A-3 torpedo carrying aircraft of KG 26 in six Vics of three in line astern. Foxley-Norris gave the order 'Attack! Attack! Attack! 'Mosquitoes were pushing shoving like housewives in a bread queue to get to get at their unfortunate targets' he said. 'When we finally got home and debriefed, we were to everybody's satisfaction credited with destroying nine [five Ju 88A-17 and four Ju 188A-3s] and we reckoned a lot more were damaged before they staggered up into the cloud cover.'

The engagement was over so quickly that Foxley-Norris never managed to get a bomber in his sights. Flight Lieutenant J. R. Keohane said, 'As soon as we saw the enemy markings, we went in to attack. They were right down on the water. I let one '88 have a burst and its starboard engine caught fire. He tried to climb away, but just stalled and went flop into the sea.' Squadron Leader Bert Gunnis DFC recorded that the sea appeared full of blazing aircraft. 'Five times I got a Ju in my sights and each time another Mosquito crew mixed in and shot it down before I could draw a bead.' 'There was naturally great rejoicing at Banff' recalled Christopher Foxley-Norris 'and much welcomed publicity that Coastal Command did not often get. My DSO, coincidentally, came through at about the same time, which called for extra drinks in the mess.' At Coastal Command Headquarters Sholto Douglas the commander-in-chief telephoned 13 Group, Fighter Command and offered his opposite number fighter escort for their Mustangs 'when and if required'!

On 22 April 404 'Buffalo' Squadron flew its first operation from Banff since replacing its Beaufighter Xs with Mosquito VIs in March. Off Kjevik one of the Canadian Squadron's Mosquitoes (RF851/H) raked a Bv 138 flying boat at her moorings with cannon and machine gun fire and it immediately exploded, sending a smoke plume to 500 feet.

On 2 May a strike by twenty-seven Mosquitoes in the Kattegat resulted in the sinking of U-2359 commanded by Oberleutnant zur see Gustav Bischoff while on passage from Kiel to Horten and was yet to be deployed on a war patrol. Primarily, the kill was achieved by Squadron Leader A. G. 'Tommy' Deck DFC on 143 Squadron, Squadron Leader D. E. Luckwell on 248 Squadron and Flight Lieutenant Geoff Mayhew DFC on 235 Squadron. At least five on 143 Squadron dived on U-2359 , firing 38 rockets and scoring at least a dozen hits, plus cannon damage. Two others on 143 hit a second boat with 16 rockets scoring two hits and then four Mosquitoes attacked with cannon and they raked the whole length of the hull. 248 Squadron led by Squadron Leader Luckwell blitzed the same boat with rockets and cannon. He was followed by 235 Squadron with Flight Lieutenant Geoff Mayhew leading and they scored between eight and sixteen rocket strikes. U-2359 sank north-east of Laeso Island with twelve hands.

On 4 May 48 Mosquitoes on 143, 235, 248, 333 and 404 Squadrons led by Wing Commander Christopher Foxley-Norris DSO, escorted by eighteen Mustangs, with three ASR Warwicks with airborne lifeboats along, sighted a very heavily armed convoy in the Kattegat, which they immediately attacked. Wing Commander Foxley-Norris reported, 'They met us with a box barrage of light and heavy flak. It was some of the heaviest we met and the convoy was unusually well protected by escort vessels.' Three Mosquitoes sought sanctuary in Sweden due to severe flak damage. With one engine shot away Flight Lieutenant Douglas Thorburn DFC and his navigator Warrant Officer Crocker attempted to land on the remaining engine when suddenly it cut out and the Mosquito struck a wall. Crocker managed to get clear through the escape hatch, with two broken legs and a head injury but as the aircraft caught fire Thorburn was burnt to death.[117]

Flight Lieutenant Gerry Yeates DFC* and Flight Lieutenant Tommy Scott on 248 Squadron were so low that when they attacked a destroyer they returned with the top of a mast-head complete with pennant embedded in the Mosquito's nose! In a separate action, in the Little Belt, U-2503 which was on passage from Kiel to Norway was attacked with rockets and cannon fire by Beaufighters on 236 and 254 Squadron - primarily by Squadron Leader S. R. Hyland AFC (NV542/A) and Flight Lieutenant T. F. Leaver-Power flying 'B'. One rocket actually burst in the control room killing the 29-year old commander, Karl-Jürgen Wächter and twelve of the crew. The stricken U-boat had to be beached on the Danish island of Fyn.[118]

These final, massive, battles were the end of the shooting war for the strike wings but patrols for U-boat crews who might be inclined to continue the fight went on until 24 May when four Mosquitoes on 143 and 248 Squadrons found only passive E-Boats.

Operations ended on 21 May when 248 Squadron supplied two Mosquitoes and 143 Squadron two for an anti-U-boat patrol between Svinoy and Terningen. Eight E-boats were the only activity recorded. The Banff Wing provided escorts for the King of Norway as he sailed back to his country under heavy naval escort. Days later a schnörkel was seen and attacked by a single Mosquito on 404 Squadron, by 25 May the rapid run down of the anti-shipping wings had begun.

The casualties in Coastal Command between 3 September 1939 and 8 May 1945 were over 8,000 killed. The Command claimed 192 U-boats sunk and 'shared' in 19 more with Royal Navy ships and 478,000 tons of enemy shipping sunk in all theatres. The cost was 5,866 aircrew killed in action and about 2,060 aircraft; 741 in the anti-U-boat campaign.

Footnotes

111 Squadron Leader Cook on 235 Squadron and 'Taffy' Stoddart on 248 were both killed as were their navigators. Warrant Officer Bob Gennoe and his navigator 'Benny' Goodman were shot down and after standing on the wing of their ditched Mosquito, they were taken prisoner by the Germans. Initially Corbin was recommended for the DFC and operations mentioned were an attack on an M-Class minesweeper on 30 June and an attack on a convoy off the French coast on 27 July, when he was hit and had to return on one engine and a punctured tyre. The recommendation, however, was changed to the CGM by AVM Sir Brian Baker KBE CB DSO MC AFC, AOC 19 Group. Flight Sergeant Webb received the DFM. *In Action With the Enemy: The Holders of the Conspicuous Gallantry Medal (Flying)* by Alan W. Cooper (William Kimber 1986). On 18 September Corbin attacked U-867 on the surface near Bergen with cannon and machine gun fire and then dropped depth charges astern of the submarine. The U-boat was sunk the next day by a Liberator on 224 Squadron.

112 *Intercom* Autumn 1987.

113 *A Separate Little War* by Andrew D. Bird (Grub St. 2008).

114 His brother 27-year old Wolfgang Herwatz had been killed in command of U-1302 on 13 March 1945 when his submarine was sunk by Canadian frigates.

115 McIntyre and Smith returned to Leuchars aboard a BOAC DC-3 after internment at Falun. On home leave they experienced VE-Day, 8 May 1945.

116 *U-Boat Fact File* by Peter Sharpe (Midland Publishing Ltd 1998).

117 Crocker was sent to Varberg hospital and recovered from his injuries. The news of Thorburn's death was communicated to his parents, Brigadier Stephen Thorburn OBE MC and Henrietta Thorburn MBE of Layer-de-la-Haye, Essex. His former master at Eton held a service of remembrance. Douglas Thorburn's remains were recovered and buried in Varberg Church New Cemetery on the south-west coast of Sweden. Flying Officer W. Moffatt and Flight Lieutenant C. Hardy landed at Satenas, damaging the undercarriage in the process. Flight Sergeants W. Shewry and J. E. Hornby landed at the airfield of the SAAB aircraft factory at Trollhattan unhurt. *A Separate Little War* by Andrew D. Bird (Grub St 2008).

118 Ibid.

Index

206